THE FOUR POWER PACT
1933

THE FOUR POWER PACT
1933

by

Konrad Hugo Jarausch

THE STATE HISTORICAL SOCIETY OF WISCONSIN
for
THE DEPARTMENT OF HISTORY, UNIVERSITY OF WISCONSIN
Madison, 1965

PREFACE

THE *ANNUS MIRABILIS* NINETEEN THIRTY-THREE has been severely neglected by diplomatic historians. Although the internal history of the major powers has been studied intensively, little attention has been devoted to the corresponding international developments. In part history herself is at fault, for the year produced few major clashes and no spectacular successes, little to attract the curiosity of the scholar. Instead, 1933 witnessed a series of failures: Japan's break with the League of Nations, the collapse of the World Economic Conference, the demise of the disarmament negotiations, and Germany's withdrawal from Geneva. Historians quickly forget ill-fated solutions. It seems unfortunate that Clio shows an inherent bias for success, since defeat can also hold the key to understanding the course of human affairs.

The failures of 1933 were the first in a chain of disasters leading to the outbreak of World War II. When assessing the causes for the breakdown of the peace, it is more fruitful to investigate the long-range reasons for the conflict than the crisis diplomacy of the last, desperate moments before the outbreak of war. Charting the initial interplay of the contesting forces, when the alignments are still in flux, often yields more insight than recording the inescapable collision after the diplomatic field has polarized. It is the purpose of this essay to study the response of the European powers to Hitler's *Machtergreifung* in order to answer the questions: Did Europe merely blunder into war? Did harsh reality force the powers inevitably into the abyss? Or did a viable alternative exist which could have prevented the renewed holocaust?

I would like to express my profound gratitude to the patient and inspired mentors who have guided my efforts. My special thanks to Professor Franz Petri for his fatherly concern; to Professor Lawrence E. Gelfand for arousing my curiosity in diplomatic history; to Professor George L. Mosse for sharpening my awareness of the importance of ideology; to Professor Chester V. Easum for directing my interest towards the Nazi period, and above all, to Professor Theodore S. Hamerow, whose kind and steady hand helped to shape the manuscript and who provided the *Vorbild* for my striving. Moreover, I wish to acknowledge a great debt to my fellow students Robert B. Dockhorn, John W. Davis and David A. Hackett for their trenchant criticism of all stages of the writing.

At the conclusion of this work I cannot escape Gustave LeBon's haunting reflection: "*Il faut considérer comme des ouvrages d'imagination pure les livres d'histoire. Ce sont des récits fantaisistes de faits mal observés, accompagnés d'explications faites après coup. Gâcher du plâtre est faire oeuvre bien plus utile que de perdre son temps à écrire tels livres . . .*"

Konrad H. H. Jarausch

Madison, Wisconsin
1965

TABLE OF CONTENTS

PREFACE . . . . *v*

ABBREVIATIONS . . . . *viii*

INTRODUCTION 3

CHAPTER
    I.   THE GENESIS OF THE FOUR
          POWER CONCEPT 8
   II. THE LAUNCHING OF THE PROPOSAL . . 24
  III. INITIAL NEGOTIATIONS 46
  IV. INTERNATIONAL PUBLIC REACTION. . . 73
    V. FINAL NEGOTIATIONS 111
  VI. THE SIGNING 160
 VII. THE FAILURE 185

CONCLUSION 219

APPENDIX 229

BIBLIOGRAPHY 242

INDEX 259

ABBREVIATIONS

BFP   Great Britain. Foreign Office. *Documents on British Foreign Policy, 1919-1945* (series C, 1933), vols. IV, V.

FBB   France. Ministère des Affaires Étrangères. *Pacte d'entente et de la collaboration paraphé à Rome le 7 juin 1933* (Paris, 1933), also called *French Blue Book*.

FRUS   U.S. Department of State. *Foreign Relations of the U.S.: Diplomatic Papers* (1933), vol. I.

GFP   U.S. Department of State. *Documents on German Foreign Policy, 1918-1945* (series C, 1933), vols. I, II.

GMF   Germany. Ministry of Foreign Affairs. Microfilms of the National Archives, Washington, D.C. For convenience the mention of the serial number was omitted in the three main collections. All frame numbers beginning with H refer to serial 7457; D refer to serial 3170; E refer to serial 6058. All other citations include serial numbers.

THE FOUR POWER PACT
1933

INTRODUCTION

> *The peoples of Europe have*
> *every reason to cease war-*
> *ring and to ally instead. Eu-*
> *rope is but a province of the*
> *world—every war between*
> *Europeans is a civil war.*
>   —Napoleon I

AS A LOGICAL ALTERNATIVE to the fleeting mirage of collective security, the idea of a directorate of the Great Powers held a continual attraction to the statesmen of troubled Europe. In the nineteenth century the "Concert of Europe," or, more precisely, the "Congress System" effectively organized the peace after the Napoleonic wars and continued to exist loosely throughout the century, resolving major international crises—more often than not short of war. Although momentarily discredited by the outbreak of World War I, and overshadowed by the brilliant spectacle of the League of Nations, the concept of a Great Power directorate continued to appear at crucial moments in the 1920's and 1930's. The permanent seats of the Council of the League of Nations; the Big Four at the Paris Peace Conference; their successor, the Conference of Ambassadors; the treaties of Locarno; the Lausanne Conference on reparations; the consultative pact of 1932; the negotiations during the Abyssinian crisis;

and climactically, the Munich agreements, expressed the attempt to preserve the peace by the co-operation of the principal European powers in the inter-war period. Whenever the issue of war and peace arose among them, the Great Powers preferred to settle the dispute by frank discussions among themselves and fell back upon the proven methods of traditional diplomacy.

With Adolf Hitler's assumption of power on January 30, 1933, the post-World War I era had ended in Europe. It is difficult to recreate the feeling of shock, doubt, and insecurity, which brutally dispelled the foggy illusions of the 1920's. The victory of National Socialism plunged Europe into a deep and prolonged crisis of self confidence from which she has yet to recover. Born in revolution, the Twenties had witnessed an astounding burst of economic progress and artistic creativity; but Hitler's rise to power shattered all euphoria. For many, a new pre-war period seemed to have begun. The Nazi takeover in Germany provoked an international crisis grave enough to threaten the diplomatic balance of Europe, although its open outbreak was postponed until 1939. Hitler's challenge to European security was too serious to be left to the ailing League of Nations. The alarmed statesmen of the West, therefore, turned to the traditional remedy of a Great Power directorate. In 1933 their solution took the shape of the Four Power Pact.[1]

---

[1]At present there is no satisfactory study of the Four Power Pact. Francesco Salata, a Fascist Senator, wrote an eulogy to Mussolini's diplomacy in October 1933, *Il Patto Mussolini*: Storia di un piano politico e di *una negazione diplomatico* (Verona, 1933). In a telegram to Berlin on October 5, German Ambassador to the Quirinal, Ulrich von Hassell, called the "publication worth attention, since it recounts the origin of the Four Power Pact fairly correctly." GMF, E 44761. A senior member of the Italian foreign service, Fran-

Basically the Four Power Pact was an attempt to meet the renewed danger of war with nineteenth-century diplomatic means. By establishing a Great Power directorate, the "Concert of Europe," whose record had probably been more creditable than that of any other system of keeping peace, would be restored. Since the League of Nations was bankrupt after Japan's defiant walk-out on February 25, 1933, Europe possessed no organization, no common forum, no tool to contain Hitler peacefully. A new initiative was clearly needed if the Continent were not to drift hopelessly once more towards the abyss. The Four Power Pact was contrived to meet the crisis by curing the principal weakness of the League. It was a more realistic project, inasmuch it took into account the fact that without harmony among the big European powers peace could not be preserved. But would not the small powers have to foot the bill for great power collaboration? In 1933 as in 1938, Europe faced an inexorable dilemma: Could a restoration of the old order, based upon power and authority, succeed in maintaining the precious peace, or would such a sacrifice of Wilsonian ideals open a Pandora's box of aggression and merely whet the appetite of the dictators?

---

cesco Jacomini, published an extended article, "Il Patto a quattro," in the *Rivista di Studi Storici* (January 1951), pp. 25-66, but without divulging any information out of Italian diplomatic files. The only treatment in English is a perceptive article by René Albrecht-Carrié, "Four Power Pacts, 1933-1945," in the *Journal for Central European Affairs* (April 1945), pp. 17-45, stressing the continuing attraction of the concept in the World War II period. In *Il Fascismo nella politica internazionale* (Modena, 1946), p. 126, Luigi Salvatorelli correctly pointed out: "Even today the significance of this initiative of Mussolini is by no means clear."

The Four Power Pact was the diplomatic expression of Europe's response to Hitler's seizure of power. The reaction of the Western nations to the Nazi menace was slow, faltering, and undetermined. Spanning the period from March to October, the pact provided the backdrop for the groping diplomacy of 1933 by which the powers sought precariously to find a new equilibrium. Intimately involved in the disarmament negotiations, in the World Economic Conference, in the first Austrian crisis, and in Germany's withdrawal from the League of Nations, the Four Power Pact revealed the nature of Hitler's early foreign policy and his typical decision pattern of brooding hesitation followed by impulsive action. The pact exposed unsparingly the tortuous vacillation between firmness and appeasement of the French and British leaders as well.

Moreover, the Four Power Pact provided a classic example for the workings of Mussolini's Fascist diplomacy, reflecting the contradictory strains of his personality, his ideological commitments, and his concessions to political reality. Conceived as his crowning diplomatic achievement, the pact represented a direct application of the hierarchical structure of the corporate state to international affairs. The making of major decisions was restricted to the four Great Powers of Europe, which, for their superior strength, should carry a heavier share of the responsibility. The Wilsonian concept of equality among nations was to be destroyed. If the League of Nations was founded upon the principles of international democracy, the Four Power Pact was an accurate expression of the rival concept of corporate hierarchy.[2]

---

[2]René Albrecht-Carrié in *Italy from Napoleon to Mussolini* (New York, 1950), p. 201, calls the Four Power Pact "a proposal which has not received sufficient attention. It is worth studying in some detail for

Finally, the negotiations for the Four Power Pact and its inglorious failure produced the shifting diplomatic alignments which set the basic pattern until the outbreak of the Second World War. Co-operation of three powers in favor of moderate revision of the peace treaties, an even division of Europe into two ideologically hostile camps, or an alliance of the three Western powers against the Nazi menace were the possible power constellations after Hitler's appearance on the international scene. The various combinations were rehearsed and executed during 1933, although the groupings were still improvised, unstable and full of mutual distrust. Only five years later, forces similar to those which led to the acceptance of the Four Power Pact opened the road to Munich and precipitated the Continent once more into the holocaust.

And yet in 1933 there was still hope. Although the League had been shaken beyond repair, the Four Power Pact, if faithfully implemented, might have sufficed to stem the tide. At least French Foreign Minister Joseph Paul-Boncour believed that it had been possible, when deploring the failure of the pact from the rostrum at Geneva: "If only this accord so diligently negotiated between the four Great Powers of Locarno, members of the Council of the League, could have been put into effect; Locarno would perhaps not been in ruins, nor the League of Nations be derailed!"[3]

---

it constitutes an excellent and typical example of the sort of thing that Fascism stood for and thus goes a long way towards revealing the true nature of that system."

[3] *Tribune des Nations* (Geneva), February 1937.

Chapter I

THE GENESIS OF THE FOUR POWER CONCEPT

MUSSOLINI'S FOREIGN POLICY from the March on Rome to the apogee of his prestige in the early 1930's provides the key to the origin of the Four Power Pact. The diplomacy of the Duce has often been described as blundering pragmatism: "If Mussolini was ill-informed, uncertain and vacillating at home, he was equally so in his conduct of foreign affairs. Here he was torn in every direction by ingrained prejudice, ignorance, passing predilections, ambition, and above all by fear." Mussolini allowed himself to drift and he appeared not only to the counselor of the British Embassy in Rome, Sir Ivone Kirkpatrick, to be more "the victim and not the master of his own destiny." But, although this psychological characterization can hardly be overstressed, it does not afford an adequate guide to the substance and the form of Mussolini's initiatives in foreign affairs.[1]

---

[1] Sir Ivone Kirkpatrick, *Mussolini: A Study in Power* (New York, 1964) is the most recent biography. For Mussolini's early foreign policy see Piero Pieri, "La politica estera di Mussolini dal 1922 al 1932," *Nuova Rivista Storica* (1956), p. 167f. and Arrigo Solmi,

Basic to a more acute understanding of the Duce's foreign policy is the constant awareness of his dictatorial hold over Italy, which made him largely independent of public opinion. Because of his autocratic powers he was able to settle the thorny question of Fiume and grant *de jure* recognition to the Soviet Union——problems which had defied solution before his takeover because no parliamentary majority dared champion such unpopular measures.[2]

A second factor determining Mussolini's foreign policy, his notorious and intense dislike of the League

---

"Zehn Jahre Faschistische Aussenpolitik," *Europäische Revue* (1932), pp. 670-675. There is no satisfactory account of his whole foreign policy in English. One has to rely on M. Macartney and P. Cremona, *Italy's Foreign and Colonial Policy* (London, 1938); Gaetano Salvemini's biting *Mussolini diplomate* (Paris, 1932); M. Missiroli, *La Politica estera fascista* (Rome, 1945); Luigi Salvatorelli, *Il Fascismo nella politica internazionale* (Modena, 1946); L. Villari, *Italian Foreign Policy Under Mussolini* (New York, 1956); E. di Nolfo, *Mussolini e la politica estera Italiana* (Padua, 1960); and the introduction to F. Siebert, *Italiens Weg in den zweiten Weltkrieg* (Frankfurt, 1962).

[2]The strength of Mussolini's position is underlined by a remark of Sir Winston Churchill on February 18, 1933, at Queen's Hall: "The Roman genius incarnated in Mussolini, the greatest living legislator, has shown to many nations, how one can resist the blandishments of socialism and has indicated the way which a nation can follow, if it is courageously led. In the Fascist regime Mussolini has created a center of orientation for those countries which are engaged in bodily combat with socialism." As retranslated from the Italian in L. Salvatorelli, *Il Fascismo nella politica internazionale*, p. 120.

of Nations, stemmed from a minor incident. Although
the Duce was friendly in his early dealings with the
Western Powers, his violent reaction to the Corfu incident soon disrupted the deceptive amiability.   In
retaliation for the murder of General Tellini, the Italian
member of the Albanian Boundary Commission, Mussolini angrily ordered the shelling and occupation of the
Greek island of Corfu. France and Britain were appalled
by such draconian methods, and the matter was brought
before the League.   The ensuing debate reflected the
almost universal disapproval of Italy's rash punitive
action, and Mussolini threatened to depart from the
shores of Lake Geneva.   But through his unrelenting
pressure the investigation was sidetracked into the
Conference of Ambassadors, the successor to the Supreme Council of the Peace Conference, which succeeded in blaming neither side for the dispute.[3]

　　From Mussolini's emotional hatred of the League
derives another characteristic of his foreign policy:
his preference for the Locarno Treaties.   Although the
Duce sulked because he interpreted his failure to secure a guarantee for the contested Brenner frontier as
a slight to his prestige, he eventually became a strong
advocate of the ideas embodied in the Locarno Pacts.
As one of the guarantors of peace between France and
Germany, Italy's position as a Great Power was reaffirmed and a closer collaboration with Great Britain
realized.   Mussolini repeatedly hailed the Locarno
Pacts as an attempt to preserve the international order
by a Great Power directorate and claimed them as spiritual ancestors of the Four Power Pact.[4]

---

[3]Kirkpatrick, *Mussolini*, p. 206f., sees in Mussolini's xenophobia the main reason for his dislike of
the League.
[4]See, e.g., Mussolini's speech before the Italian
Senate on June 7, 1933:   "The Locarno Pact was ini-

Mussolini's ideas on foreign policy were dominated by two basic tenets: imperialism and revisionism. In most instances the desire for expansion and the call for amending the peace treaties went hand in hand, but where they clashed, as in the South Tyrol, imperialism prevailed. The striving for empire runs as a *Leitmotiv* through Mussolini's entire career, dating already from his break with the Socialists over Italian intervention in World War I. Imperialism served as the rallying point for the otherwise so heterogeneous *fasci di combattimento* in 1919, and after the seizure of power it became the avowed goal of the Fascist state to unify Italy at home to make her more powerful and respected abroad. The Duce's imperialism bore a heavily histrionic tinge. In mapping out his plans for conquest, the Duce strove for nothing less than the resurrection of the glory of the ancient Roman Empire. His territorial goals, therefore, lay in three directions: in *Italia irredenta*; in the Balkans on the other shore of the Adriatic, Italy's *mare nostrum*; and in the desert sands of the North African colonies. A chauvinistic nationalism, fused with a mystical belief in the mission of Rome, was grafted upon the restless activism of the blackshirt cohorts. Tiny Albania was the first to suffer from the revived vigor of Fascist Italy, when Mussolini gradually established a protectorate and in-

---

tialled in October 1925. The Four Power Pact constitutes its logical and necessary development. . . . In the Pact of Locarno the position of the Four Powers was clearly defined, thus establishing a premise from which in the course of time definite consequences could result." Translated in J. Wheeler-Bennett, Ed., *Documents on International Affairs*, 1933 (London, 1934), pp. 267—77. Official Fascist historiography also stresses the connection; cf. V. Gayda, *Was Will Italien?* (Leipzig, 1941), p. 135 *passim*.

stalled a puppet government during 1926-1928. His
imperialism sprang from a curious mixture of sincere
devotion to Italian greatness and from the unfulfilled
craving for personal prestige. It was the most powerful and constant motive force in the Duce's foreign
policy.[5]

More important for the European scene was Mussolini's championship of revisionism. As one of the
most violent critics of the *vittoria mutilata*,[6] the Duce

---

[5]Material on Mussolini's political thought can be
found in the biographies by Gaudens Megaro, *Mussolini in the Making* (Boston, 1938); Giorgio Pini and
Duilio Susmel, *Mussolini: l'uomo e l'opera* (3 vols.,
Florence, 1953–1955); Georges–Roux, *La Chute de
Mussolini* (Paris, 1961); Laura Fermi, *Mussolini* (Chi-
cago, 1961); Christopher Hibbert, *Benito Mussolini*
(London, 1962); and Ivone Kirkpatrick, *Mussolini*. For
a more complete listing see Elia Festa, "I biographi
di Mussolini," *Nuova Rivista Storica* (1961), pp. 467–
513, and Charles F. Delzell, "Benito Mussolini: A
Guide to Biographical Literature," in the *Journal of
Modern History* (Dec., 1963), pp. 339–353. Treatments
of Fascism in general are G. Ferrero, *Four Years of
Fascism* (London, 1924); D. Sturzo, *Italy and Fascismo*
(London, 1926); P. Alatri, *Le Origini del Fascismo*
(Rome, 1926); L. Salvatorelli, *Storia d'Italia nel periodo fascista* (Turin, 1956); A. Tasca, *Nascita e av-
vento del Fascismo* (Fiume, n.d.); Roy MacGregor-
Hastie, *The Day of the Lion* (London, 1963); and F.
Chabod's classic, *A History of Italian Fascism* (Lon-
don, 1963).

[6]According to Ennio di Nolfo the phrase originated
with Gabriele d'Annunzio, who published on October 24,
1918, the appeal in the *Corriere della Sera*: "Vittoria
nostra non sarai mutilata." *Mussolini e la politica
estera*, p. 5.

opposed the peace treaties from their inception. Already in the founding statutes of the *fasci* Mussolini called for the revision "of all those treaties, which carry within themselves the seeds of future wars." The theme recurs in a speech in Trieste on February 6, 1921: "Fascism believes that Italy has to conduct a European policy of balance of power and of reconciliation between the powers. The treaties have to be revised and changes made in those clauses, which have turned out to be inapplicable and whose application can be the well spring of monstrous hatred and new wars."[7] Or more epigrammatically: "Treaties are not eternal. They are not irreparable. They are chapters, not epilogues of history."[8]

But when in power, Mussolini's espousal of revisionism proved to be sporadic and opportunistic. Although he affirmed the principle in his first foreign policy pronouncement on November 16, 1922, he was preoccupied with more immediate tasks in the early years of his regime. Only after having consolidated his position at home, the references to revision became more frequent, and his polemics against the "mummification of mankind by treaties" grew more caustic. On June 5, 1927, he reiterated the demand for revision in a widely publicized speech before the Ital-

---

[7] As cited in Virginio Gayda, *Was Will Italien?*, p. 138.

[8] *Scritti e Discorsi*, VIII, 126. In a contemporary pamphlet on the Four Power Pact, Asvero Gravelli attempted to show that "The historical importance of Mussolini and Hitler consists exactly in the fact that their teachings bring the peoples closer to revision. Their thesis is that Fascism shows itself in the manifold forms of international justice, an influence which has been lacking until now. *Hitler, Mussolini und die Revision* (Detmold, n.d.), p. 44.

ian Senate. In the early 1930's Italian attacks on the peace treaties became more outspoken and began to include criticism of the League as an institution. Mussolini's hostility to the status quo was evident in the eventful first session of the Disarmament Conference. On the whole, he supported the German stand, even though he enjoyed his role as mediator in bringing about the Five Power Declaration of December 11, 1932, which opened the door to Germany's return to the deliberations by an ambiguous compromise formula.[9] During the negotiations Mussolini entered the fray with an article on "Equality of Rights," stating clearly his attitude towards the resurgent strength of Germany: "It is naive and ruinously illusionary to believe in stopping the course of history, to believe that one can repress until eternity a people with such a high civilization as the Germans, who—after Russia—are the

------

[9]When the Disarmament Conference reached a deadlock in mid-1932, Germany withdrew temporarily, claiming that parity of arms had been denied to her. The Five Power Declaration, sometimes also called the No—Resort—to—Force—Pact, patched up things sufficiently to allow for a resumption of the negotiations. (Acc. to BFP, IV, 377-8). Its most important passage reads: "The Governments of the United Kingdom, France, and Italy have declared that one of the principles that would guide the Conference on Disarmament should be the grant to Germany . . . of equality of rights in a system which would provide security for all nations, and that that principle should find itself embodied in the convention containing the conclusions of the Disarmament Conference." A feeble compromise between the German demand for equality of rights and the French desire for security, it also provided for the renunciation of war, but it never entered into effect, since the Disarmament Conference failed.

most numerous in Europe. To break open the door of the future one cannot forever remain enshrined in the past! "[10] Although he was not interested in replacing hegemony with German domination in Central Europe, Mussolini decided to throw in his lot with revisionism, the wave of the future. His basic aim was to restore the balance of power on the Continent, which alone provided the opportunity for Italy's advantageous position as arbiter, wooed by both sides, a role infinitely attractive to the vainglorious Duce.[11]

In the fall of 1932 Mussolini hinted for the first time that a new plan for international co—operation was taking shape in his mind. The failure of the consultative pact, suggested by MacDonald as complément to the Lausanne Conference,[12] the disturbing probability of the complete breakdown of the Disarmament

---

[10]The article appeared in the Popolo d'Italia on September 13, 1932. *Scritti e Discorsi*, III, 105f.

[11]In *Italy from Napoleon to Mussolini* Albrecht-Carrié stresses (p. 198f.) Mussolini's preference for the role of the "not so honest broker."

[12]The British suggested a general consultative pact as political counterpart to the reparation agreement of Lausanne. On July 13 British Foreign Secretary John Simon explained its purpose in the Commons: "Indeed it is not a substantative agreement at all, but it is an invitation to adopt candid and open relations and discussions to which we hope all the leading European powers will respond." Although MacDonald had originally only a meeting of the Great Powers in mind, France insisted on the participation of her minor allies. When the Little Entente and the small revisionist powers joined the agreement, the original scheme became inflated beyond recognition and lost all political influence. In more ways than one it foreshadowed the fate of the Four Power Pact. GMF, D 675598-676723.

Conference, the crippling shadow of the Great Depression, and Italy's virtual diplomatic isolation at Geneva
stimulated the Duce to concoct a scheme which would
cure all these ills by one magic stroke.[13] On October
23, 1932, Mussolini voiced for the first time in public
the idea of four power co-operation.   In a long, dramatic speech to the workers of Turin he invoked the
consecrated blood of generations of gallant Italian
soldiers to plead: "If tomorrow . . . through the conditions necessary and sufficient for the collaboration of
the four Western powers. Europe could become peaceful from the political point of view, then the economic
crisis that torments us, would approach its end!" The
ideas were still vague and unformed, but all essential
features of the pact were implicit in the call. The appeal to justice and to sacred Italian rights was a dis-
creet promise of revision. "The conditions necessary
and sufficient for the collaboration of the four Western
powers" represented a veiled reference to a Great
Power directorate, while at the same time implying
German parity of rights.[14]

Only three weeks later the ideological basis of
four power co-operation was elaborated.   During the
spectacular celebrations of the tenth anniversary of

----

[13]For this reason Mussolini reorganized the direction of Italian foreign policy by sending Dino Grandi,
who had "become too enamoured of Geneva and the
League of Nations," as ambassador to London. Kirkpatrick, *Mussolini*, p. 286. He personally took charge
of the ministry of foreign affairs and made Fulvio Suvich
his permanent Undersecretary of State.   E. di Nolfo,
Mussolini e la politica estera, p. 305.

[14]*Scritti e Discorsi*, VIII, p. 126. For Mussolini's
rhetoric see the dissertation by Frank Iezzi, *Selected
Political Addresses of Benito Mussolini* (Madison,
1954).

the Fascist regime, a Congress of the Italian Royal Academy was called "to shed light on the spiritual cause of the European crisis, to define the subject 'Europe' and the value of her civilization for the present and the future ... and, if possible, to crystallize a uniform European consciousness of the European problem." This Congress of Volta was an assembly of *savants* from all European nations, who were lavishly entertained from November 14 to 20 by the King and State of Italy. The implicit purpose of the congress was to create "admiration for the political order of our country, for the creative virtue of Fascism and for the political genius of the Duce."[15]

The German conservative philosopher Prince Karl von Rohan, and Alfred Rosenberg, his National-Socialist counterpart, played the most active roles among the dignitaries, despite the handicap of meeting minds both morally and intellectually superior. Rosenberg indulged in a verbose and mystical discourse on the necessity of preventing the decline of Europe by a renewal of faith despite the challenge of Bolshevism, the rising

---

[15]For the proceedings see R. Accademia d'Italia, Fondazione A. Volta, Atti dei Convegni. *Il Convegno di scienze morali e storiche, 14-20 Novembre 1932.* Tema: l'Europa (Roma, 1933), vol. I, 272, 288. A skeptical description of the Congress is by Maurice Pernot, "Au Congress Volta: La Crise Européenne" *Revue des Deux Mondes*, XII (1932), pp. 909-916; an eulogy by Ugo Andrea, "I Congressi" *Nuova Antologia*, CCCLXIV (1932), pp. 532-535. For Karl Anton Prince of Rohan's cultural philosophy and political commentary see his essays in *Europäische Revue* (1933), which he edited, especially pp. 93-106, 595-602, 719-725. Cf. Francesco Salata, *Il Patto Mussolini*, pp. 329-332. If one can believe the latter account the aim of the Congress was fully achieved.

tide of anti-colonialism, and the pseudo-idealistic
internationalism of the United States. This inner regeneration could only come about through a return to
the fountainhead of racial nationalism: "Today Europe
can realize ... the most profound law of its existence:
the fourfold spirit of its civilization, and each of its
vital branches will assure itself, corresponding to its
strength, the growth and the flowering which is its
right and its obligation. ... Europe contains four Nations: Germany, Italy, France and England. Each possesses its own destiny, each its own center of happi-
ness: Italy its state, France its territory, Germany its
race and England its society. ... The destruction of any
one of these would not result in the unification of Europe, but in chaos in which the other nations shall
also perish." The unity of Europe, Rosenberg claimed,
could only be realized by "shoulder to shoulder" co-
operation between Germany looking towards the east
and northeast, France towards the south, Italy towards
the southeast, and Great Britain towards the oceans.
Here was a grandiose scheme for a National-Socialist
reorganization of Europe, an almost mythical division
into realms.[16]

----

[16]*Ibid.* Rosenberg elaborated his ideas on Europe
in greater detail in the collection of essays *Blut und
Ehre* (Munich, 1934), pp. 296-311. Hitler delighted
in similar statements: "Whenever in Western or Middle Europe a nation falls under the sway of Bolshevism,
this poison corrodes further and destroys the oldest
and most beautiful culture on earth. By taking this
struggle upon herself, Germany now fulfills, as she has
done so often in her history, a truly European mission."
Taken from a speech to the SA and SS on September 3,
1933. Max Domarus, *Hitler: Reden und Proklamationen, 1932-1945* (Würzburg, 1962), I, 299. Cf. also
Paul Kluke, "Nationalsozialistische Europaideologie,"

Mussolini was thinking along similar lines. While waiting in the Palazzo Venezia for members of the Volta Congress, he uttered this "profound" remark to the Italian diplomat Francesco Jacomini: "This is Europe— Europe exists only insofar as the four great currents of energy which compose it exist, which in their variety and emulation determine its progress." The idea of a hierarchical four-power domination over Europe was more than a matter of political expediency for Mussolini; it was an expression of his fundamental beliefs.[17]

The Fascist concept of a four-power directorate over Europe was more clearly and rousingly formulated by Asvero Gravelli, a veteran *squadrista* and a leading contributor to *Gioventū Fascista*, *Ottobre* and *Mattino*. As director of the theoretical journal *Anti—Europa*,

---

Vierteljahreshefte für Zeitgeschichte, III (1955), pp. 240-74. For a summary of the Volta Congress in German see Francesco Orestano, "Gesamtbericht über die Verhandlungen des Volta Congresses in Rom, November 1932," *Europäische Gespräche* (1933), pp. 125-187.

[17] Fr. Jacomini describes the incident in "Il Patto a quattro," p. 27. Emil Ludwig tried to induce Mussolini to commit himself to the idea of a United Europe: "Mussolini as founder of Europe: You could become the first man of this century...! He looked at me as King Philipp at the curious fanatic. Then he replied quietly and coldly: Yes, I am now closer to this idea than five years ago. But the time is not yet ripe. The crisis first has to reach its nadir. New revolutions shall come. Only they will form the new type of European man." This conversation took place in mid-1932. *Mussolinis Gespräche mit Emil Ludwig* (Berlin, 1932). Another source for the Duce's ideas on Europe is the semi—official *Geschichte des Faschismus* (Berlin, 1942), by Giorgio Pini, p. 240f.

which had been founded in response to Briand's abortive scheme, he served as the mouthpiece for Mussolini's ideas for a Fascist reconstruction of Europe. During the protracted negotiations for the Four Power Pact, Gravelli hastily penned a pamphlet defending and clarifying the Duce's original ideas, which he published shortly after the signing under the title of *Hitler, Mussolini und die Revision*. Following the Führer's clarion call ("Italy and Germany have the same enemies: it is their mission to advance the cause of *Kultur*!") the publicist heralded a fascist rebirth of the continent: "There will be no tranquility for honourable old Europe until she has become, or has been forced to become fascist. . . . Our common ideal must be a fascist Europe, a European *Bund* of fascists."[18]

Like Mussolini, Gravelli believed that every race had its special task in building the new Europe, and

---

[18] According to Count Coudenhove-Kalergi, *An Idea Conquers the World* (New York, n.d.), p. 188, the journal *Anti-Europa*, far from being devoted to anti-European propaganda "was in fact a rather cunning attempt by Mussolini to win over the Italian intelligentsia for the idea of Pan-Europe without any loss of face on his part." On May 10 the indefatigable Count managed to be received by Mussolini, and in a wide-ranging conversation they discussed every aspect of European politics except for Mussolini's latest initiative, the Four Power Pact. Before leaving the Eternal City, the Count also paid a visit to Gravelli, whom he described, perhaps over-enthusiastically: "This youthful protege of Mussolini turned out to be a staunch supporter of Pan-Europe, who had read every line of my writings and was in fact a secret disciple of mine. He had made it his aim to win over public opinion in Italy to my ideas and to organize with Mussolini's approval an Italian branch of our Union." Pp. 192-193.

that Europe as a whole was to assume the leadership towards a better world. But before the world mission could be shouldered, all European states had to be equal. Denying the insinuation that the Duce's championship of German equality was merely a Machiavellian move, Gravelli snorted: "Well, Herr von Freytag-Lohringhoven! You did not give the whole picture: Italy wants to destroy the criminal status quo, the malignant consequence of the Peace Treaties. For the security of Europe, it is gladly willing to sacrifice the immediate advantages, which a rapprochement with France could offer. This is the true goal of Mussolini's policy, because Germany and Italy have a mission to fulfill in the history of Europe and the world." But merely political revision would not be enough: "The question of European peace is above all a revolutionary problem, a problem of the revolutionizing of ideas. . . . It does not suffice that Italy be Fascist and Germany be National-Socialist. The new ideas have to conquer Europe and the world. Only then can there be complete understanding and peaceful and friendly collaboration." The triumph of fascism was approaching with giant strides: "Europe is on the path towards fascism. Only fascism creates the possibility for an ever widening, more rational and more human cooperation. A new outline appears more and more clearly on the horizon: the fascist international! "[19]

---

[19]If the above be impressionistic and incoherent, this is due to Gravelli's style which is rapturous rather than analytical. His ideas seem to float, one stirring image follows the other, and logical exposition is almost entirely missing. But Gravelli is clever enough to engage in a bit of fascist dialectics, when turning around the charge that the Four Power Pact was a Great Power directorate: "We further reject that the four powers together form a 'directory' in the true sense of

For the Fascist thinkers all traditional cures for Europe's ills had failed. "The needs and necessities of the European nations must supplement each other. ...We want to be idealists, we want to say it again and again, and we want to cry it out into the world that the present situation is unbearable...!" Only an inner regeneration of the four principal peoples through fascism could rescue Europe from its decline. "Fascism wakens the natural powers, brings the nations to the highest civilization and drives their culture to perfection." Until now, "European politics were lacking the organ which could ensure to them a steadfast direction." The spiritual revolution then must find expression in a new system of international relations. Gravelli, at least, knew the right path: "The technique of Mussolini [and this clearly was the Four Power Pact] will decide the tomorrow. Mussolini unites in himself the qualities which mark all men of fate. He can mold the not yet existing!"[20]

Mussolini's suggestion of four-power collaboration in his October 23 speech at Turin was, therefore, something more than an accident. It was the logical

---

the word. This label was invented by the democrats. The collaboration between the four powers is nothing but a passing phase in the better solution of the European questions. The overpowering position of the four countries follows exactly from our thesis that the rights of all states must be equal." *Hitler*, pp. 13, 14, 23, 31, 60, 62, 68, 117, 124.

[20]*Ibid.*, pp. 41, 120, 129, *passim*. For a suggestive critique of the concept of corporatism in its historical, its philosophical and its totalitarian meaning see Wilhelm Röpke, *Civitas Humana* (Zürich, 1946 ed.), p. 96n. Professor Röpke distinguished 1) private or guild corporatism; 2) feudal state corporatism (*Quadragesimo Anno*); 3) and fascist totalitarian corporatism.

complement to his notions of corporate organization at home. The sham equality of Geneva was to be rejected in favor of a hierarchy based on power, function, and responsibility. The Great Powers, and among them Italy, would once again determine peace and war. At home and abroad there was but one remedy for Europe: Fascism. "In one decade Europe will be fascist or fascitized! [*sic*] The antitheses into which contemporary civilization is dissolving can be overcome only in one way: by the doctrine and wisdom of Rome!" At the end of 1932 the basic outlines of the Four Power Pact had taken shape in Mussolini's mind. The idea was maturing. Only a stimulus from the outside was now required to make it come alive.[21]

-----

[21]Spoken by Mussolini at his oration of October 25 in Milan. *Scritti e Discorsi*, VIII, p. 132.

Chapter II

THE LAUNCHING OF THE PROPOSAL

"**B**ADLY LED EUROPE drifts towards a new world war. Sapped by misery, it is driven by hate. No political leader desires this war, but nobody opposes it with vigor. The failure of the Disarmament Conference threatens to become the signal for the outbreak of the conflagration; it poses an ultimatum for Europe, it means the bankruptcy of political intelligence, it heralds the decisive struggle between peace and war. . . . For the European peoples, it is of no interest who will be man enough to put out the flaming torch of war, but only who will do so energetically. The times cry for a man who will stamp out aggression once and for all!" Thus lamented the journal *Pan Europa* in March, 1933.[1]

Despite repeated assurances of German Foreign Minister Count Constantin von Neurath, Europe was profoundly alarmed by the advent of Hitler.[2] A violent

---

[1]As cited in Gravelli, *Hitler*, pp. 108-9.

[2]Sir Horace Rumbold's dispatches from Berlin reflect the growing apprehension. They are classics of diplomatic reporting in their lucid and prophetic analysis. BFP, IV, 232, 235, 238, 240, 243, 244, 247, 253, 258, 265, 270 *et seq.*

press campaign began in the West against National Socialism and ominous incidents began to occur. Marshal Pilsudski strengthened the Polish garrison on the Westerplatte, controlling the harbor of Danzig; Japan, enraged over the Lytton report, withdrew from the League of Nations; a mysterious arms shipment was discovered at Hirtenberg in Austria; the SA brandished swastika flags in Kehl, part of the demilitarized zone opposite Strassbourg. French General Maxime Weygand was reputedly plotting a preventive war against Italy, and the Poles looked menacingly towards Germany.[3] War clouds began to collect on the horizon.[4]

The fears generated by Hitler's seizure of power now seem exaggerated. For once, the world could have taken the Führer's protestations of peace at face value. When outlining his cabinet program on February 1, Hitler stated the immediate aims of the government: "In the realm of foreign policy the national government will see as its highest mission the defense of the basic rights and the regaining of freedom for our people. We are fully conscious of the importance of the duty of working for the maintenance and strengthening of the peace with a free and equal nation; a peace which the world today needs more than ever before. May the sympathy and understanding of all other [nations] help that our sincere desire for the welfare of Europe and

---

[3]Z. Gasiorowski, "Did Pilsudski attempt to initiate a preventive war in 1933?" in the *Journal of Modern History* (1955), pp. 135-151, and *infra* p. 102n.

[4]*London Herald*, March 13: "WAR CLOUDS GATHER OVER EUROPE." Dominions Secretary Thomas was reported to have remarked: "I don't remember any period since 1914 when more war talk was about than in the last ten days." *New York Times*, March 19. All newspaper citations refer to the year 1933, unless indicated otherwise.

of the whole world will be fulfilled." But the declaration had little effect at the time and the diplomatic crisis worsened steadily during February and the first half of March.[5]

The internal consolidation of his regime ranked first among Hitler's immediate concerns. The surprising inactivity or even timidity of his early foreign policy can best be understood through a parallel with Russia after 1917 and Italy after 1922. The need for a breathing spell dampened the revolutionary ardor of Lenin and Mussolini as well as that of Hitler. Repudiation of Versailles provided a common ground with Mussolini, especially since Hitler had renounced all claims to the South Tyrol in *Mein Kampf* and the *Zweites Buch* in favor of friendship with the admired Duce. In an interview with the *Giornale d'Italia* three days after his victory, Hitler emphatically repeated that "both nations naturally find themselves on the same ground and strive for identical aims. . . . Everything will be undertaken from the German side to insure such understanding." His professed desire for an alliance with Great Britain also fitted Mussolini's scheme. In a group of four Great Powers, a majority of three would favor moderate revision and take a stand which would aid Hitler in accomplishing his third aim peacefully: German expansion.[6]

---

[5]M. Domarus, *Hitler*, p. 193. French Ambassador Andre Francois-Poncet supports the view that Hitler "judged it opportune to avoid conflicts which would risk provoking a foreign intervention capable of forcing his retirement or even of reversing the regime." *Souvenirs d'une ambassade à Berlin* (Paris, 1946), p. 139.

[6]For Hitler's early foreign policy see M. Beer, *Die Auswärtige Politik des Dritten Reiches* (Zürich, 1935); Freytagh-Loringhoven, *Deutschland's Aussenpolitik*,

French reaction to the new danger was typical. Not since Gustav Stresemann's death had the moment seemed so propitious for a Franco-German rapprochement. Premier Edouard Herriot, heading a left-center coalition, had been willing to go a long way towards reconciliation, although "until his death he did not cease to denounce the danger of a renaissance of German military might."[7] Hitler's rise to power produced a sudden revulsion of feeling against the eternal *Boche*, which was aggravated by border incidents at Kehl and by the incorporation of the SA into the auxiliary police. In French eyes these events constituted a clear violation of the Treaty of Versailles. At the same time the caretaker government of Joseph Paul-Boncour was replaced by Edouard Daladier. The new cabinet was dis-

---

1933–1941 (Berlin, 1942): E. M. Robertson, *Hitler's Pre-War Policy and Military Plans, 1933-1939*; and the articles by K. D. Bracher, "Das Anfangsstadium der Hitlerschen Aussenpolitik," in *Vierteljahreshefte für Zeitgeschichte* (1957), pp. 63-77; H. Lutz, "Foreign Policy in the Third Reich," in *Current History* (1955), pp. 222–235; Th. Vogelsang, ed., "Hitler's Brief an Reichenau vom 4. Dezember 1932," *Vierteljahreshefte für Zeitgeschichte* (1959), pp. 429-437. The best description of Hitler's attitude is perhaps the phrase with which he repudiated Schleicher's suggestion of a German-French-Russian combination: ". . . and I shall do the very opposite!" Norman Baynes, *The Speeches of Adolf Hitler, April 1922-August 1939* (London, 1942), p. 1001. Cf. also *infra*, p. 74.

[7]V. Michel Soulie, *La Vie politique d'Edouard Herriot* (Paris, 1962), p. 588ff. Unfortunately Herriot's memoirs *Jadis: D'une guerre à l'autre, 1914–1936* (Paris, 1952) are very sketchy for the year 1933 and yield little if any insight into Herriot's attitude towards the Four Power Pact.

couraged and hesitant. Unwilling to follow the clamor
of the Right for intervention, it could no longer continue the policy of concessions. A growing defensive
feeling appeared, and France began to lean more and
more on British support.[8]

In Great Britain the response was slower but more
far-reaching. To be sure, Labour papers such as the
London *Daily Herald* and the left wing *Manchester
Guardian* denounced Hitler from the very beginning,
but conservative and semi-official circles remained
uncommitted while Lord Rothermere's reactionary press
openly welcomed National Socialism as a defense
against Bolshevism. In Prime Minister MacDonald's
mind two objectives were dominant: to save the Disarmament Conference and to make substantial progress
towards alleviating the sufferings of the Great Depression. The mildly pro-German leaning of the British
government continued during the first month and a half
after Hitler's assumption of power, and it was not until late in March that the full impact of the change
was felt across the Channel.[9]

---

[8] British Ambassador Lord Tyrell's penetrating dis-
patches, BFP, IV, 266. Cf. also German Ambassador
Koester's analyses in GMF, D 675808 and almost daily
thereafter. J. M. d'Hoop "Frankreichs Reaktion auf
Hitler's Aussenpolitik 1933-1939" in *Geschichte in
Wissenschaft und Unterricht* (April 1946), pp. 211-222.
It is important to note that at the very moment of Hit-
ler's takeover France was without a government!

[9] For MacDonald's goals see BFP, IV, 290, 303.
British Public opinion was analyzed approximately
once a week by German Ambassador Hoesch in GMF,
D 675835ff. and by junior members of the embassy
like Bernstorff, GMF E 447112, E 447219. Cf. also
infra, p. 55, and Rolf Kieser, *Englands Appeasementpolitik und der Aufstieg des Dritten Reiches im Spie-*

Hitler's victory deeply disturbed the countries of the Little Entente: Czechoslovakia, Yugoslavia, and Rumania. During a conference in Belgrade on December 18-19, 1932, they had already decided to create a permanent council of their foreign ministers which was to meet three times a year and possess a permanent secretariat. Every new political treaty, every unilateral act changing the actual political situation, every economic agreement involving political consequences, was to be entered only with unanimous consent of the council. The disquieting news from Germany spurred them into quicker action, and on February 16, 1933, they drew up in Geneva the statute of a permanent "unified international organization" to put the previous agreement into practice by co-operating with respect to statutory, political, and economic affairs. In effect, they attempted to create a "fifth great power in Europe."[10]

---

gel der britischen Presse (1933—1939) (Winterthur, 1964), pp. 19-26, 36-40, who develops a triple division of the British press into the Establishment papers who were hostile to Hitler's internal but favorable to his foreign policy; the Left dailies who rejected Nazism categorically; and the Rothermere and Beaverbrook sheets who were tolerant if not well-disposed towards the "New Germany."

[10]The most detailed study of the Little Entente in the inter-war years is Victor Arnold's unpublished dissertation, "The Little Entente and the Revisionists" (Wisconsin, 1958), pp. 446ff. For a contemporary description, see Arnold Toynbee, *Survey of International Affairs*, 1933 (London, 1934), pp. 203-22. Gravelli suspected ulterior motives in the consolidation of the Little Entente: "It is a lie to maintain that the last treaty of alliance with its secret clauses [*sic!*] was concluded because the Little Entente was endangered. It was rather concluded to isolate Mussolini's policy which is directed towards the pacification of Europe." *Hitler*, p. 42.

Mussolini himself was not a little uneasy about Hitler's accession to power. The first enthusiasm over this new international success of Fascism soon wore off, and the Duce became aware of the need for taming Hitler's dynamic expansionism by small voluntary concessions before the latter would be strong enough to dictate his price. While publicly stressing the similarities of Fascism and National Socialism, Mussolini privately moved closer to the British point of view of making timely compromises, but of standing firm against any exorbitant demands.[11]

In view of the Four Power Pact, the most significant result of Hitler's victory consisted in the quickened pace of the Franco-Italian rapprochement, which it produced, although its first traces could already be detected in the fall of 1932. Hitherto the problems of Tunisia, the colonial settlement in fulfillment of the Treaty of London, the question of Italian immigrants into southern France, the successive waves of anti-Fascist refugees, and finally the naval rivalry had blocked any continued co-operation between the two

---

[11]Mussolini's numerous statements to this effect can be taken at face value. BFP, IV, 44. See also Baron Pompeo Aloisi's diary, which in the absence of Italian diplomatic documents possesses source value if used with discretion. *Journal*: 25 Juillet 1932-14 Juin 1936 (Paris, 1957). I. Kirkpatrick, *Mussolini*, p. 169 stresses the Duce's cowardly fear of National Socialism.

Naturally the Fascist press played up more to Hitler: "The momentous analogy between National Socialism and Fascism has, to be sure, escaped the French journalists, who continue to write that Fascism and National Socialism are two opposites, while they are rather the two standard bearers of the new Europe." Gravelli, *Hitler*, p. 83.

"Latin sisters." The ideological antagonism between the Third Republic and Fascism exacerbated the existing tension. On May 17, 1931, Mussolini had spoken defiantly: "Fascist Italy, strongly armed, poses the simple alternative: either precious friendship or implacable hostility!"[12]

Nevertheless, there had always been political leaders in France who desired a rapprochement with their southern neighbor. During Germany's temporary withdrawal from the Disarmament Conference, France felt isolated and suddenly awoke from her illusions about-collective security and began extending feelers towards Italy and Russia.[13] In the fall of 1932, Premier Herriot made a conciliatory speech on the Congress of the *Parti Radical Socialiste* in Toulouse. Henry Berenger, chairman of the Foreign Affairs Commission of the Senate, attended the Volta Congress and after his return dwelt with renewed fervor on the need for better Franco—Italian relations. Alie Bois, editor of the *Petit Parisien,* Charles Dupuy, Louis Gentizon and a number of other prominent journalists descended upon the Eternal City and began to strike a friendlier note towards Mussolini in their editorials.[14]

More important than these visits was the firm conviction of Joseph Paul-Boncour, for a short time

---

[12]As cited in Gaetano Salvemini, *Mussolini Diplomate,* p. 290.

[13]The result was a treaty of non—aggression with the Soviet Union which was ratified in May, 1933, by the Chamber with a vote of 520-0!

[14]Elizabeth Cameron, *Prologue to Appeasement* (Philadelphia, 1942), p. 29. Hubert Lagardelle, *Mission à Rome: Mussolini* (Paris, 1955), pp. 6-7. Baron Aloisi expressed skepticism at these methods, calling for "less words and more acts" to speed the rapprochement. *Journal,* p. 55 *passim.*

Premier and then Foreign Minister of France throughout 1933. He approached relations with Italy quite
realistically and was willing to make substantial concessions if he could secure co-operation in return. In
his memoirs he declared: "I have always been a warm
partisan of an entente with Italy, since I was convinced
that—more than just our proximity—an accord between
the Latin countries is a useful counterweight against
the Germanic and Anglo-Saxon powers in Western Europe."[15]

On December 18, 1932, Paul-Boncour nominated
Senator Henri de Jouvenel Ambassador Extraordinary to
the Quirinal. The foreign minister was convinced that
it would be best to send a politician, a man who had
been High Commissioner to Syria and Minister of Education, since he could act more independently and
stand a better chance than a career diplomat of breaking the ring of suspicion between the two countries.
The choice proved fortunate; Mussolini and de Jouvenel
soon established cordial relations, allowing the newly
appointed ambassador to make progress towards exe-
cuting Paul-Boncour's simple directive: "To fix a dur-
able entente, which will associate the two countries
for a long time." The major French and Italian dailies
were little impressed, however, by the newly estab-

---

[15]Joseph Paul-Boncour, *Entre deux guerres* (Paris,
1945), p. 338. For a more detailed statement of Paul-
Boncour's attitude towards Italy see Charles Serre,
ed., *Commission chargée d'enquêter sur les événe-
ments survenu en France de 1933 à 1945* (Paris,
1948), vol. III, pp. 790-3, where he asserted: "Preoccupied with Germany's attitude... because of Hitler's triumph in having been named Reich chancellor in
January, I saw as my principal object a rapprochement
with Italy." Paul-Boncour regarded Jouvenal as capable and hoped he would restore the tradition of French
diplomacy of such figures as Chateaubriand and Barrère.

lished intimacy and continued their nationalistic hate campaigns. De Jouvenel initiated a private and personal diplomacy, conducted in direct negotiations, man to man. Mussolini soon took a special liking to the flamboyant *bon-vivant*, especially since both agreed that an excess of egalitarianism was the fundamental weakness of the League.[16]

In the first days of March, Mussolini summoned the French ambassador for his official welcome reception in order to test French reaction towards his new plan for peace. De Jouvenel was surprised to hear his host suggest that they should not quibble over Franco-Italian differences, but rather concern themselves with a more general European settlement involving all the Great Powers. With great frankness and friendliness Mussolini broached the touchy subject of treaty revision, recommending some changes in the Polish corridor and in Hungary's frontiers. If some small concessions could be made to Germany now, the dangerous principle of revision could be limited and confined to a narrow application. The matter of disarmament was also briefly touched upon.[17]

---

[16]The most graphic, if not always reliable description of the tenure of de Jouvenel at the Palazzo Farnese is the account of his syndicalist friend Hubert Lagardelle, *Mission à Rome,* who attributed the rapprochement to the *grande peur* of Germany. More scholarly is R. Binion, *Defeated Leaders: The Political Fate of Caillaux, Jouvenel and Tradieu* (New York, 1960). Cf. Vl. d'Ormesson's article in the *Revue des Vivants* (Nov. 1935), p. 1687ff.

[17]There is no unanimity on the date of the conversation, but from Aloisi's evidence, March 2 seems most likely. The only eyewitness transcript was apparently made by Aloisi, pp. 77-80 in his *Journal*, which is borne out by the reports of the British and German Ambassadors in BFP, V, 37 and GFP, I, 68.

A professional diplomat would have been highly suspicious of such a broad offer, but de Jouvenel eagerly grasped the chance in order not to bypass the precious opportunity for effecting a quick rapprochement and making his appointment a success. A week later he wrote to his friend Emile Roche: "Concerning the negotiations here, it is no longer a matter of a Franco-Italian accord, but rather of a complete European settlement. My feeling is that one can make progress today better than tomorrow." Almost instantly he reported Mussolini's demarche to Paris and was soon encouraged to follow it up. The favorable response of de Jouvenel in the exploratory discussion induced Mussolini to put his ideas into writing. Their meeting constituted, after the vague allusion in the Turin speech, the first concrete move towards the launching of the Four Power Pact.[18]

The next step followed on March 4, when Mussolini jotted down a first draft. The exact circumstances surrounding this document are still shrouded in uncertainty, but what is known about its origin in summed up by British Ambassador Sir Ronald Graham and helps to explain the mystery: "I have no reason to doubt that the proposed pact was the work of the Duce's own hand. He is reported to have said that he required a short holiday and to have gone away himself in a small village in the hills not far from Rome whence he returned after a brief weekend with the draft in his own handwriting."[19] This evidence is supported by Salata's account and by Aloisi's diary.[20] It is further substantiated by such circumstantial proof as the dating

---

[18] Emile Roche, *Caillaux que j'ai connu* (Paris, 1949), p. 65.

[19] BFP, V, 45.

[20] Fr. Salata, *Il Patto Mussolini*, p. 23; P. Aloisi, *Journal*, p. 81.

of the draft, March 4; the place, Rocca della Cam-
minate, a castle which was Mussolini's favorite hideout; and his general habit of withdrawing and making
his decisions alone.[21] According to Francesco Jacomini, the first person to see the project was the permanent Undersecretary of State Fulvio Suvich, to whom
it was communicated the same day.[22]

Some of the motives in Mussolini's mind can be
inferred from an interview published on March 5 in the
Berliner Börsencourier. Invoking the statesman's
responsibility before God and describing the general
fear of a new war, the Duce asserted: "It [is] time to
move on from the armistice to peace. The armistice
has now lasted for fifteen years and we are still up
against the simple but terrible dilemma: to take up
arms once more or to conclude peace."[23] It seems
plausible that Mussolini was sincere in his desire for
peace at that time. Italy was not yet fully armed and
the economy could not have withstood the strains of a
modern war. In a speech before the Grand Council of
Corporations on March 9, the Duce re-emphasized his
peaceful intentions, without, however, so much as
hinting at his new plan.[24]

The last hurdle for the diplomatic launching of
the Four Power Pact was removed by Ramsay Mac-
Donald's frantic effort to save the tottering Disarmament Conference, which prompted him to travel to
Geneva via Paris and to continue on to Rome. The ill-

---

[21]For a touching description of Mussolini's personal habits, see his wife's published diary: Rachele
Mussolini, *La mia vita con Benito* (Verona, 1948), p.
119

[22]Fr. Jacomini, "Il Patto a quattro," p. 28.

[23]As cited in Luigi Villari, *Mussolini's Foreign
Policy*, p. 99.

[24]GFP, I, 109.

fated Conference had reopened on February 2, 1933,
only to be shaken severely by Japan's unexpected withdrawal from the League of Nations three weeks later.
A deadlock immediately developed between the French
demand for security, arms control, and a short-term
militia (which would emasculate the small but professional Reichswehr), and the German insistence on parity of armaments, already conceded in the Five Power
Declaration of December 11, 1932. Once again everything seemed lost. But the British stepped into the
breach and proposed drastic measures to avert a final
breakdown.[25]

Questioned in the House by Labour spokesman
Lansbury about the "hasty decision" to go to Geneva,
MacDonald spelled out the purpose of his trip on March
6: "At the present moment we think it a piece of work so
important that it should be done. Our purpose in going
to Geneva is to try and get some kind of agreement as
to how the Disarmament Conference can do its business
in the best way at the moment. There is no new policy.
We are going to try and use whatever influence we may
have to get the Disarmament Conference to a point
when agreement, although not reached, is well within
sight."[26] Two days earlier British Foreign Secretary

---

[25]On March 4, the British Cabinet had taken the
decision to attempt to save the Disarmament Conference on Anthony Eden's urgent recommendation. Cf.
London *Times*, March 11: "The Conference Appears
to be on the Verge of Breakdown"; *Deutsche Allgemeine Zeitung*, March 14: "The Conference has Col-
lapsed"; *Völkischer Beobachter*, March 16: "Awaiting
the Fiasco of the Disarmament Conference." For the
French thesis see Colonel Jaques Minart, *Le Drame
du désarmement français: la revanche allemande
1918-1939* (Paris, 1959), pp. 40-66. Cf. *infra*, p. 55.
[26]House of Commons, *Debates*, vol. 275, pp. 220-
223. A. C. Temperley, *The Whispering Gallery of Eu-*

John Simon had denied to German Ambassador Hoesch that Britain was about to propose a five-power conference. It was only the wish of His Majesty's Government to contribute to the resolution of the present difficulties as the good friend of all concerned. Of course, the possibility of five-power talks in Geneva could not be excluded entirely. But he left the German diplomat with the distinct impression that the "British really went to Geneva without any programme." On March 9, Prime Minister Ramsay MacDonald and his Foreign Secretary John Simon boarded the train to Paris.[27]

The mood in the French capital was irritated and uneasy, although no clear course of action against Hitler had yet emerged from the anxious discussions. Public opinion had been shocked by Nazi excesses, and even the former advocates of closer co-operation with their neighbor across the Rhine suddenly rediscovered the dangerous depths of the Germanic soul. Ambassador Roland Koester warned Neurath from Paris: "I cannot deny that the thought of a forceful preventive strike against the threatening danger is gaining ground. ... The conviction that a German-Italian bloc is forming could create a situation here which will subject

---

rope (London, 1938), p. 234: "We were by February reduced to the desultory work of some interminable committees and failure stared us in the face. In these depressing circumstances the British delegation made the last effort. Our task was to prepare a complete Convention *with the figures filled in.*" The British were caught between their 'guilt complex' towards Germany and their traditional entente with France. Since they understood both countries' arguments only too well, they were in the best position to offer a compromise which might save the conference.

[27] Neurath circular to all embassies GMF, H 17604; Hoesch report, H 176405; Nadolny's reaction, H 176411.

Franco-German relations to a test, like we have not experienced since the occupation of the Ruhr."[28]

The conversations between the British and French Ministers at the Quai d'Orsay on March 10 reflected the anxiety and the futility of the Western efforts to meet the crisis. While MacDonald pressed for some kind of agreement to save the Disarmament Conference, Daladier pictured the fear of the French people, especially of those *départments* which had suffered so terribly during the first war. The British Prime Minister replied with the telling statement that "he was out to get peace and meant to use whatever method seemed calculated to give the best results." MacDonald denied categorically that he was planning a four, five, or six-power conference. He merely intended to exchange views privately with some of the important people, and was therefore willing to continue his pilgrimage to Geneva.[29]

The stage was now set for Mussolini to explore the British and German reactions to the idea of the Four Power Pact, before the public launching of the proposal. In order not to be rebuffed, he instructed Baron Aloisi, the Italian representative at the League and his chief of the Cabinet of Foreign Affairs, in general terms of the purpose and content of the draft. Aloisi was to sound out MacDonald and Nadolny, the head of the German delegation, and procure their general assent before the Duce would formally begin negotiations in Rome. Aloisi met with MacDonald and Simon for several discussions between March 11 and 24. Skilfully the Italian delegate prepared the ground for Musso-

---

[28] GMF, H 176428. Koester further reported that "In the meeting yesterday the British seem to have brought up the suggestion of a five power conference, but the French rejected the idea categorically." Cf. text below.

[29] BFP, IV, 290. GFP, I, 46.

lini's project without disclosing any details of the plan. Aloisi strongly seconded Graham's suggestion for a trip to Rome by the British Prime Minister in order to discuss the tangled issues of German equality, French security and the fate of the Disarmament Conference with Mussolini in person. He intimated that these problems should be treated outside the stifling atmosphere of Geneva and that they actually were a four-power matter. Piece by piece he extracted from the British affirmative answers to some questions of boundary revision and greater equality for Germany. Although Sir John repeatedly interjected the French reluctance for any concessions, the wily Italian goaded MacDonald into the assertion that "in fact, a four-power meeting was the only way of settling these questions."[30]

---

[30]BFP, IV, 293, 297, 301. Mussolini also instructed Aloisi not to reveal too much of the plan to allow for preliminary negotiations with the Germans. During the Geneva conversations the Italian delegate also pledged support for the British disarmament plan, which had been drawn up by Whitehall and which eventually became known as the MacDonald Plan. BFP, IV, 284-285 contain the first outlines of the proposal. The plan was officially launched by MacDonald on March 16 in a stirring speech before the plenum of the Disarmament Conference. The British Prime Minister proposed concrete arms figures and attempted to remove the debate from the realm of nationalistic oratory to the discussion of details. He was successful insofar as his initiative gave the Conference a new lease on life, but even his sincere gesture could not stave off its final collapse. GMF, H 176434 and Anthony Eden's memoirs, *Facing the Dictators* (Boston, 1962), pp. 35-41. Cf. also A. C. Temperley, *The Whispering Gallery of Europe*, pp. 234-233 for a thorough exposition of the MacDonald plan by the chief military advisor to the United Kingdom delegation.

At the same time Aloisi dealt with Nadolny to prevent the Germans from becoming suspicious of the
Anglo-Italian discussions.   Before his first meeting
with the British he hinted to the German delegate that
"one should ponder, if one should not decide for an
interim solution, such as the postponement of the conference, since otherwise one would have to fear its
complete collapse."   On March 12 Aloisi finally revealed his hand, telling Nadolny that "he had proposed
to MacDonald his idea . . . that the decisive questions
should be removed from the Conference and be posed
for decision directly with the cabinets involved (Germany, France, Italy, and England). . . . Meanwhile the
Conference could be kept busy with minor matters.
MacDonald had asked him to contact [Nadolny] regarding this suggestion."   Caught by surprise, the
German ambassador immediately inquired if the demarche had Mussolini's approval. When the question
was answered affirmatively, Nadolny declared that
"the proposal did not make any sense to him at first
glance," but that he "wanted to think it over." Although Nadolny was skeptical about the idea, he reported it to the Wilhelmstrasse, which shared his
doubts. Neurath thought it utopian to believe that the
British would support Germany in the concrete question of arms material, but he was cautious enough not
to reject the offer out of hand. Neurath only stressed,
as did Nadolny in a second conversation with Aloisi,
that Germany would under no circumstances be tied
down to the status quo forever and that it had to receive full equality in armaments.   Clearly both the
British and the Germans had misjudged the scope of
Mussolini's proposal and had shown little enthusiasm.
But they had not reacted violently against it, and the
Duce refused to be discouraged by the inconclusive
result of the first skirmish.[31]

---

[31]GMF, H 176415, H 176422, H 176426; H 176431,
H 176438 *passim* and GFP, I, 78, 79ff.

In order not to alarm the French unduly, Mac-
Donald telephoned Ambassador Lord Tyrell in Paris and
asked Daladier to come to Geneva for a last exchange
of views to present a common front to Mussolini.[32] The
French Premier was reluctant to leave the capital, but
he was sufficiently alive to the danger of excessive
British concessions to Mussolini to hurry to Geneva
and commit MacDonald to a clear line. Upon British
assurances that they were only out to establish closer
co-operation between Paris, London, and Rome against
Hitler, Daladier expressed "in general his entire approval of the Rome visit and sincerely trusted that it
would have a happy result." When MacDonald and
Simon wearily climbed aboard two salon cars on March
17 in Geneva, they fervently hoped that this unprecedented step would somehow overcome the diplomatic
crisis. At most, they expected a fresh disarmament initiative from Mussolini, but they did not foresee its
form, nor did they know that the Duce was ready to
launch the Four Power Pact.[33]

---

[32]BFP, IV, 303, 306, 310. On March 17 MacDonald
and Simon also had two long conversations with Polish
Foreign Minister Josef Beck and his Czech colleague
Edouard Beneš, in which the British statesmen tried to
reassure them that "no commitments would be taken [in
Rome], but that there would be time for each government to learn the general policy in mind of the other."
Beneš and Beck stressed the danger of any revision of
the peace treaties, while MacDonald insisted on the
harmlessness of his visit to Mussolini.

[33]BFP, IV, 310. In the light of the preceding analysis, there seems to be no validity in Furnia's blanket
generalization about the origin of the Four Power Pact,
Prologue to Appeasement (Washington, 1960): "Here,
of course, we encounter a cardinal objective of British
diplomacy which runs like a thread through British
policy during the nineteen thirties. This objective

The origin of the four-power concept and the exploratory moves accompanying the diplomatic birth of the pact were as haphazardly opportunistic and yet as predetermined as the character of its creator, Mussolini: "The man who had committed, to be sure errors and sins, but who had been all of one piece, mono-

was the Four Power Pact. MacDonald believed that, if the four Western Powers could be grouped together in a cooperative relationship, not only could the Franco-German difference be settled, but Soviet Russia could be isolated from the councils of Western Europe." Pp. 65-66.

"Mussolini has been given credit for the original conception of the Four Power Pact, but British documents prove otherwise" (p. 66), or "With the evidence available in British and American documents, there should be little doubt remaining that the genesis of the Four Power Pact originated with the MacDonald government" (p. 80).

Not only does Furnia's strong anti-appeasement bias make the interpretation of MacDonald seem highly one-sided, but his historical scholarship appears to be open to serious doubt. Analyzing his "evidence" one finds that he relied primarily upon dispatches of American diplomats who were not involved in the negotiations and whose testimony is little better than hearsay. He does not consult the German diplomatic documents readily available in English translation, and even in the British documents there is no shred of evidence to support Furnia's contention. The *British White Paper* (the most detailed summary of the negotiations from the British side) contains no hint of a MacDonald initiative. The memorandum BFP, IV, 301, cited in a footnote by Furnia, proves, if anything, only Aloisi's skill in manipulating MacDonald. It is impossible to conclude from such "evidence" that MacDonald was

lithic... strong, self-assured, intelligent to the point
of almost being a genius, gave way to a far more complex personality, full of contradictions, of unanswered
and probably unanswerable questions."[34] Yet despite
the enigma one can suggest a few lines of motivation.
Benito Mussolini was incurably vainglorious and
wanted to become the savior of Europe, having already
been hailed as the regenerator of Italy. An anecdote
told by Francesco Jacomini lends support to this interpretation. When this diplomat brought the original of
the treaty to the Duce for his signature, the latter made
him leave it and procure another copy, since Mussolini
wanted to give the original to Edda, his favorite daugh-
ter, "as a record of that European organization which
I have initiated today in Rome."[35]

Fused with the personal motive was Mussolini's
desire for the greatness of Italy. Poland was just below and Italy barely above the fine dividing line be-

---

the principal, and deliberate author of the Four Power
Pact.

The British Prime Minister did make some general statements to the British press before his departure from Geneva: "It is not a matter of negotiating
an accord with the Head of the Italian government, but
of seeking to assure peace and mutual trust in Europe.
It is a question of looking how one can constitute a
group of powers of good will in search of easing the
situation...." As cited in Fr. Salata, *Il Patto Mussolini*, p. 34. Does this vague statement represent an
unequivocal announcement of the dominant theme of
British foreign policy in the inter-war years? Cf. *infra*,
p. 55ff.

[34]Laura Fermi describing her experience when
working on her biography of the Duce. *Mussolini* (Chicago, 1960), pp. v-vi.

[35]Fr. Jacomini, "Il Patto a quattro," p. 27.

tween the small and the great powers. Through the
Four Power Pact, Italy's place among the directors of
Europe's fate would be permanently assured. By an
almost Bismarckian expedient, Rome would no longer
have to chose between allegiance to Paris or to Berlin,
but together with London it could exert a decisive influence in the direction of moderation and peace. The
balance of power would be restored, and Italy could
resume that subtle game of blackmail for which she
was justly famous.[36]

Another compelling factor for the launching of the
Four Power Pact was Mussolini's very real apprehension of war. A Franco-British rapprochement would
leave Italy in Hitler's arms and might encourage General Weygand's aggressive designs in Paris. The consolidation of the Little Entente threatened to stop Italian expansion in the Balkans. With Hitler's victory
the dreaded *Anschluss* became a concrete possibility.
And, above all, Europe might once more be split into
two hostile blocs of powers and a new pre-war situation be created.[37]

---

[36]S. William Halperin, *Mussolini and Italian Fascism* (Princeton, 1964) even calls a subheading: "Using
Hitler for the Purposes of Blackmail, 1933-1935," p.
74. According to Gravelli, "Mussolini wants a Europe
which is in balance, a Europe in which no victors and
vanquished, rulers and ruled can be distinguished. An
entente with Germany has to go hand in hand with an
understanding with France, and an entente with France
cannot be entered without an understanding with Nazi
Germany. Only then will Europe enjoy tranquillity,
when the peace between the four Western Powers will
be restored, and they possess equal rights and duties
in the life of the European nations." *Hitler*, p. 21.

[37]The fear of war was the most prominent argument in Mussolini's arsenal of persuasion, whenever

The final force which guided Mussolini's hand in proposing the Four Power Pact was his political realism, which demanded the emasculation of the League and its replacement with a Great Power directorate. Moreover, his initiative would bring the frozen diplomatic fronts into motion again and allow the waters of change to flow freely—as long as they would benefit Italy by providing a safe outlet for Fascist activism. At the same time Mussolini attempted to channel these waters lest he unleash a flood which might wash Fascism and his rule along with it, leaving only debris in its wake. This dual purpose of the Four Power Pact was encapsulated in the Duce's earlier dictum: "The dilemma is this: treaty revision or a new war."[38]

---

he wanted to gain a new concession from the Germans. It seems to have been the typical mixture of cunning and sincerity which characterized the diplomacy of the Duce also on other occasions. GFP, I, 109, 120; Cf. also Fr. Jacomini, "Il Patto a quattro," p. 41, and P. Aloisi, *Journal*, p. 81f.

[38] As quoted by Villari, *Mussolini's Foreign Policy*, p. 5.

Chapter III

THE INITIAL NEGOTIATIONS

URING THE LONG AND DREARY negotiations for
the Four Power Pact, Mussolini proved a more
skillful diplomat than one might have expected from
his journalistic and demagogic past. He delighted in
the task of mediating between the opposing French and
German views and must be given considerable credit
for the final settlement. The decision to restrict Italy's
role to reconciling the extremes rather than pressing
his own wishes amounted to a sacrifice of the Duce's
personal vanity, but it produced fortunate results in
the long run. "Once Mussolini had made his proposal
... he stepped aside and allowed the other three powers to come to an agreement without interference on
his own part." Although the spotlight of international
attention focused on London, Paris and Berlin, the Duce
was in a better position to urge the other governments
to accept the compromises than if he had been more
directly involved. In dealing with the French, Mussolini showed himself surprisingly conciliatory; with the
British there was more common ground but less intuitive
rapport; even with the Germans, the most stubborn partners, Mussolini was successful by dealing personally

with Hitler through telephone, letter, and special messenger.[1]

Something of Mussolini's shrewdness is revealed in his method of initiating the actual negotiations for the Four Power Pact. Having sounded out the three prospective participants in informal conversations during the first two weeks of March 1933, the Duce formally proposed the Four Power Pact to the Germans on the fourteenth of the same month. But even then he shied away from public disclosure of his initiative and the French journalists, usually so suspicious of any Italo-German plots, did not hint at the possibility of such a move, while the British public similarly seems to have been in the dark.[2] The reason for the clandestine procedure was Mussolini's calculation that by informing Germany first he could procure Hitler's acceptance before the pact would be subjected to the crossfire of French and British criticism. By such a show of special confidence, the Führer would be more inclined to favor the project and Mussolini would be protected from unwelcome surprise moves from Berlin while negotiating with Paris and London.[3]

---

[1]FRUS, p. 422. Francesco Salata goes too far in praising Mussolini's accomplishments as a diplomat, since the very flexibility and resourcefulness which made him a successful negotiator made him too unsteady, too moody, and limited his trustworthiness. *Il Patto Mussolini*, p. 136f.

[2]The most precise summary from the British point of view is BFP, V, 216, published as *British White Paper* on June 8 (Cmd. 4342).

[3]The best accounts from the German side are the circular written by Secretary of State Bernhard von Bülow on April 20, GMF, D 676100, and Hassell's extensive analysis of the negotiations in GMF, E 447221.

Immediately after his return from a briefing session with Mussolini, Signor Cerruti, the Italian ambassador to Berlin, formally proposed the Four Power Pact to German Foreign Minister Neurath. After a general *tour d'horizon* in which he vividly portrayed the strength of the French and Polish armaments, the danger of a preventive war, and the impending collapse of the Disarmament Conference, Cerruti presented the original draft of the pact, explaining that in order to meet MacDonald's wish of revamping the moribund Conference "Mussolini had drafted a plan which, in his opinion, would be calculated, if the four principal powers could agree on it, to bring about a considerable *detente* in Europe and ultimately also satisfy the desire existing in all quarters for peaceful development."[4]

In simplest terms, the Four Power Pact was a "Political Pact of Understanding and Cooperation Between the Four Western Powers," Italy, France, Britain and Germany. This object was defined more precisely in the first article. Mussolini spoke of an "effective policy of cooperation" in order to maintain the peace in the spirit of the Kellogg Pact and the 'No-Force-Pact.'"[5] The four powers were engaged to act "in such a way that this peace policy, if necessary, will be adopted by others." So far the proposal seemed perfectly innocuous, and many observers were, indeed, deceived by the pacific language. But the failure to mention the League of Nations in the first Article, and the hint at possible Great Power coercion in the last phrase implied a return to the idea of a Great Power directorate. Although referring to the earlier treaties

---

[4]Memorandum by Neurath, March 14, GFP, I, 83.

[5]This treaty was identical with the Five Power Declaration of December 11, 1932, assuring Germany parity of arms. Cf. *supra*, p. 14n.

of the 1920's and using the phraseology of Geneva,
Article One could be (and was frequently) regarded as
the formal restoration of the old-fashioned Concert of
Europe.[6]

The specific content of this Great Power framework was elucidated in Articles Two and Three, where
the principles of the revision of the peace treaties
within the League of Nations and the grant of equality of rights to Germany in case of the failure of the
Disarmament Conference were openly set forth.[7] The
other vanquished powers, Austria, Hungary and Bulgaria, were to be treated in a similar fashion. These
two suggestions were loaded with political dynamite.
They would mean the end of the French system of alliances and of French military hegemony over Europe.
Revision would allow the territorial verdict of Versailles to be lifted, and German equality of arms would
undermine France's military superiority on the Continent—upon which her system of alliances rested.[8]

Article Four was equally provocative. Mussolini

---

[6]The original Italian draft is in GFP, I, pp. 162-3.
For a synoptic comparison with subsequent texts, see
the Appendix, col. i. In *France Europe and the Two
World Wars* (New York, 1961), p. 236f., René Albrecht-
Carrié stresses this idea.

[7]The inclusion of the reference to the League represented the fruit of the exploratory discussions between Mussolini and Jouvenel in early March and it
did not agree with the general spirit of the rest of the
proposal. Cf. *supra*, pp. 26-27.

[8]The dangerous implications of these clauses were
immediately recognized by *L'Europe Nouvelle*, who denounced it as "codified insecurity" and warned that it
"constitutes a regression, a return to the unconcealed
rule of brutal force, and the extinction of hope." March
25, 267f.

suggested that the four powers should adopt a "common line of conduct in all political and non-political, European and extra-European questions, as well as with regard to the sphere of colonies." This clause was aimed at restoring the mandates to Germany and giving Italy a free hand in Abyssinia. Here, Great Britain would potentially be the chief sufferer. The duration of the agreement was fixed at ten years, with a provision for automatic renewal for the same length of time. Finally the pact was to be registered with the Secretariat of the League of Nations.[9]

To nobody's particular surprise, Germany warmly welcomed the proposal. In an *aide-mémoire* for the Italian ambassador, probably drafted by Neurath and approved by Hitler himself, the plan was called "an inspired conception which might afford a solution to the difficulties of the present political situation." If the wording of Article Two on revision should be sharpened a bit, and if German equality in Article Three would be given immediate practical expression "the German Government could declare its agreement with the other provisions of the draft without further reservations."[10]

The German ambassador to the Quirinal, Ulrich von Hassell, agreed with the positive evaluation in a

---

[9]A howl of protest arose in London over the colonial clause. The *Daily Herald* led the attack with the headline: "BRITISH COLONIES FOR GERMANY? Premier's bait to Hitler to join new pact." March 22.

[10]Hitler's attitude towards the Four Power Pact is examined in some detail by John Davis, *Hitler and the Versailles Settlement*, pp. 109-115, and more generally pp. 150-162. The *aide-mémoire* of March 15 remained despite all second thoughts of the professional diplomats the basic German policy towards the Four Power Pact. GFP, I, 95; GMF, D 675749.

long private letter to Neurath: "I think one cannot doubt that the pact, as Mussolini has envisaged it, would be of the largest and the most pleasant importance for us." For the first time a concrete scheme for closer co-operation between the four west-European powers had been proposed for negotiation. The restrictive influence of the small French satellites would be thrown off in Italy's and Germany's interest. The control of economic and political decision-making was placed in the hands of a directorate, in which the balance of power would operate in Germany's favor. Hassell was pleased about the "moral victory" which even a discussion of revision and equality would represent in the eyes of world opinion. But he was not blind to the dangers of an emasculation of the proposal, of the possibility of a Franco-Italian bilateral understanding at Germany's expense, and of the probable disapproval of the Soviet Union. These drawbacks could only be overcome if the pact were used to strengthen the "inner relationship" between Berlin and Rome and by closer economic co-operation in central Europe. But considering all the pros and cons, Germany should at least negotiate over the proposal.[11]

Foreign Minister Neurath and the Wilhelmstrasse were less enthusiastic about the Four Power Pact. In several memoranda and discussions with the Italian ambassador Cerruti, Neurath and Bülow criticized the project severely. Skeptical of the chances of approval for the pact, and doubtful of Italian steadfastness in supporting the German claims, the German Foreign Office feared the possibility of a common front of the Western powers against Germany and was hesitant to limit its freedom of action. Secretary of State Bülow ob-

---

[11]GFP, I, 87, 98, 101, 102, 109 and GMF, D 675773, D 675777. In his letter Hassell gave a cogent analysis of the pre-history of the pact.

jected mainly to the link between treaty revision and
the Covenant of the League, since the famous Article
XIX had proved utterly ineffective in the past. Perhaps
the wording could be changed to: revision should be
accomplished "through mutual agreement with the co-
operation of the organs of the League"——a slight but
important change of emphasis. He similarly welcomed
the idea of German equality, but he insisted on its
immediate practical application. Typically enough,
the Wilhelmstrasse sought to strengthen all sections
favorable to Germany, while weakening all restrictions
included to pacify the French.[12]

The Italian diplomats tried their best to dispel
German doubts and hesitations. Mussolini, Cerruti,
Aloisi, and Suvich kept up a steady fire to impress
Berlin with the attractiveness of the pact. The Italian
ambassador assured Bülow that the duration could be
shortened to seven years in order not to perpetuate restrictions on rearmament unduly. Revision would be
carried out by the Four Powers and merely confirmed
by the League. Any further German objections should
be clothed into the form of amendments and they would
be taken into account during later discussions. The
Duce stressed to Hassell that his foremost aim had
been to grant Germany a respite, a breathing spell for
rearmament without interference from the West. He
had intended "on the one hand to give France the al-
legedly needed security force or deprive her of this

---

[12]GFP, I, 84, 88, 95, 115. In answer to Hassell's
letter Neurath stated the reservations of the German
foreign office in detail. GMF, D 675784. Cf. also the
instructions to Dirksen in Moscow of March 28, which
link the Four Power Pact to the "truce of God" pursued
by Britain and France in 1931-1932. GMF, D 675853.
Nadolny also remained skeptical and was willing to regard the pact "only as a last resort." GMF, D 675761.

pretext, and on the other hand to have the two basic principles of revision and equality of armament officially recognized and established by the four leading powers." Suvich reiterated to Hassell that the extraordinary anxiety of the moment had to be dispelled somehow, and that the Duce intended to use the trump which Hitler's victory had dealt him to press for revision, German parity, and the resumption of Italy's traditional position as mediator and arbitrator of European affairs.[13]

For the time being the Wilhelmstrasse had to be content with these profuse assurances. In order to make believe that Germany had received the pact at the same time as England and France, Hassell and Mussolini enacted a diplomatic comedy, which was rehearsed and performed so well that the deception came off. Preliminary assent had been secured from the Germans, although the going had been tougher than Mussolini had expected. Now the Duce had to test his diplomatic wile against a more formidable opponent, the British. The second round of negotiations was about to begin with MacDonald's widely publicized visit to Rome.[14]

Hope, fear, and anger heralded the British Prime Minister's trip. Scores of rumors about four, five or six—power conferences swept through the European press, and MacDonald's recent announcement of a new, comprehensive plan for disarmament was almost submerged in the wild speculations about the result of the meeting between the two ex-Socialist prime ministers.[15]

---

[13]GFP, I, 87, 95, 98; GMF, D 675773, D 675777.
[14]GFP, I, 101.
[15]The more moderate papers looked forward to MacDonald's visit with hope (London *Times*, *Deutsche Allgemeine Zeitung*, *Le Temps*, *New York Times*, *Vossische Zeitung*, and even the rabid *Völkische Beo-*

The external course of the visit belied all apprehensions: the pleasant flight from Genoa in a seaplane
piloted by the dashing General Balbo; the arrival at
Ostia on an enchanting spring morning; the spectacular
drive up the Tiber valley to the Eternal City; the colorful receptions by Pope, King, and the Roman people;
the splendid banquets and the crowded press conferences. The welcome was genuine, and Rome had dressed
in all her charms to assist Mussolini in the art of persuasion. [16]

According to the Havas report, Ramsay Mac-
Donald and Sir John Simon were confronted with the
draft for the Four Power Pact for the first time in the
state limousine immediately after their landing at
Ostia. It had been officially transmitted to London,
Paris, and Berlin during the same morning of March 18.

---

bachter). A tone of honest admiration for the tireless
efforts of the Prime Minister to ensure peace was evident throughout, although the degrees of skepticism
about concrete results varied widely. On the other
hand, apprehension was marked in the British Labour
press, as in the London *Daily Herald*, and in the French
Right and in the pro-League organs such as the *Journal
des Débats, l'Europe Nouvelle* and *L'Illustration*. Only
the Tory *Daily Telegraph* supported MacDonald's trip
unreservedly and professed to expect momentous results.

[16]For the external course of the visit see GFP, I,
109, 120; BFP, V, 45; and Aloisi, *Journal*, pp. 97-100.
The possibility of an extension of MacDonald's trip
to Geneva to include Rome and a meeting with Mussolini was mentioned as *ballon d'essai* on March 9 (in a
leader in the London *Times*), and when the British Public showed no particular opposition to the idea Mac-
Donald decided in favor of a *rendezvous* with the Duce.
GMF, D 675766, H 176420.

The British visitors were taken completely by surprise, although they had been vaguely prepared by Aloisi in their previous discussions in Geneva. They hardly had time for a cursory reading before their arrival in Rome. And yet MacDonald and Simon did not reject the project out of hand, since both had been moving into a similar direction before encountering Mussolini's proposal.[17]

Ramsay MacDonald's devotion to the ideals of the League of Nations had been above any question. Together with Herriot he had fathered the first Geneva protocol in 1924 and, once again in power in 1929, he had championed a reasonable compromise on reparations. In his comments on the King's speech on October 28, 1930, he reaffirmed the cabinet's adherence to the ideals of Geneva: "In foreign policy we are laying emphasis on arbitration and disarmament, for only by arbitration and disarmament are you going to establish peace."[18] But in the early thirties he became increas-

---

[17]The biography by B. Sacks, *James Ramsay MacDonald in Thought and action* (Albuquerque, 1952) is rather thin on foreign policy for 1933. Cf. its review by Paul Knaplund in the *Saturday Review* (May, 1950), which calls MacDonald "a Victorian Liberal" and a "conservative, human, bewildered and lonely man." An earlier work by L. M. Weir is very bitter, blasting MacDonald and Simon as "harlequins on their way to Rome." *The Tragedy of Ramsay MacDonald* (London, 1938). Eden states in *Facing the Dictators* that MacDonald had agreed to a four-power meeting before his departure from Geneva, but the memoirs are to be treated with care since Eden resented strongly what he considered MacDonald's betrayal of his own "MacDonald Plan" for disarmament, p. 35f. For a kinder assessment of the British Prime Minister see A. C. Temperley, *The Whispering Gallery of Europe.*, p. 240ff.

[18]House of Commons, *Debates*, vol.244, cols.22-32.

ingly frustrated with the ineffectiveness of the League's methods and procedures which proved bitterly wanting when confronted with the problems of the Great Depression and the reintegration of Germany into the European system. "Until the position of Germany as a factor, as an element in world trade . . . not only of Germany itself . . . but . . . as a factor of the British condition, is understood and settled, there is no recovery for us."

In order to supplement the organs of the League, MacDonald said: "We must strive to get the [differences] removed by mutual assistance by getting the great nations of Europe more and more to apply the spirit of the Covenant of the League of Nations to come together in a great council of those who help and of those who wish to help. We shall certainly continue to cooperate and use our good offices for peace."[19] When reminiscing on the ephemeral success of Lausanne, the British Prime Minister struck a different chord: "I am certain . . . that if, before the politicians had met in Lausanne, experts had been put in charge of the conflicting interests . . . we should still have been sitting at Lausanne. . . . The reason is that the politicians . . . the direct representatives of this government, and the other government, brought face to face, will much more quickly find a recommendation . . . knowing the tremendous importance of getting an agreement."[20] Although still firmly holding to the ideals of the League of Nations, by early 1933 MacDonald was casting about for a new method of combatting the

---

[19]MacDonald's report on the result of the Lausanne Conference in House of Commons, *Debates*, vol. 248, cols. 1132-1147. Cf. also the other debates on the King's Address in vol. 229, cols. 47, 66-67, and in vol. 259, cols. 61-71.

[20]House of Commons, *Debates*, vol. 272, cols. 35-38.

European crisis. His awareness of the importance of the German problem, his preference for Great Power cooperation, and his liking for personal diplomacy made him receptive to Mussolini's panacea. But at no time did he see the Four Power Pact as conflicting with the spirit of Geneva. Rather, MacDonald viewed the pact as complementing and strengthening the League by creating a more efficient machinery through which its ideals could be realized in practice.[21]

Although he has been perhaps even more maligned than his Prime Minister, Foreign Secretary Sir John Simon judged Mussolini's proposal in the light of a sincere pacifism which had induced him to resign his cabinet post during the World War. Speaking in the Committee of Supply on February 27, just two days after Japan's withdrawal from the League, he defined the government's attitude towards the crisis: "There

---

[21]Dwight E. Lee in *Ten Years: The World on the Way to War, 1930-1940* (Boston, 1942), p. 46, gives the most plausible explanation of the apparent paradox of MacDonald's acceptance of the Four Power Pact: "MacDonald was only too glad to cooperate with Mussolini since his proposal contained just the right mixture of idealism and realism."

The misleading interpretation which credits MacDonald with the authorship of the Four Power Pact, probably stems from some rumors current at Geneva. Moffat, Chief of the Division of Western European Affairs wrote in FRUS, pp. 396-8: "The idea of a four power grouping seems to have originated not with Mussolini, but with MacDonald. Prior to the latter's departure for Rome he discussed the idea in confidence at Geneva, notably with certain Polish officials of the League Secretariat, who subsequently told Mr. Gibson about it. According to these informants. . . ." Cf. GMF, E 447295.

is one great difference between 1914 and now, and it
is this: in no circumstances will this government
authorize this country to be a party in the struggle."
But rather than deserting the League now, Simon declared: "I have shown the House and the Country, and,
I think, I may ... show the world that this government
and this country really do desire to see what they can
do effectively for the purpose of promoting the position
of the League and the peace in this world." It is, of
course, impossible to fathom the hidden depths of Mac-
Donald's and Simon's souls. But whatever the unin-
tended results of their actions, one can safely assert
that they flowed from a passionate committment to
peace.[22]

In the first, somewhat cold and formal conversa-

---

[22]House of Commons, *Debates*, vol. 275, cols. 50-
59, 152-156. Cf. also Sir John Simon's memoirs, *Retrospect* (London, 1952). They contain no reference to
the Four Power Pact, but from his general attitude towards Germany one can infer that he sincerely supported the scheme. Simon has fared ill with the historians
and journalists who condemn him for his appeasement
policies and who call his tenure at Whitehall an un-
relieved failure. A. L. Kennedy, one of the editors of
the London *Times,* judged "Lord Simon as Foreign Secretary," *Contemporary Review* (March 1954), pp.136-
141, simply: "As foreign secretary he totally failed."
Stephen Watson, *History Today* (April 1955), p. 234ff.,
in an article on the British Lord Chancellors remarked,
"He seems in retrospect to have been born for the Great
Seal," but found no kind words for his foreign policy.
A. L. Rowse, *Appeasement: A Study in Political Decline, 1933-1939* (New York, 1963) draws a biting character sketch of Simon, stressing his unlimited ambition, his punctiliousness, and his unpopularity as a
fellow of All Souls, pp. 16-20. Martin Gilbert and

tion on March 18 the British accepted Mussolini's proposal in principle. The visitors could only agree that the international situation was highly explosive and could best be dealt with by friendly co-operation between the four Western powers. Simon was delighted that the thorny issues of German arms parity and revision were to be handled within the already existing framework of the League, and that France would receive greater security in return for these concessions. Mac-Donald emphasized the resemblance of Mussolini's scheme to his own disarmament proposals and expressed the hope that he would be able to procure French adherence on his return trip to Paris.[23]

After these first soundings had produced a substantial measure of agreement, the conversation turned to concrete examples of probable areas of revision. Mussolini was adamant on the Polish corridor, calling it one of the "great mistakes" of Versailles. According to the British Foreign Secretary, all nations had two obligations under the Covenant: "Firstly to respect treaties, and secondly to recognize that treaties were not of perpetual character. These two points were not irreconcilable." But on the touchy subject of revision, when applied to concrete cases, Simon raised the first objection. Article Two would have to be redrafted to include the observance of already existing treaties,

---

Richard Gott, *The Appeasers* (Boston, 1963), pp. 5ff. merely add a few strokes to the general condemnation. A. C. Temperley, *The Whispering Gallery of Europe*, pp. 216-220 makes a sincere attempt to judge the Foreign Secretary fairly, but a more balanced evaluation of both MacDonald and Simon remains to be written.

[23]BFP, V, 44. In MacDonald's opinion Daladier was more "liberal minded" than most other French statesmen and, therefore, the chances for acceptance were not too bad. For the Havas report see GMF, D 675791.

and therefore to anticipate French criticism. Mussolini, the host, rejected this request by pointing out
that such a reference would have to be very vague to
be accepted by Hitler, and would then lose all value
for the French.[24]

The next point on the agenda was German equality
of rights. The Duce promised not to allow Berlin to
push its demands too far in order not to raise too many
well-founded fears. The British guests then inquired
about the possibility of enlarging the number of participants in the directorate, to which their host replied
that it would be better to keep the body small in order
not to make it too unwieldly. In conclusion the Duce
restated the fundamental purpose of his proposal:
"Firstly, it would guarantee peace; and secondly, it
eliminated from the European scene the idea of opposing *blocs* of powers. The sensation of isolation which
some powers now felt could be eradicated. His project
had many points of resemblance with the settlement of
Locarno, especially in putting Germany on the same
footing as the other powers." This argument fell on
willing ears, and the British visitors later used it repeatedly to defend the Four Power Pact at home.[25]

The second day of conversations, though conducted in a more intimate atmosphere, showed a sober
and critical attitude on the part of the British. The effect of Mussolini's persuasive hospitality began to
wear off, and some of the drawbacks of the proposal
became apparent. Overnight the visitors had worked
out a first redraft, which bore witness to their concern

------

[24]In this connection Mussolini made the notorious
quip: "Treaties are holy, but not eternal."

[25]This line of reasoning became the key argument
in MacDonald's defense of the pact in the Commons on
March 23 and eventually even found its way into the
British White Paper (Cmd. 4342).

for public reaction in Paris and in London more clearly than their previous reservations.[26]

The British amendments contained five major modifications, although they were still surprisingly close to the spirit of the original proposal. First, as a matter of style, the obscure reference to the Five Power Declaration of December 11, 1932, was cleared up. Second, a sentence calling for "scrupulous respect to all existing treaty obligations" was introduced into Article Two to sweeten the pill for the Quai d'Orsay. Third, the article on disarmament was modified, since MacDonald could not simply abandon his own draft convention by writing the probable failure of the Disarmament Conference into the Four Power Pact. Fourth, since the signatories were not seeking to exclude other powers, the last phrase of the same article should be worded more loosely. And fifth: "What, for instance, did the reference to 'colonial sphere' signify?" Here Mussolini had hit a sensitive British nerve, since MacDonald was acutely aware of the protest this clause would arouse on his return to England. Mussolini, therefore, had no choice but to retreat as gracefully as possible by dropping the reference and by rewriting the article to include the less controversial because more elusive "economic cooperation." The word "political" was also omitted from Article Four.

The visit concluded with an ambiguous commique and the customary press conference for Italian and foreign journalists, in which the British Prime Minister made an impassioned plea for peace.[27] The text of the

---

[26]A résumé of the second conversation is in BFP, V, 44 and in Aloisi, *Journal*, p. 98f. Cf. Simon's account of the discussions to German Ambassador Hoesch in London, GFP, I, 113.

[27]The London *Times*, March 20. For the origin of the communique, See Aloisi, *Journal*, p. 99. Cf. Fr. Salata, *Il Patto Mussolini*, pp. 193ff.

proposals was kept secret, at least for the time being,
until a French indiscretion revealed it to the international press.[28] Mussolini could well congratulate himself on his success, remarking complacently to his
wife Rachele: "It seems that the English government
has finally understood the necessity for revising the
treaties. MacDonald and I have an almost complete
identity of views. He understands that Italy is no longer
the same as in the immediate post-war era. He must
be thanked for that and for his charming cordiality."[29]
MacDonald, too, was bewitched by Mussolini's imag-
itive ingenuity, and he left for Paris to procure French
adherence much impressed with his host.[30]

Despite de Jouvenel's soothing dispatches, the
French capital was growing more and more anxious.
Daladier hastily called a cabinet meeting on the nineteenth, but it seems to have decided nothing more than
to wait for the British explanations about the Four Power Pact.[31] The rightist press raved, whereas moderate

---

[28] R. Binion in *Defeated Leaders*, p. 181, suggests
that de Jouvenel was responsible for the leak to quiet
the exorbitant rumors then circulating in Paris.

[29] An entry under March 18 in Rachele's *La mia
vita con Benito*, p. 119.

[30] Ivone Kirkpatrick, *Mussolini*, p. 189. Gravelli
even stated enthusiastically: "It is an immediate consequence of the meeting between MacDonald and Mussolini that England now belongs in the camp of the
revisionists, and that the idea of revisionism no longer
exhausts itself in sterile polemics but turns into action." *Hitler*, p. 115.

[31] The documentation on the French side of the Four
Power Pact negotiations is most unsatisfactory, since
the publication of the diplomatic documents has not
yet reached 1933. For the public correspondence there
is the *French Blue Book* (Paris, 1933). Much can be

and left-wing papers desperately struggled to maintain some semblance of objectivity towards the project.[32] The Daladier government rested on a slender parliamentary base, since "Daladier, like Herriot, had failed in his attempt to create a real majority. Parliament was henceforth patently unworkable." The cabinet existed more by default than by virtue of a positive program, since it was clear "that the Radical electorate, if it demanded anything, demanded a left-wing foreign policy and a right-wing financial policy, a contradiction that was to be the source of many troubles." The fundamental ambiguity of electoral support and the party platform of the Radical Socialists prevented them from a clear-cut alliance with either the right or the left and contributed fundamentally to the *immobilisme* and the political sterility of the Third Republic.[33]

Premier Daladier's position on the Four Power

---

reconstructed out of the reports of the British, American and German diplomats in Paris. There is also a plethora of memoirs by Paul-Boncour, Tardieu, Herriot, de Monzie, Gamelin, etc., but they have to be used with caution. This fragmentary picture has to be supplemented by the French press, which was usually better informed than the foreign diplomats.

[32] E.g. the different headlines of the *Journal des Debats* and *Le Temps* on March 19: "L'APOTHEOSE DE L'IMPERIALISME" vs. "L'ENTENTE A QUATRE."

[33] Apart from the multi-volume histories of the Third Republic by Edouart Bonnefous, *Histoire politique de la Troisième République* (Paris, 1962), vol. V, and by Jaques Chastenet, *Histoire de la Troisième République* (Paris, 1962), vol. VI, the most trenchant analysis of French politics from 1932 to 1934 is Peter Larmour, *The French Radical Party in the 1930's* (Stanford, 1964), pp. 110, 130 *passim*.

Pact was no more clearly defined than that of his party.
Described by the vitriolic Pertinax as "dictator despite
himself," he was good-willed, well-educated, but lacking in forcefulness and direction.   "He does not mark
others with his imprint; he is more molded by them.
He is not a convex personality like Clemenceau: he
is concave. His political line is hammered out by contradictory forces, which put pressure upon him, and
with some trickery he tries his best to explain away
any deformations."[34] Although Pertinax' biting portrait
is anything but disinterested, it contains some grains
of truth. Daladier received the office of Premier on
his record within the Radical Socialist Party, especially since Herriot, its nominal leader, had made himself *persona non grata* in the debate over inter-allied
war debts, and the short-lived Paul-Boncour government had never been anything but a caretaker cabinet.
Hence it was not too surprising that Daladier's first
declaration on foreign policy contained nothing beyond
the obligatory rhetorical platitudes of a radical Repub-
lican: "Anxious for our fatherland, the Republic, anxious for international peace, our foreign policy strives

---

[34]Because of Daladier's involvement in Vichy there
exists no satisfactory biography of this enigmatic
French politician. Pertinax (Andre Geraud), *Les Fossoyeurs: Défaite militaire de la France* (New York,
1943), vol. I, p. 107ff., is always entertaining but not
very reliable. The polemics by Pierre Mouton and J.
Rinaldi, *Le Mesonge de Daladier* (Paris, 1942) and
James de Coquet, *Le Procès de Riom* (Paris, 1945) are
of no value for the study of Daladier's reaction to the
Four Power Pact. Cf. also Daladier's testimony to *La
Commission chargeé d'enquêter sur les évènements
survenus en France de 1933 à 1945*, ed., by Ch. Serre
(Paris, 1947), vol. I, p. 11f.

for these two goals. We want our security and the security of all those peoples who should—to receive equal rights—carry equal obligations. (Very good! Very good!) Without it there can be no confidence in the world, no economic restoration, no effective plan for disarmament, and even less for general arbitration, the only method which permits now the peaceful evolution of Europe and the world. (Applause at the Left). ... With our allied powers, with all nations of good will, we desire to strengthen or to form anew close and trustful relations of mutual respect of our institutions."[35]

Baffled by the rapid rise of Hitler and confronted with Mussolini's suggestion for the Four Power Pact, transmitted to him in glowing terms by Jouvenel, the French Premier hesitated. Chatting with the American chargé Marriner, he remarked that, while Mussolini's project "negativated [*sic*] the principles at the base of the League of Nations, namely the equality of nations and contained nothing new, nevertheless at the present moment it had a valuable psychological effect, since it indicated clearly that Mussolini had no intention of tying himself too closely with Germany alone." Edouard Herriot, the chairman of the *Parti Radical Socialiste* and the head of the majority behind the cabinet, opposed the pact in occasional articles in the press, while refusing to commit himself in public. Foreign Minister Joseph Paul-Boncour, once won over to the proposal by de Jouvenel, favored it cautiously. No clear parliamentary alignments had

---

[35]Annales de la Chambre des Députés. *Débats Parlementaires*, vol. 149, pp. 399ff, 414. February 3, 1933. In this policy declaration Daladier dwelt mainly upon internal reforms and upon the necessity to prevent the loss of the dynamic of French democracy.

yet formed and the situation was completely in flux
when MacDonald and Simon arrived in Paris late on
March 20.[36]

Conversations began the next morning and were
scarcely interrupted for lunch. The discussion between the British and French ministers was heated,
but it was carried on in the frank tone which prevails
only among friends. The British acted as *rapporteurs*
and presented Mussolini's proposal as well as their
own redraft, which had been accepted by the Duce as
basis for further negotiation. MacDonald and Simon
were quick to point out that they had by no means accepted the Four Power Pact in its entirety. Their redraft should only be regarded as a starting point for
debate. To calm French apprehensions and to create
a favourable climate for an exchange of opinions, Mac-
Donald stressed three general points. First, he was
deeply impressed with Mussolini's genuine desire for
peace. Second, he agreed with the Duce's attempt to
prevent the creation of two hostile blocs in Europe and
to avoid the return of a pre-war situation. And last,
he did not intend to create a directorate of the Great
Powers; he only favored an agreement among the powers
which wished to act along similar lines in the general
interests of European peace.[37]

---

[36]FRUS, pp. 64-66. Herriot's attitude towards the
Daladier cabinet is described by his biographer Soulie:
"Herriot did not engage himself, but he assured his
support. As a matter of fact, although he was somewhat displeased to see another personality from the
party over which he presided preferred by the President of the Republic, he upheld him with his loyal efforts." *La Vie politique d'Edouard Herriot* (Paris,
1962), p. 422. For French public opinion see Koester's
analysis in GMF, D 675770.

[37]The Paris discussions are in BFP, V, 46. Cf.
also GFP, I, 113. The overriding importance of the

After reassuring their hosts of Mussolini's sincerity, the British visitors broached the touchy subject of revision. MacDonald declared with conviction that some change of the peace treaties must come sooner or later, and that it would be better to create a framework for keeping it within the confines of the League than to force Hitler into unilateral repudiation of Versailles. Daladier quickly posed the uncomfortable dilemma: "Supposing that M. Beneš or M. Beck opposed revision, what would happen?" Simon could only counter that the present machinery for revision contained in the Covenant, the famous Article XIX, was too vague to allow for any effective action. The question would have to be faced. Would it not be better to determine the methods of revision now, while there was still time?

At this point Paul-Boncour asked the crucial question for the French: "How could the idea of a four-power agreement be justified before the rest of Europe?" Even if France were willing to agree to the proposed pact, this query would have to be answered if France was not to lose face all over the Continent. The French Foreign Minister also shrewdly indicated a solution by suggesting that it was the responsibility of the four states with a permanent seat in the Council of the League to confer outside Geneva as well. But might not this rationale also serve to strengthen Polish and Czech resistance? MacDonald had to concede that "this was perfectly true. How long, however, could they stand in this position? Would it be possible to do so for twelve months, or for two or three years un-

---

Four Power Pact at that time is evident from the postponement of any debate on the MacDonald Plan in its favor. The French also raised the question of vetoes within the pact, but the British glossed over the issue, declaring that no such eventuality would arise.

til their hands were forced by Germany? What they
were facing at the moment was the means of getting
the machinery of revision into order. . . . They would
like to get the threat of trouble removed. How could
they do so? "

Daladier well understood this point. But he did
not want to give Germany a victory in revision and
disarmament without adequate *quid pro quo*. The French
Premier started from the assumption that there were
already two blocs of powers in existence; one should,
therefore, consider the methods of revision more care-
fully. One had to disarm first; then one could revise
the treaties, if—and only if—French security would
be safeguarded. Better yet, one should omit any reference to revision entirely. It was one thing to revise
the peace treaties in a period of calm, but was it opportune to advance such a dangerous proposal during
a time of turmoil?

These spirited entreaties prompted the first British
concession. Sir John Simon was now willing to con-
fine German equality to the terms of the Five Power
Declaration of December 11, 1932, thus retreating considerably from Mussolini's bolder project.[38] Even Mac-
Donald began to waver under the pressure: "Would
German equality not lead to German rearmament? "
He began seeing more and more objections. It would
be better to postpone discussion of this point. Could
the French, he asked, submit a redraft of the article?[39]

---

[38] Simon's concession in effect robbed Article Two
of any significance. Cf. Aloisi, *Journal*, pp. 20-36,
for the "No-Force-Pact. "

[39] At the same time Whitehall also harbored second thoughts on the Four Power Pact. In a detailed
memorandum F. O. Sargent spelled out the British reservations: "Cooperation between the four Great Powers represents the realistic and perhaps in the cir-

Since no further difficulties arose about the last article, the British Prime Minister returned to the fundamental problem. Were the French "prepared to accept the idea of the collaboration of the four powers, and secondly, if so, could we think out and agree to a method by which it could be carried out?" MacDonald was well aware that this course of action would raise two additional questions: what would be the relationship between the Four Power Pact and the League, and how could the text be made public without causing Poland and the Little Entente to raise untold objections? Since these problems accounted for Paris' distaste for Mussolini's scheme, the French were reluctant to suggest compromises. Paul-Boncour asked devastatingly: "First, if the idea were well founded, and secondly, if it was opportune to bring it foreward now?" Daladier was more specific, making acceptance a question of France's eastern allies. France had treaties with these states and was obligated to inform them of any new commitments. Moreover, could one trust the new militant spirit of Germany and Italy?

But these objections produced an unexpected result. Afraid of losing Mussolini's bold initiative in

---

cumstances the only effective method for dealing with Europe's present problems. . . . [But] the policies and the outlook of the four governments must be capable of being so adjusted as to be brought to bear on a common object." Was this condition fulfilled among the four powers? Sargent insisted on the Anglo-Italian role as mediators "provided that these two intermediaries enjoy the confidence of both the other powers. . . . Great Britain fulfills this qualification, Italy definitely does not. . . . Unless she [does] any written agreement between the four powers is likely to be stillborn." A remarkably clearsighted assessment! BFP, V, 49.

the quagmire of French tergiversations and complaints, and prompted, moreover, by the strong fear of unilateral German action, MacDonald returned to his basic question: How could Great Britain forestall Hitler's twin demands for revision and rearmament? For him the special attraction of Mussolini's proposal was that, if the four powers agreed, these questions were not left to the Fascist dictators to deal with alone. In his inimitable manner he concluded: "We have told you all we know. It is possible that the Cabinet will be unfavorable to the scheme: we would certainly like to consider it further."

But MacDonald's oratory left his hosts unmoved. Their suspicion of Hitler's designs blocked any chance of concession for the moment. Pouring out his heart to President Roosevelt's special envoy, Norman Davis, Daladier stated the fundamental reason: "Had he been in power when Brüning had been in power in Germany, he might have obtained something along these lines, but faced with Hitler and Hitlerism, the whole project was difficult."[40] After MacDonald's flow of words had subsided, Paul-Boncour denounced Hitler's breaches of the Treaty of Versailles, especially the use of the SA as auxiliary police in the demilitarized zone at the French border. The French Foreign Minister bluntly posed the unanswerable question: "How could France agree to a policy of disarmament and revision, if treaties are being disregarded by Germany every day?"

The communique which issued from the animated discussion was remarkable not so much for its haziness as for the French assertion, however vague, that Paris desired "to see established in the interest of

---

[40]FRUS, pp. 82-84 (memorandum by Davis). Daladier also declared "that this idea would bear considerable reflection, since he felt that the diplomacy of Machiavelli was still the rule in Italy."

peace, within the framework and spirit of the League of Nations, a loyal cooperation between the Four European Powers who are permanent members of the Council of the League." This statement spelled French acceptance of the pact in principle, at least for the purpose of further discussion. In retrospect it seems surprising that Paris even went this far. But it was evident from the initial discussions of the Four Power Pact that France was still diplomatically isolated among the Great Powers in the spring of 1933. The British and the Italians favored moderate revision and greater equality for Germany, while the Soviet Union pressed for an extension of the Treaty of Berlin. Daladier and Paul—Boncour saw as their highest objective not to alienate the British statesman by a blank refusal, especially since the idea seemed to have captured Mac-Donald's imagination. They rather preferred to let Hitler do his work on Western public opinion, and to allow the British to return to their own position, after cooling off their enthusiasm on the banks of the Thames. The French statesmen could not but accept the proposal in principle and trust the skillful hands of the Quai d'Orsay to render it harmless from within.[41]

MacDonald and Simon travelled back to London to face a divided Cabinet, a hesitant Foreign Office, and a hostile Commons on the next day. The French min-

---

[41]How grossly Hitler misjudged the French mentality is evident from a remark to General E. von Hammerstein on February 3, 1933: "The most dangerous time is during the rebuilding of the *Wehrmacht*. Then it will become clear, whether France possesses *statesmen*: if so, she will not leave us the time, but fall upon us (presumably with her Eastern satellites)." In Thilo Vogelsang, "Neue Dokumente zur Geschichte der Reichswehr, 1930-1933" *Vierteljahreshefte für Zeitgeschichte* (1954), pp. 377-436.

isters remained behind, uneasy, baffled, and perplexed by Mussolini's unexpected proposal. Slowly the first effects of the Four Power Pact began to make themselves felt. The diplomatic crisis caused by Hitler's appearance on the European stage stopped short of breaking into an open conflict. Mussolini's suggestion provided the chancelleries, the foreign offices, the journalists and the street corners with a positive issue over which they could momentarily forget the Nazi menace. In the recent discussions the Four Power Pact had weathered the first searching criticism and had been approved in principle by all participating governments. Its future now depended upon the response of the European public.

Chapter IV

INTERNATIONAL PUBLIC REACTION

THE SUCCESS of Mussolini's bold initiative in proposing a Four Power Pact between the principal European states depended primarily upon the response of public opinion in the countries directly involved.[1]

---

[1]Any assessment of public opinion, especially on a Europe-wide basis, is fraught with great difficulties. In *The Art and Practice of Diplomacy* (London, 1962) C. K. Webster states: "If it is difficult to estimate the influence of Parliament on foreign policy, that of public opinion presents still a more complicated problem. No technique has yet been discovered to assess it quantitatively. A large number of studies have appeared in Britain and the U.S. on this subject, but for the most part they are mere compilations, derived mainly from the press, and leading to no certain conclusions." (P. 94.)

For the purposes of the present discussion the working definition developed by Vernon O. Key in *Public Opinion and American Democracy* (New York, 1961) seems most useful: "Public opinion . . . may simply be taken to mean these opinions held by private persons which governments find it prudent to heed. Governments may be compelled towards action or inaction by

Among them, Germany was the first to express its position openly. Speaking in the Reichstag on March 23 in support of his bid for emergency powers, Adolf Hitler welcomed Mussolini's suggestion enthusiastically. In a few parenthetical remarks on National Socialist foreign policy he reviewed the MacDonald Plan in a friendly but reserved manner, adding: "More comprehensive yet is the plan of the head of the Italian government, who generously and farsightedly attempts to secure a tranquil and even development for Europe. We consider this plan of the highest importance. We are willing to collaborate on this basis in full sincerity in the endeavor to unite the four powers Germany, Italy, England and France in a peaceful political cooperation, a plan which approaches boldly and resolutely the tasks upon which the fate of Europe depends (Applause on the right)." Mussolini could hardly have expected a more generous compliment than: "For this reason we are especially grateful for the understanding and cordiality with which the national rising of Germany was greeted in Italy (Stormy applause and clapping from the National Socialists)."[2] Yet even such praise

---

such opinion; in other instances they may ignore it, perhaps at their peril; they may attempt to alter it; or they may divert or pacify it. So defined opinion may be shared by a few people. It may be the eeriest whim or may be a settled conviction." (P. 14.) When dealing with such a diverse subject as Europe, another caveat should be heeded: "The range of opinions that enter into the calculation of governors obviously varies among societies with their political norms and customs." *Ibid.*

[2]*Verhandlungen des Reichstags,* (VIII Wahlperiode, 1933), vol. 457, p. 30. Germany in the spring of 1933 is a case in point for the difficulty of using the concept of public opinion. The freedom of the press

did not suffice to appease the Duce's vanity.[3] The foreign press hardly noticed this passage in Hitler's speech, which led to a Nazi charge of its deliberate suppression by the British cables and a somewhat forced protest of the German correspondents in London.[4] Where it was commented on, it caused little surprise, since German acceptance of the Four Power Pact had been a foregone conclusion. Only Hitler's strong stress on peace encouraged some favorable press remarks abroad.[5]

More important than German public reaction was Great Britain's response to the Four Power Pact. During the previous decade much sentiment had developed

---

and of discussion was gradually rescinded. Hitler's attitude alone was politically relevant, although for a few precarious months other political figures and newspapers still dared to disagree with the party line. (Cf. the suspension of the *Deutsche Allgemeine Zeitung* on May 31, 1933). On the Four Power Pact there was little or no discussion. The *Völkischer Beobachter* mentioned the "friendly reception of Mussolini's pact in Berlin's political circles." (March 21) While still in operation, the *Deutsche Allgemeine Zeitung* called the "proposed ten years truce ... an ideal to be desired most strongly." (March 28) Only the *Vossische Zeitung* cautioned: "We do not want another patched-up peace."(March 20) Cf. also Adolf Grabowsky, "Aussenpolitik und nationale Revolution," *Zeitschrift für Politik* (April, 1933), pp. 1-6. Grabowsky called for a favorable response to the initiative, "since even if the Mussolini pact can only be a basis for something more that we must reach, it still provides a springboard, which we did not possess until now."

[3]GFP, I, 128.
[4]*Völkischer Beobachter*, March 28.
[5]*Le Temps* and London *Times*, March 25.

in support of the German claim for the re-consideration
of the Peace Treaties. The humanitarian tradition of
the Labourites, the fair-play outlook of the Liberals,
and the good business sense of the Conservatives
made them receptive towards German propaganda, made
them lean towards championing the German cause in
opposition to France. There was a remarkably high
degree of continuity in the British attitude towards
Germany in the 1920's and 1930's. Hitler's seizure of
power was greeted with some apprehension in Liberal
circles, but Prime Minister MacDonald believed he was
still reflecting his country's opinion accurately when
he rose to report in the House on his trip to Paris, Geneva, and Rome,—on the same day on which Hitler
had spoken in Berlin.[6]

---

[6]For British policy towards the Four Power Pact,
consult R. W. Seton-Watson, *Britain and the Dictators*
(New York, 1938); W. N. Medlicott, *British Foreign
Policy since Versailles* (London, 1940); Arnold Wolfers, *Britain and France Between the Wars* (New York,
1940); W. M. Jordan, *Great Britain, France and the
German Problem* (London, 1943); and Philip L. Reynolds, *British Foreign Policy in the Inter-war Years*
(London, 1954).

The British press was split on the Four Power
Pact. The *Daily Express*, the *Daily Telegraph* and
the London *Times* championed it in editorials such as
"Peaceful Revision," (March 27) calling it "the biggest
and most immediate problem with which [Europe] has
to deal." Labour papers like the London *Daily Herald*
and the independent liberal *Manchester Guardian* opposed the scheme from the start, because of its hostility to the League. On March 29 the *Daily Herald*
blasted it as "a monstrous apple of discord." The periodicals were also divided between the *Fortnightly
Review* in favor and the *New Statesman and Nation*
critical, while the *Saturday Review* carried a bitter
editorial by "Audax" entitled "Ramsay Romanus Sum."

James Ramsay MacDonald began his account with a muddled defense of his disarmament plan. In his groping and emotional style he conveyed the gloomy atmosphere of Geneva: "I felt day after day, whilst there as though I was looking upon a stage with something moving immediately behind the footlights, but as if there was something else there of a different character——an ominous background full of shadows and uncertainties." Without giving any details of Mussolini's suggestion, the Prime Minister recounted the course of his visit to Rome. On his arrival he had received "a short document, which roughly gave Signor Mussolini's views . . . on an effective collaboration between the four Western Powers to maintain peace in the spirit of the Kellogg Pact and the No-Force-Pact." Thus far the project had seemed innocuous enough, but it also contained a clause on the controversial question of revision. MacDonald endorsed the Duce's assertion that Article XIX of the Covenant had been utterly ineffective in the past, and even went so far as to repeat Mussolini's dictum: "Every treaty is holy but none are eternal!" This phrase created a sensation in the foreign press since for the first time a British minister had openly espoused the dangerous principle of revision in Parliament, although that body had been acting on it for years.[7]

---

[7]House of Commons, *Debates*, (5th series, 1933), vol. 276, p. 511ff. MacDonald also defended his disarmament plan before the House: "We decided to assist the Conference by the production of a plan that would cover the whole field and deal with questions like security, consultative pacts, land armaments, naval armaments and air armaments; that would deal with the use of poison gases, that would embody the rules of war, the complete effect of which was disarmament and security." The two essentials of the plan were: "First of all it contained for the first time figures regarding various arms," and second, "we are pledged to give

The British Prime Minister was shrewd enough to know that a blanket assertion of revisionism would produce furor abroad, and he quickly limited the statement by reassuring the public that "these smaller States have a right to be consulted, whenever their special interests are concerned and that will be done." Mac-Donald also denied the allegation that there had been talk of restoring Tanganyika to Germany. Nothing had been settled yet. The plan would undergo some re-drafting and would have to be discussed with Britain's friends. Summing up the attitude of the cabinet, the Prime Minister concluded: "The government welcome Signor Mussolini's idea. . . . There is no greater imme-diate danger to Europe than that, when the inevitable nationalist revival occurs, the Peace Treaties may be subject of a challenge initiated by only one under con-ditions which will only renew enmities and ruin the prospect of a friendly accommodation. . . . Meanwhile, the unsettlement will keep Europe unwilling to disarm." After this penetrating portrayal of Europe's ills, Mac-Donald ventured to suggest a solution: "I express no opinion, though I entertain strong hopes of the result, but I say that were any of the four powers to reject it for their self-regarding purposes, immeasurable may be the responsibility for what may follow."

Even the London *Times* called the speech "not al-together illuminating, nor very precise."[8] Yet in his

---

equality to Germany." (Telegram by Bernstorff) GMF, H 176443. It is interesting to note that even the Mac-Donald Plan still envisaged concessions to Germany some one and one half months after Hitler's assump-tion of power.

[8]London *Times*, March 24. In its editorial the paper was more favorable, stating that the speech was "in substance enlightening and satisfactory" and the policy "as brave as it is wise."

peculiar way MacDonald had expressed the British stand rather clearly: moderate treaty revision and greater equality for Germany were still welcome, although they were no ends in themselves and would be sacrificed when they began to collide with the higher aim, peace. The House responded less than enthusiastically to the Prime Minister's speech, but the government regulars stood firm, supported by the Liberals of most shades. Both Churchill and the Labour Party were opposed, though for different reasons. Only a sensitive ear could detect the first rumblings of the brewing storm.[9]

The prize of the debate went to Winston Churchill, who delivered a blistering attack on MacDonald's foreign policy. He began bluntly: "During the last four years [MacDonald] has directed our foreign policy, and no one can pretend that the results are satisfactory.... He has actually aggravated the state of affairs at the present." Churchill savagely criticized the national government's disarmament policy for being unrealistic and out of step with the times. It would have been wise to make concessions to a weak Germany, but now, when under Hitler's spell the tide of nationalism was rising again, one could only repeat, what he, Churchill, had been saying for years: "Thank God, for the French army!" Moreover, MacDonald was only a recent convert to the idea of a four-power pact, and had launched it at the most inopportune moment. The climax of the speech came in a devastating mixture of allusions and comparisons: "No doubt it gave the right honourable gentleman a great deal of pleasure to see Mussolini; the same sort of pleasure that

---

[9]In the absence of Lansbury, the Labour specialist for foreign affairs, Grenfell led the attack on the pact from the left side of the House. London *Daily Herald*, March 23.

one thousand years ago was given to a Pope when an Emperor paid a visit to Canossa. . . . We have got our modern Don Quixote home again with Sancho Panza at his tail, bearing the somewhat dubious trophies, which they have collected among the nervous titterings of Europe." The Commons was aghast, and Colonel Spears rushed to MacDonald's defense. Yet the charges contained a good deal of truth and were not easily forgotten.[10]

The most perceptive comment came from the radical maverick Colonel Josiah Wedgewood. "It is remarkable what a revolution has come about in public opinion in the last fortnight, and it is noteworthy that during the last ten days at least, the Prime Minister and the Foreign Secretary have been out of this country. . . . What has taken place in Germany has completely converted a pro-German England into a pro-French England, and that change has not yet become obvious to the Prime Minister." MacDonald's attempts at Geneva and Rome had been supported by most Eng-

----

[10]Commenting on Churchill's vitriolic oratory, German Ambassador Hoesch remarked: "Public opinion, Parliament and perhaps the Government itself are only now becoming aware of the importance, the possible repercussions and the daring nature of the recent political exploits of MacDonald and Simon." Mussolini's proposal had initially caused the British ministers "a headache," but they were persuaded by the prospects of German and Italian participation in a system of peace. Only gradually did the magnitude of their step dawn upon MacDonald and Simon, especially after they had encountered such strong reservations in the French capital, and open criticism at the League. Hence Simon once again left for Geneva to allay the fears of the smaller powers after the end of the debate in the Commons. GMF, D 676040.

lishmen at his departure. But while he was away, public opinion rapidly slipped away from him, and upon his return he faced a sullen House. Hitler's political and racial policies had produced a swift and complete reversal in British opinion. Roles were now suddenly reversed between Opposition and Government. Previously the Labour Party had been most vocal in demanding reconciliation with Germany. Now the Government was out of step with the public in advocating revision and German equality at a time when the British people had already turned away from these issues in disgust.[11]

The results of this rapid shift were soon apparent. Only a week later, on March 30, Lord Hailsham, Minister of War, had serious difficulties defending the Four Power Pact as a "cabinet decision" against the violent attacks of Lord Cecil in the Upper House.[12] During the Easter Adjournment Debate, Clement Atlee, Herbert Samuel, Colonel Wedgewood, Winston Churchill and many lesser lights assailed MacDonald's championship of revision. Sir Austen Chamberlain joined the general attack by expressing his profound anxiety about the unrest which had been created by the Four Power Pact in Europe and by condemning revision as a "dangerous word... and singularly inappropriate at the moment." The House was in agreement as seldom before in deploring Hitler's actions. Simon's and MacDonald's defense of the pact was only halfhearted,

---

[11]The *New York Times* mirrored this reversal of British public opinion: "Britain is Aroused by Hitler's Methods" (April 2); and "Nazi Rise May Aid British Liberalism: Mass of Nation Aroused—Backers of Democracy, Long Germany's Friends, Shocked into Change of Attitude—Tories Aware of Drift" (April 9).

[12]House of Lords, *Parliamentary Debates* (1933), vol. LXXXVII, p. 192f.

since their position had become untenable in the face
of such moving protestations. The government was
forced to modify its stand on revision to such an extent that Mussolini's original proposal lost all its
force: "So far as any question of revision is concerned,
revision as it has been considered, is a revision of
peace, and revision not away from the League of Nations, but in the League of Nations, and by the machinery of the League of Nations; a revision in the
consideration of which the small powers interested
will have just as much to say as the large powers."[13]
British reaction to the Four Power Pact had been devastating. Frightened and revolted by Hitler, England
had temporarily moved to the side of France.[14]

In Paris, the organs of opinion reacted even more
quickly and violently; there vocal opposition was over-

---

[13]House of Commons, *Debates* (5th ser., 1933),
vol. 276, p. 2739.

[14]On April 10 MacDonald was pushed even further
into the defensive, when Cocks asked: "Will the Prime
Minister bear in mind that any pact which involves any
concessions to the present German government will
instantly be repudiated by the British people?" Mac-
Donald could only reply: "I am sure that the House
will be aware that there is no such pact under con-
templation." House of Commons, *Debates* (5th ser.,
1933), vol. 276, p. 2176f. Two days later MacDonald
warned the German ambassador Koester "that as a friend
of Germany he had to state objectively that Germany
had lost extraordinarily much ground in England during
the last weeks." He also admitted his unpleasant surprise that Simon and he "at their return . . . had found a
radically changed atmosphere and they had been forced
to realize that their actions in Geneva and Rome did
not find the favorable reception which they had expected." GFP, I, 152.

whelming from the beginning. The press, with the exception of a few venal government journals, ranted against the proposal. Through the whole political spectrum every editor and columnist was in a state of near frenzy. Yet the general public took the issue more calmly than the newspapers. The Four Power Pact drew universal opposition from the *bloc national* and the Communists, while nearly all of the *cartel des gauches* supported Mussolini's proposal, despite its suspicion of the author and its almost equally strong distaste for the scheme. As in Great Britain, the issue illuminated a partial shift in opinion towards foreign policy in the 1930's. Faced with Hitler, the non-"philofascist" Right became a staunch supporter of the League of Nations, subordinating its ideological distrust of Geneva to the exigencies of defending French security. The noncommunist, internationalist Left grew more willing to sacrifice Wilsonian methods in favor of traditional diplomacy, as long as the latter would be more successful in assuring its supreme goal: peace.[15]

---

[15]GMF, D 675808 (Koester's analysis); BFP, IV, 266 (Tyrell). The unanimity of opposition in the French press was overwhelming. Such heterogeneous papers as *Le Temps*, *Le Journal des Débats*, *Le Matin*, *L'Echo de Paris*, *Le Figaro*, *L'Humanité*, *L'Europe Nouvelle*, *L'Ère Nouvelle* and *La Revue de Deux Mondes* never tired of inventing new invectives for Mussolini's pact. Pertinax, Pinon, Bernus, d'Ormesson, Buré, Tabouis, Fabry, Kerrilis—one would have to name the whole roster of luminaries of French journalism—combatted the proposal. Even politicians like Herriot and Tardieu opposed the project in editorials in *L'Ère Nouvelle* and *L'Illustration*. The few sheets daring to support the Four Power Pact, such as *Le Petit Parisien*, *La Volonté*, *L'Aube* and *L'Oeuvre*, were notoriously venal and dependent under government subsidies. E. Lautier

The gradual regrouping was evident in the parliamentary struggles for the Four Power Pact. On March 28 the nationalist spokesmen Franklin—Bouillon and Louis Marin used a general budget debate to submit an interpellation on French foreign policy forcing the government to commit itself on a fixed date for a full dress debate on the subject. Franklin-Bouillon called the pact and the MacDonald Plan "terrible political mistakes" and warned the government not to let itself be trapped by "English pressure." Unwilling to face a discussion as long as things were still in flux and the cabinet had not yet decided on its position, Daladier opposed the motion and carried the day with a resounding vote of confidence, 368-212.[16]

But because of the increasing clamour of the press, the issue could not be avoided much longer. Franklin-Bouillon and Louis Marin repeated their attacks on March 31 deploring the lack of official information on the state of the negotiations and calling attention to the dangers of the proposal: "As far as the plan itself is concerned I demand to know why France should want to revive these anti-democratic forms of diplomacy?"

---

was the most bitter, writing: "The Four Power Pact— that means war" and terming it "a club of butchers." Cf. also Aloisi, *Journal*, p. 101f.

For the political transformation see Ch. Micaud, *The French Right and Nazi Germany* (Durham, N.C., 1943); J.M.d'Hoop's article "Frankreich's Reaktion..."; and P. Larmour, *The French Radical Party*, p. 110ff.

[16]Chambre des Députés, *Débats Parlementaires* (s.o., 1933), vol. 149, cols. 1610-1617. Even the most critical papers endorsed Daladier's attempts to reintegrate the Four Power Pact into the framework of the League and, according to Koester, "MacDonald was the prime target for press attacks during the last few days." GMF, D 675808 (March 24).

(A strange argument from a conservative nationalist!)
To the public it looked as if the government were dodg-
ing the issue, and Daladier was finally forced to consent to a full-scale debate on foreign policy on April
6 in order to quiet the rumors and suspicions.[17]

A few days earlier, on March 28, the French public had received the first official comment of the government on the pact in a speech which Foreign Minister
Paul-Boncour made at a press banquet appropriately
given by *les amis de la paix*. He assured his listeners: "A very close and continuous cooperation... between the four Great Powers, which are permanent members of the Council [of the League]... in the framework and in the spirit of the League of Nations and
applied to questions which concern themselves—this
field is sufficiently broad—can aid their solution before its [the League's] regular organs." But the general public was not reassured until the official text
of the treaty appeared three days later in the press.[18]

During the first week of April Paris witnessed a
three-cornered struggle between the British Ambassador, Lord Tyrell, who presented the second English
counter-draft; the Rumanian Foreign Minister Titulescu,
who had rushed to the Seine to block the pact in the
name of the Little Entente; and the French Ambassador
to the Quirinal, Henry de Jouvenel, who suddenly returned from Rome to consult with the Quai d'Orsay and

[17]Chambre, *Débats*, vol. 149, col. 1703f.

[18]For Paul-Boncour's speech see *Le Temps*, March
28. The Foreign Minister's position was buttressed by
an article in *L'Europe Nouvelle*, "The Covenant of the
League and the Revision of the Peace Treaties." (April
8, p. 315f.) Although the journal's editorial policy was
severely critical of the pact, it admitted that France
could not reject the project outright, but rather had to
render it innocuous by patient negotiation.

to drum up support for the original proposal by holding press conferences. Public anxiety reached a peak, when the Chamber finally met to debate the Four Power Pact on April 6.[19]

Léon Blum, veteran leader of the S.F.I.O., led the attack: "The Four Power Pact is unacceptable for a multitude of reasons." He sharply rejected the recreation of the Holy Alliance and feared any grant of parity of arms to Nazi Germany, since no peace could be made with Hitler. Blum only needed to point out the treatment of the German Social Democrats to drive home his point. Even the Communist Peri supported Blum with the slogan: "The real pact of peace is neither a three power nor four power nor any other pact: it is the alliance of the revolutionary world proletariat!" The arch-nationalist Henry Franklin-Bouillon found himself in strange company, when his turn came to denounce the pact once more: "What is this pact? It is the expression of the will of three powers... which above all are resolved to organize the revision of treaties against us."[20]

---

[19]To counteract the criticism in the French and Little Entente papers de Jouvenel gave "an authorized version" of the pact. Stressing the dangers of a divided Europe, he stated: "It is necessary to save Europe from such a danger by uniting the four powers into one force to lead the Disarmament Conference to a positive conclusion. In case the powers should not come to any agreement, one should create, on the basis of Mussolini's suggestion an insurance society against the risks of such a failure and against the dangers of an attempt at revision by the use of force." Cf. also Fr. Jacomini, "Il Patto a quattro," p. 43; P. Aloisi, *Journal*, pp. 102-107; GMF, D 675919.

[20]Chambre, *Débats*, vol. 149, col. 1935ff. Jouvenel's entreaties later changed Blum's mind and made the eventual passage of the pact possible.

The fate of the Four Power Pact in the Chamber depended upon Edouard Herriot, the leader of the Radical Socialists, who, although not in the government, controlled the majority of votes behind the Daladier cabinet. As long as possible he straddled the issue, at first defending the general idea of four power cooperation against nationalist attacks, but then admitting that the proposal was singularly inopportune at the present moment. Only in one way could the pact be made acceptable to the French public: it had to be completely integrated into the machinery of the League by mentioning Articles X and XIX. Unanimity in all decisions affecting revision and German equality of arms had to be required, a stipulation which would give France a veto against any disadvantageous projects. The feeling of most deputies was summed up by Herriot's conclusion: "I have always said: the Covenant, the whole Covenant, and nothing but the Covenant."[21]

-----

[21]Edouard Herriot's position remained ambiguous until the last day of the negotiations. His biographer Michel Soulie choses to emphasize exclusively that Herriot "pronounced himself unequivocally against the Four Power Pact." *La Vie politique*, p. 425. But it is difficult to rationalize, that "at Marseille on May 14 in a great speech, and later in the Chamber during the debate on general policy, Herriot never delivered a direct attack against the government." (P. 429.) Soulie sees the solution to this apparent contradiction in Herriot's "loyalty to a government headed by a Radical Socialist." This may be a sufficient explanation, but it is possible that there were other factors as well. Because of the parliamentary position, Herriot was always the potential leader of another cabinet should Daladier fail. Hence he probably thought it wise to criticize Daladier to a certain extent while not incurring the blame for his rival's fall. The Italians

Daladier's speech marked the climax of the debate. It was a moderate, clear, and well-balanced exposition of the French readiness to collaborate in Mussolini's scheme, if the price were not too high. In defense of his cabinet's decision to submit a French counter-draft, Daladier called the pact "a project of high inspiration" and emphasized that France "has to practice a positive policy, a constructive policy conforming to its real traditions." Nevertheless, he assured France's allies that the Great Powers did not intend to impose their will on the small powers and paid rhetorical tribute to the spirit of the League. But he admitted the theoretical possibility of treaty revision and concluded on a positive note: "I believe that it was our duty to accept this invitation, which was extended to us, in order to affirm our will for cooperation and organization of the peace, while safeguarding all our rights." The vagueness of this statement was the outcome of the conflicting pressures operating on the French government. Britain, Italy, and Germany pushed for acceptance of the pact, whereas French public opinion was almost solidly opposed, save for some halfhearted support in the government press. Daladier found a clever solution to the impossible:

---

suspected also a feeling of hurt pride since Mussolini failed to respond to Herriot's invitation at the Congress of the Radical party at Toulouse in the fall of 1932. Aloisi, *Journal*, pp. 25, 28, 107 *passim*, stressed that Herriot was dismayed over Mussolini's condition for a rapprochement, i.e. that an *entente à quatre* should precede an *entente à deux*. The philosophy behind the Four Power Pact was thoroughly uncongenial to Herriot, who preferred a united front of the democracies against Hitler, but his political attitude remains in doubt, especially in light of the open attacks in the press. On March 30, he cautioned in *L'Ère Nouvelle* "to guard oneself against provoking war by pretending to assure the peace."

while staking his cabinet on the pact's approval, he was content to leave it to the Quai d'Orsay to emasculate it by negotiation.

Henry Bergery's and Joseph Paul-Boncour's orations could only be anticlimactic to Daladier's brilliant exercise in ambivalence. Both defended the pact while insisting on considerable modifications. The Chamber was reassured, trusting the skill of French diplomacy to remove the dangers of Mussolini's proposal. Louis Marin's motion of no confidence was, therefore, defeated by the margin of 430-107, a surprising endorsement of Daladier's moderate policy, considering that the normal governmental majority could at best count on 350 votes. With such solid backing the French government proceeded to elaborate a counterdraft, which was presented to London and Rome on April 11.[22]

Public reaction in the countries not immediately concerned also left a definite imprint on the final form of the Four Power Pact. Only Italy's smaller satellites Austria, Hungary, and Bulgaria openly welcomed the

---

[22]The evolution of French public opinion towards Daladier's position is sketched by Koester's telegrams. Cf. GMF, D 675928 (April 3), D 675931, D 675938 (April 4), D 675941, D 675977 (April 5), D 675994 (April 7), D 676007 (April 8). Criticizing de Jouvenel's eager support for the proposal, the French press hoped that the spread of protest abroad would remove the burden of criticism from Paris, while France, acting as mediator, would have to concede nothing and could maintain the facade of reconciliation. Koester judged the press clamour as largely artificial, believing that a solid majority of Frenchmen shared Daladier's position who wanted "to avoid the impression that he intended to torpedo [the pact]. On the other hand the desire to water down the pact was "undeniable." On the eve of the vote in the Chamber, the prospects for passage had seemed doubtful, since "there was a split in the Radical [Socialist] group itself. Herriot was opposed to

proposal, expecting gains through revision and parity of arms which they were to be accorded in the pact.[23] The Hungarian Foreign Minister Kanya, when informed by Mussolini in a general manner of the project, expressed his warm approval. Hungary had been following so closely in Italy's wake that a rumor of a secret tripartite pact between Mussolini, Horthy, and Hitler arose, and this Kanya had to disown publicly.[24] The

---

the entry of France in the Four Power Pact. Caillaux and the others advocated entry, if the pact were brought within the League of Nations framework. It would be assumed that the view of Caillaux and his friends would prevail." Since there was no group which advocated the acceptance of the pact without modifications, the bargaining position of the French diplomats was strengthened considerably.

The size of the governmental majority when compared to domestic votes, and even the first ballot on March 28, is baffling. Only the Communists and the extreme Right voted against the cabinet. Perhaps the phenomenon has to be understood as a rallying of all moderate elements around the French government to stand united in the coming negotiations with Hitler and Mussolini.

[23]According to Hassell's information the Little Entente was exerting considerable pressure on Hungary, Austria and Bulgaria to bring about "a kind of uprising of all the small nations against the idea of a four power pact," but the efforts were in vain. GFP, I, 126. For Bulgarian reaction see Susmel-Pini, *Mussolini*, II, 270.

[24]The Hungarian response was the most enthusiastic one among the small Italian satellites. GFP, I, 100; Stephen Kertesz, *Diplomacy in a Whirlpool* (Notre Dame, 1953); P. Aloisi, *Journal*, p. 100f. The denial of the Balkan Pact rumor is in GMF, D 676267.

Austrian Chancellor Dollfuss visited Rome over the Easter holidays, ostensibly to pay hommage to Pope Pius XI and to celebrate the Holy Year. The real purpose of his trip was to seek Mussolini's backing against Hitler and to obtain an Italian guarantee of the continued independence of Austria. Hence nothing but acclaim could be expected from this quarter.[25]

The other small European states continued to stand aloof. Because of her traditional friendship with England, Greece welcomed the suggestion with some reservations.[26] Spanish Foreign Minister de Madariaga also gave his qualified approval.[27] Turkey was apprehensive of anything which seemed like a revival of the traditional Concert of Europe, since it had not forgotten its past treatment.[28]   Speaking for the small neutrals, Sweden expressed its doubts, and the Portugese suffered night-

---

[25]The Austrian question is discussed in greater detail *infra*, p. 165f. For Hassell's political report of the Dollfuss visit see GFP, I, 173.

[26]*New York Times*, March 23. Francesco Jacomini, "Il Patto a quattro," p. 52f., presents a vivid picture of the reactions of the smaller powers.

[27]*Le Temps*, March 27. Cf. also Welczeck's telegrams from Madrid, GMF E 447003 and E 447013, who quotes an interview of the Minister of State Zulueta with the *Heraldo de Madrid* (March 23) and a resolution of the Spanish Council of Ministers: "According to this [decision] the Spanish government sees in it the basis for far-reaching international agreements."

[28]According to German Ambassador Fabricius the Turkish government condemned the proposal. Foreign Minister Tewfik Rüschtü Bey doubted whether France would agree, and Italian Ambassador Lojacono was equally unsuccessful in changing Mustafa Kemal (Atatürk's) mind. GMF, D 676367, E 446975. Pini-Susmel, *Mussolini*, II, 270.

mares about the possible loss of Angola and Mozam-
bique to Italy.[29]

As insignificant as these weak voices was the reaction of the United States. The Italians were afraid
that the Four Power Pact would be misinterpreted in
Washington as an attempt to create a united front
against America in the question of inter-allied debts.
Italian diplomats stressed in their conversations with
American officials the peaceful intent of their proposal
and extended a cordial invitation to join the four European powers.[30] This move was mainly intended to
disarm American suspicions, since it was highly im-
probable that the American public could be aroused.[31]

An anecdote illustrates the degree of American concern about Mussolini's project. On March 22 Roosevelt was asked by an eager White-House correspon-

---

[29]London *Times*, March 27.

[30]There was some momentary confusion in Washington about Italy's invitation to have the United States
join, but the Italian Ambassador Signor Rosso quickly
dispelled the doubts. GMF, D 676019. The Italians
also stressed constantly that the pact was no attempt
to create a united front, and they apparently even
succeeded in convincing Senator Borah of the harmlessness of the proposal. FRUS, pp. 400, 403f; GFP,
I, 119.

[31]The American press carried little coverage of the
Four Power Pact. The *New York Times* reflected the
benevolent attitude of the administration, but opinion
in the periodicals was divided. Generally speaking
the Liberal and pro-League journals like the *New Republic* and *World Tomorrow* denounced the proposal
as "Hitler's anti-Russian Plot" whereas moderate and
isolationist organs such as the *Survey Graphic* and
the *Christian Century* supported it.

dent whether he intended to join the "peace club."
After the President had informed himself that such a
thing existed and had ascertained its general character, he leaned back in his chair, smiled, and asked
what the dues were. The chorus of laughter which
followed the quip, ended further questioning on the
subject. The State Department did not take any more
definite stand on the matter, but stressed that it was
interested in anything which contributed to the pacification of Europe. Senator Pittman, Borah's successor as chairman of the foreign relations committee of
the U.S. Senate, similarly assured Jules Sauerwein of
the *Paris Soir*: "At this moment of disquiet it seems
to me an excellent idea to negotiate between the four
European big powers.... I assume that we shall not
raise any objections against a consultation treaty."
Contrary to French hopes, this policy of non-engage-
ment actually furthered the Four Power Pact, since by
its vague approval the United States had ratified its
own exclusion from European affairs.[32]

The reaction of France's allies was more important
in shaping the Four Power Pact. All were unanimously
opposed. But the strength of their rejection varied almost inversely with their dependence upon French power. Belgium displayed immediate apprehension. Although government circles had viewed Hitler's rise to
power with considerable restraint, in Belgium, as in
France, journalists immediately took up the battle. The
Belgian people were deeply disturbed and viewed the
pact with suspicion, because they feared that their
colonies, and especially the Congo, might be threatened, since the small powers usually had to foot the
bill for Great Power co-operation. Brussels was also

---

[32] As cited in *New York Times*, March 25 and
Vossische Zeitung, March 22, morning edition.

afraid that another Locarno directorate might be established, but this time without Belgian participation.[33]

On April 4, therefore, the Belgian government
drafted a memorandum, which was immediately dispatched to London and Paris. In friendly terms Brussels welcomed the co-operation of the four principal
powers in Europe as long as it unfolded within the
framework of the League. "A collaboration among the
four greatest powers can perfectly well be reconciled
with the dispositions of the Covenant," since their
responsibility was recognized by the possession of
the permanent seats in the Council. Even the possibility of revision was included in Article XIX, but made
contingent upon two conditions: first, on "the scrupulous observation of all obligations of the treaties,"
and second, on "the fundamental rule ... that no question which concerns a member of the League is resolved
without it." These mild reservations only strengthened
the French position, since the Quai d'Orsay could insist on their inclusion into the pact because of France's
treaty obligations to her allies. But Belgium was ready
to acquiesce in Paris' acceptance of the project, after
it had received renewed assurances from the British
and French that its demands would be respected.[34]

The response of the Little Entente was at once
more vigorous and more difficult to reconcile with the
French position. The gravity of the threat presented
by the Four Power Pact, was clearly recognized by

---

[33]For an analysis of Belgian public opinion see
Count Lerchenfeld's dispatches GMF, D 675943 and D
676068. Cf. also *Le Temps*, April 16 *et seq*. O. de
Raeymaeker, *Belgie's International Beleid* (Brussels,
1945); Pierre van Zuylen, *Les Mains libres* (Paris,
1950); and Jane K. Miller, *Belgian Foreign Policy* (New
York, 1951) supplement the contemporary accounts.

[34]The memorandum is in BFP, V, 68 and in the FBB,
No. 7.

Edouard Beneš, when speaking in Prague on April 25:
"What is at stake for us, is our vital political, eco-
nomical, cultural, even national interest; what is at
stake is the maintenance and defense of the new order
in Europe; what is at stake is our whole existence!"[35]

The Little Entente immediately called a meeting
of their permanent council of foreign ministers at Geneva which issued a lengthy communique. After a per-
functory welcome to the endeavor of the Great Powers
"to regulate all questions which concern themselves
exclusively," Beneš, Titulescu, and Yevtitch vigor-
ously assailed the Four Power Pact: "Since nobody
can dispose of someone else's property, the states of
the Little Entente formulate, at present, their most
expressive reservations concerning the eventual conclusion of these accords, in any way in which they
could enfringe upon their rights and policies." They
rejected the idea of a Great Power directorate mainly
because they would be excluded and could have little
hope to influence its decisions. The second, equally
vehement protest concerned revision: "The states of
the Little Entente also regret that... the idea of a revisionist policy had been emphasized.... They con-

---

[35]*Sources   et   Documents   Tchechoslovaques*,
(Prague, 1933), No. 21, p. 24. The same day the Czech
Foreign Minister poured out his heart to John Simon in
Geneva, who tried his best to calm Beneš' exaggerated
fears. But Beneš remained unresponsive and was not
to be dislodged from his objections: "In the first place
he feared that to enunciate the theory of the desira-
bility of revision would create *blocs* in Europe which
would react violently against the idea.... In the second place he did not believe that Germany—or Italy
for that matter—would ever dare to attempt revision
by force." The firm belief in the efficacy of democratic
world opinion was to be the tragic undoing of Czech
independence twice within ten years. BFP, V, 54.

sider it their duty to call attention to the fact that such
a policy of revision, which necessarily causes strong
reactions, is not such as to calm the spirits of the nations and to enforce the sentiments of confidence which
alone permit mutual cooperation."[36]

The memorandum of March 25 was only the opening
gun for a vigorous campaign in all the capitals of Europe. Titulescu, the Rumanian Foreign Minister, was
dispatched to Paris where he arrived in early April to
plead the cause of the Little Entente. He then proceeded to London to work on Vansittart and the British
Foreign Office.[37] The Czech Foreign Minister remained
in Geneva and bombarded Simon with his fears. Yev-

---

[36]BFP, V, 54, Appendix. Unfortunately the recently
published Czech diplomatic documents do not contain
any material on the Four Power Pact. One, therefore,
has to resort to the older, often unreliable Friedrich
Berber, *Europäische Politik im Spiegel der Prager
Akten* (Essen, 1941); Emil Strauss, *Tschechoslowakische Aussenpolitik Eine Geschichtliche Einführung*
(Prague, 1936); Felix J. Vondraceck, *The Foreign Policy of Czechoslovakia* (London, 1937); Robert Machray, *The Struggle for the Danube and the Little Entente* (London, 1938). Cf. also Paul E. Zinner's essay
on "Czechoslovakia: The Diplomacy of Edouard Beneš,"
in Craig and Gilbert, *The Diplomats*. The exchange of
notes with the French government is in the *French
Blue Book*, Nos. 10, 12-16.

[37]Before leaving Geneva after the meeting of the
Little Entente Council, Titulescu expressed his "grave
concern" about the Four Power Pact to Sir John Simon.
The Rumanian Foreign Minister was even less impressed
than Beneš by the gravity of the international situation
and retreated into a purely legalistic and moral defense,
harping on "his right" to oppose treaty revision. BFP,
V, 56. According to Koester his visit to Paris was quite
successful in strengthening the back of the anti-pact
party at the Quai d'Orsay. GMF, D 675907.

titch, his Yugoslav counterpart, besieged the British and French embassies.[38] The ministers of the Little Entente cleverly couched their attacks upon the pact in the language of the League and, since Western opinion tended to be sympathetic to the grievances of small states, the continuous stream of propaganda left a remarkable imprint upon the final version of the Four Power Pact.[39]

The chorus of dissent swelled to such proportions

---

[38] On March 27 Simon also conferred with the Yugoslav representative at Geneva, Foitch, and attempted to allay Belgrade's fear of Italian revisionism in the Istria. BFP, V, 57, 70. German Ambassador Dufour reported that "the excitement, which is shown in the press at command, does obviously not exist in government circles. . . . Jevtitch is not disturbed." The *Politika* and the *Vreme* carried editorials warning against "the conspiracy" of the Four Power Pact, and asking to beware of "Mussolini as savior of Europe." But the lack of real opposition in government circles helps to explain the ease of the later reversal of the Little Entente's policy towards the pact. Cf. GMF, E 446978, E 44676987. See also the extensive treatment by the Yogoslav journalist Lazare Marcovitch in *La Politique extérieure de la Yougoslavie* (Paris, 1935), pp. 53-92.

[39] The agitation was so effective that it misled the *New York Times* correspondent in Warsaw to report on April 25: "FIVE POWERS IN PACT TO BAR REVISION OF PEACE TREATIES——Combat Mussolini's Plan—— France, Poland, and the Little Entente Join Hands at Warsaw—Paris Cordial to Moscow," a canard which was disavowed the next day. For a concise treatment of the reaction of Germany's eastern neighbours to the Four Power Pact see also Christian Höltje, *Die Weimarer Republik und das Ostlocarno-Problem 1919-1934* (Würzburg, 1958), pp. 222-226, since the Four Power Pact was the diametrical opposite of the Eastern-Locarno plans in the inter-war period.

that Mussolini dropped all diplomatic pretense and on April 13 published through the Universal Service News Agency a scathing counterattack on the Little Entente. It was not enough to conclude a political pact in order to become the fifth great power in Europe, since the states of the Little Entente had nothing but their problems in common. Their military establishment was overrated, and they acted like the *nouveaux riches* of European politics. In one of his few touches of humor, the Duce gibed: "Seen from close by this 'fifth great power' is nothing but the individual states of the Little Entente, having climbed on top of a billiard table to increase their height and stature."[40]

The replies of the Little Entente were hardly less outspoken, but their position did not remain unshaken. Czechoslovakia, Rumania, and Yugoslavia were too dependent upon France to follow an independent policy. Since it became clear, after the dust of the first objections had settled, that the Quai d'Orsay would negotiate the Four Power Pact, the Little Entente was forced to revise its stand grudgingly and accept the project. The first sign of weakening came with a three-hour speech of Beneš on April 25 in Prague. The discourse was spirited, statesmanlike, and surprisingly realistic. Unsentimentally Beneš admitted that it was in the interest of the Little Entente to ally themselves with the largest military power on the Continent. He deplored the recent initiative of the Duce, since it came at a time when Europe was in chaos, but he recognized its value as clarifying the problem of revision.

---

[40] *Opera Omnia*, vol. XXV, p. 21. Aloisi admiringly called the diatribe "undisputably a journalistic masterpiece and perhaps one of the best papers that Mussolini has ever written," although even he could not but notice its unfortunate international repercussions. *Journal*, p. 109.

Despite strong reservations the Czech Foreign Minister was flexible enough to concede the remote possibility of revision without outside pressure, in an
atmosphere of tranquility, after several years of co-
operation, and as long as it would not amount to a
capitulation of one of the parties concerned. Only the
frontiers should be immutable, since they guaranteed
the postwar order and with it the existence of the succession states. An undertone of conciliation ran through
the speech, which opened the door for the eventual reluctant acceptance of the Four Power Pact: "The Czech
government considers the idea of collaboration among
the great powers sane and just. It would consider the
initiative of M. Mussolini extremely useful, if the final
negotiations would produce terms acceptable for all."[41]
On May 30 the permanent Council of the Little Entente
issued another communique in which it acquiesced in
the Four Power Pact in return for renewed French assurances.[42]

Poland proved to be the most obstinate of France's
Eastern allies and refused to swallow her pride in the
end, preferring to follow the maxim of *fara da se*, as
Beck called it, and go it alone. The Polish response
was so vehement that the British Ambassador Erskine
noted: "In their first reaction the Polish government
appear to have lost their head."[43] Recognizing that the

---

[41]*Sources et Documents Tchechoslovaques*,
(Prague, 1933), No. 21 *passim*.

[42]FBB, Nos. 10, 12-16.

[43]BFP, V, 58. To Erskine "the prospect of securing
acceptance by the Polish government for the proposals
in anything like their present form seems to me extremely remote. They affect them on the two points on
which beyond all others the Poles always show extreme
sensitiveness—the creation in any form of a concert
of powers from which they are excluded and [the] threat

implicit purpose of the Italian scheme was to divert
German expansion towards the northeast to preserve
Austrian independence and Italian hegemony over the
Adriactic, Marshal Pilsudski became the implacable
foe of the Four Power Pact. The Polish Ambassador to
Rome was so alarmed over the proposal that he is ru-
mored to have died of heart-failure as a consequence.[44]

---

of revision of their frontiers." Cf. also Simon's conversation with Ambassador Skirmunt on April 4 in London, BFP, V, 67 and German Ambassador Moltke's detailed dispatches GMF, D 675843, D 675909 and his
political reports GMF, Serial 8902 H / E 621659 and
GFP, I, 167. An editorial in the *Gazeta Polska* (April
5, 1933), evidently inspired by the Polish foreign office, sarcastically stated: "The Polish government
could never declare its acquiescence to the offer of a
little stool, while the representatives of the four Great
Powers are sitting in comfortable armchairs. . . . Poland
at any rate would never sit down. . . since it could not
feel bound by agreements which these had reached
within their clique."

[44]The literature on the Polish reaction to the Four
Power Pact is as extensive as it is controversial. In
the absence of more reliable documentation the Polish
White Book, *Official Documents Concerning Polish—
German and Polish—Soviet Relations, 1933–1939*
(London, 1941); Josef Beck, *Dernier rapport* (Geneva,
1951) and *Beiträge zur europaischen Politik*: Reden,
Erklärungen, Interviews, 1932-1939 (Essen, 1939); Jean
Szembeck, *Journal* (Paris, 1953); and Jules Laroche,
La Pologne de Pilsudski (Paris, 1953) assume source
value. The major secondary works include Zygmunt
Wierzbowski's essay in *Pologne 1919-1939*, Vol. I:
Vie politique et sociale, pp. 96-149 (n.p., n.d.); Henry
Roberts, "The Diplomacy of Colonel Beck," in *The Dip-
lomats*; Roman Debicki, *Foreign Policy of Poland*,

Pilsudski immediately mounted a diplomatic counterattack. He protested in London and had Foreign Minister Beck's planned visit to Paris postponed *sine die*. In a demonstratively offensive manner he instructed the new ambassador to the Quirinal, Count Potocki, to resign as a gesture of defiance against Mussolini. The old marshal even approached Prague to sound out Beneš about closer co-operation—a hitherto unprecedented step.[45] But his main attention was focused on Hitler. The uproar against the pact could be used for a preventive war against Germany to secure East Prussia and to strengthen Polish borders once and for all. The general diplomatic situation looked favorable for such a venture, since Poland could count on the support of France, the Little Entente, and even Russia. A vehement press campaign was mounted in Poland, incidents increased in frequency and vio-

---

1919-1939 (New York, 1962); Richard Breyer, *Das Deutsche Reich und Polen, 1932-1939* (Wiesbaden, 1955); Hans Roos, *Polen und Europa, 1931-1939* (Tübingen 1957); and Josef Korbel, *Poland Between East and West—Soviet and German Diplomacy towards Poland, 1919-1933* (Princeton, 1963).

[45]In Marcovitch's mind this rapprochement even raised hopes of a greater South-Western Slav federation, and he entitled one of his chapters "Towards a Pact of the Slavic Powers." *La Politique extérieure*, p. 71ff. In his unfinished recollections Beneš stated repeatedly that these demarches took place, while reserving a full treatment for a later section which was never written before his tragic death. *Memoirs of Eduard Beneš*, ed. by Godfrey Lias (London, 1954). The Czech Foreign Minister also maintained that the Four Power Pact provided the impulse for the Polish-German rapprochement and for Moscow's move towards the League of Nations. See pp. 10, 22-24, 38, 44n.

lence, and troops were shifted towards the border.[46]

Berlin was highly alarmed by these ominous developments. A preventive war by Poland was the last thing that Hitler expected to result from the Four Power

---

[46]There exists a considerable controversy over this point between Zygmunt Gasiorowski, "Did Pilsudski Attempt a Preventive War in 1933?" *Journal of Modern History*, (XXII, 1955), pp. 135-151; Boris Celovsky, "Pilsudskis Präventivkrieg gegen das Nationalsozialistische Deutschland," *Welt als Geschichte*, (XIV, 1954), pp. 53-70; and Hans Roos, "Die Präventivkriegspläne Pilsudskis von 1933," *Vierteljahreshefte für Zeitgeschichte*, (III, 1955), pp. 344-363. All three authors agree on a high degree of probability for at least one attempt in October-November after Germany's withdrawal from the League. The debate about the March and April attempts remains inconclusive for lack of sufficient documentation.

C. A. Macartney and A. W. Palmer, *Independent Eastern Europe* (London, 1962) attribute the "legend of Pilsudski's preventive war" to the German Communist Otto Katz, who under the pen name Andre Simone is to have written another *J'accuse*. They are on firmer ground when pointing out that Pilsudski only aimed at the occupation of East Prussia and part of Upper Silesia "as pledges of Germany's observance of the Treaty of Versailles." (P. 301ff.)

The question will probably never be settled to everybody's satisfaction, since, even if there was a feeler to the French military by Pilsudski, its existence cannot expected to be found on paper. There is, however, overwhelming evidence to support the contention that Hitler, the Wilhelmstrasse, and the General Staff feared such a possibility and acted accordingly. Based on Hans Roos' monograph, *Polen und Europa*, the above sketch is written from the German documents in order to explain Hitler's sudden concessions.

Pact. Neurath and the Foreign Office were transigent, but Minister of War Blomberg counselled caution since German rearmament was then only in its infancy.[47] Marshal Pilsudski counted on two possibilities: either France would back him in a swift preventive strike, or if not, Hitler might be sufficiently intimidated to come to terms. Since the French military was reluctant to repeat the Ruhr debacle, the marshal was forced to turn to the second alternative.[48]

On May 2, Adolf Hitler received Polish Ambassador Wysocki for a memorable interview in Berlin. The Führer was surprisingly conciliatory, and repeatedly stated his abhorrence of war and his love for peace. As a true nationalist he understood the nature of Polish nationalism, and, although he regretted the boundaries of Versailles, he was willing to repudiate the use of armed force to revise them. On the express desire of Wysocki, Hitler even agreed to the publication of a joint communique in which both governments declared their intention to "keep their attitudes and actions strictly within the framework of the existing treaties."

---

[47] Due to his one-sided documentation Georges Castellan, *Le Réarmement clandestin du Reich, 1930-1935* (Paris, 1954) tends to overrate the strength of German rearmament in 1933. A more balanced picture emerges from Thilo Vogelsang, "Neue Dokumente zur Geschichte der Reichswehr, 1930-1933" *Vierteljahreshefte für Zeitgeschichte* (II, 1954), pp. 377-436; Gerhard Meinck, *Hitler und die deutsche Aufrüstung, 1933-1937*; and the magnum opus of Jaques Benoist-Mechin, *Histoire de l'armée allemande*, vol. III: *l'Essor* (Paris, 1964).

[48] Zygmunt J. Gasiorowski, "The German-Polish Nonaggression Pact of 1934," in the *Journal for Central European Affairs* (1955), pp. 3-29, underestimates the Four Power Pact as a factor in the gradual cooling of relations between Paris and Warsaw.

Hereby Hitler in effect renounced all possible gains in the East from the Four Power Pact, and Pilsudski emerged as the victor in the first round of the diplomatic struggle.[49]

But Polish hostility to the Four Power Pact continued undiminished. After the threat of revision in the corridor had been banned by Hitler's timely concession, the issue was one of pride alone. "Poland in all objectivity was a great power. . . . It was therefore evident *a priori* that this system was unacceptable. . . ." As a self-respecting nation Poland could never agree to be excluded from the inner circle of a European directory. When France refused to be swayed by Polish protests, Colonel Beck even threatened to leave the League.[50] In an interview with the *Excelsior* on May 7, Beck made little attempt to hide the feeling that he would prefer Polish isolation to being a powerless pawn of the Great Powers. "It is quite clear that, if the pact would be accepted in its original form, without any doubt, a deterioration of the Franco-Polish relations would have been the result." Even profuse declarations of friendship from Paris did not allay the Polish Foreign Minister's fear of a deal between Daladier and Hitler at his expense. The altercations between Warsaw and Paris over the acceptance of the Four Power Pact weakened the Franco-Polish alliance and made Pilsudski more willing to lend an open ear to Hitler's advances, which culminated in the sensational

---

[49]*Polish White Book*, No. 1; J. Laroche, *La Pologne*, p. 123ff. Beck declared angrily to Jules Laroche, the French Ambassador to Warsaw: "Even if the Little Entente caves in, we will remain firm!" The communique can be found in Norman H. Baynes, *The Speeches of Adolf Hitler*, p. 1139.

[50]Josef Beck, *Dernier rapport*, pp. 40, 268ff.

signing of the German-Polish non-aggression pact on January 26, 1934.[51]

The last, and in the long run perhaps the most important reaction to the Four Power Pact, came from the Soviet Union. During the initial conversations in Rome, Hassell has already been keenly aware of the probable detrimental effect on Russo-German relations and had implored the Wilhelmstrasse to keep Moscow fully informed of the proceedings. Dirksen at the Kremlin and Neurath in Berlin had heeded the advice and repeatedly tried to impress Maxim Litvinov with the harmlessness of the proposal. Similarly Mussolini attempted to dispell Soviet suspicions; but these efforts were not crowned with success. Moscow's perception of the ideological causes and the hidden goals of the Four Power Pact served to reinforce the growing Soviet neutrality towards Fascism and the Democracies during 1933.[52]

---

[51]This does not, of course, imply that the Four Power Pact was the sole or even the most important reason in the sudden diplomatic *volte face*. However, the memory of the Franco-Polish disagreements over the pact was still alive on April 23, 1934, when French Foreign Minister Barthou asked in hurt innocence: "Do you have anything to reproach us with?" And Pilsudsky answered bluntly: "The French policy regarding the Four Power Pact raised many reservations here." J. Szembeck, *Journal*, 1933-1939, p. 35f.

[52]GFP, I, 109, 120. According to Hassell's Italian sources, the "Soviet government was . . . in very bad humor." The Four Power Pact was only one of a number of reasons for the growing estrangement between Berlin and Moscow and probably not even the most important one. But in the light of the parallel of Munich, and because of the dating and content of Radek's ar-

Hostility against the "bug bear of a four power pact," by which the capitalist powers would compromise their outstanding differences to turn eastward, was deeply rooted in the Soviet mind, since it raised unpleasant memories of Western intervention in the Civil War. On Spril 4, Maxim Litvinov shared his concern with Ambassador Dirksen in the Narkomindel. The People's Commissar for Foreign Affairs "regarded Mussolini's plan with heavy qualifications and certain reservations. The original aims of the pact might be limited, but with such political agreements one never knew where they would lead in the long run." Litvinov proposed that the Soviet Union act as observer without being directly involved. As Dirksen cynically noted in his report, such an arrangement would kill two birds with one stone: it would satisfy Moscow's craving for prestige while serving as a check against secret Western designs.[53]

---

ticles, a case can be made that the Four Power Pact contributed significantly towards Moscow's shift to neutrality. The final consequences of the realignment were no longer connected to Mussolini's pact, since it was not until December 12, 1933 that Soviet support of collective security became the official party line. Cf. Stalin's speech at the 17th Congress of the CPSU: "Our orientation in the past and our orientation in the present is towards the USSR and the USSR alone." Jane Degras, *Soviet Documents on Foreign Policy* (London, 1953), vol. III, pp. 65-72. See also Maksim Litvinov, *Vneshnaia Politika SSSR* (Moscow, 1935), p. 58f. For the deterioration of Soviet German relations during 1933 see also Herbert A. Dirksen, *Moskau — Tokio — London* (Stuttgart, n.d., probably 1949), pp. 120-130.

[53]The fear of four-power co-operation is stressed by Max Beloff, *The Foreign Policy of Soviet Russia*,

In response to the Four Power Pact, Karel Radek, a veteran propagandist of pre-Rapallo fame, gradually accomplished the shift away from advocacy of revision to a more ambivalent attitude towards the capitalist camp. In a series of articles from March to July, Radek announced the ideological re-evaluation of the world situation and the Soviet role in the columns of the *Izvestia* and *Pravda*. "As a world power the Soviet Union cannot remain indifferent at the sight of the conflicting currents on the world stage and the efforts to create a so-called concert of four powers that arrogates the right to direct the destiny of all nations." If this article of March 30 expressed only Moscow's general concern with the negotiations, a few days later Radek more explicitly denounced "The Revision of the Treaty of Versailles." In Radek's eyes "already the simple fact that the revision of the Versailles Treaty is connected with the victory of Fascism shows that this revision can only be evaluated from the viewpoint of the national interests of the mass of nations destined by the Fascists for servitude." And more strongly yet: "The path to the revision of the vengeful, predatory Treaty of Versailles leads through a new world war.... The word revision is but another expression for a new world war."[54]

1929-1941 (London, 1947), vol. I, pp. 89-93. For Dirksen's telegram see GFP, I, 121. Speaking in Paris on July 7, Litvinov gave a clear definition of Soviet neutrality: "We are not advocates of political groupings in the sense of opposing the aggressiveness of one group by the aggressiveness of another. We want to maintain the best relations with all States which have no design against our interests and whose peaceful policy coincides with our own."

[54]It is ironical that Radek was entrusted with this ideological about-face, since he had been the father of

In these articles Radek clearly repudiated the Rapallo policy. But was the Soviet Union in 1933 already willing to arraign herself with the democratic powers of the West against Fascism? Could the West be a trusted partner as long as Radek summarized the origin and goal of the Four Power Pact in these terms: "It is clear that British Imperialism, the principal director of the Four Power Pact, wants to give the pact the meaning of an instrument in the fight against the U.S.S.R." As much as Adolf Hitler, the city of London was still the villain, the Four Power Pact the devious tool, and the Soviet Union the innocent victim.[55]

---

close Russo-German collaboration in the early 1920's and had coined the 'national-Bolshevik' slogan of the "Schlageter line." Lyman Legters, "Karl Radek als Sprachrohr des Bolschewismus" *Forschungen zur Osteuropäischen Geschichte*, (VII, 1959), pp. 196-323. Radek's articles appeared in *Izvestia*, March 30; *Pravda*, May 10; *Izvestia*, May 12, 14, 18, June 2, 10 and several lesser, unsigned items.

[55]*Ibid*. Radek even traced the idea of the four power pact back to World War I: "But the fact is clear that the British imperialists already during the World War thought of a four power pact against Russia." *Izvestia*, May 19. The same hostile suspicion of the capitalist world is still rampant in recent Soviet historiography on the Four Power Pact. According to the 1961 edition of the study handbook of the highest party school in Moscow: "The Four Power Pact was supposed to serve only for the refusal to create a united front against aggression, and even to stimulate it. The project envisaged the full liberation of Germany from the stipulations of the post-war treaties; it would give her the right to arm for offense as well as for defense. ... By concluding the Four Power Pact the imperialists of England and France sought to strengthen the main-

The international reaction to the proposed Four
Power Pact was out of all proportion to its intrinsic
importance. If Mussolini's aim had been to calm Europe's nerves, he achieved the very opposite result.
The pact served as a catalyst for crystallizing the op-

_____

tenance of their interests and to direct the aggression
of Fascist Germany and Italy against the USSR. However, the Four Power Pact was a failure. Through the
active participation of the Soviet diplomats the plans
of the imperialists were foiled." No shred of evidence
warrants such a conclusion, but it explains the psychological and ideological reasons for the Soviet hostility against Mussolini's pact.

Vl. Potemkine, *Histoire de la diplomatie* (Paris,
1947); I. F. Ivashin, *Ocherki istorii vneshnei politiki
SSSR* (Moscow, 1958); Moscow Institute for International Relations, *Istoria mezdunarodnykh otnoshenii
i vneshnei politiki SSSR* (Moscow, 1961); CPSU. Vysshaia partinaia shkola. *Mezdunarodnye otnoshenia i
vneshnaia politika SSSR*, *1917-1960* (Moscow, 1961);
and M. E. Airapetian and G. A. Deborin, *Etapi vneshei
politiki SSSR* (Moscow, 1961). Airapetian gives as the
date for Soviet adherence to the policy of collective
security the 12 December 1933 on which "the Central Committee of the VKP (b) made the decision to un-
roll the fight for collective security in Europe." pp.
202-206.

One is more tempted to agree with A. J. P. Taylor's clever explanation: "Soviet historians claim that
Great Britain and France wished to win Germany for a
European crusade—a new war of intervention against
Soviet Russia; and some Western historians allege
that the Soviet leaders constantly stirred up trouble in
international affairs in the hope of fostering revolution. This is what each side ought to have done if it
had taken its principles and beliefs seriously. Neither

position, for voicing the fears and anxieties which had risen with Hitler's accession to power. In some cases it initiated profound changes, in others it reinforced existing prejudices. Except in the United States, public opinion was everywhere violently engaged. Governments, parliaments, politicians, generals, columnists, and even the mythical man on the street were thrown into great commotion. What would the international public reaction mean for the future of Mussolini's scheme? Would it hasten the conclusion, or would it force changes in the original draft so severe that they bore out Wheeler-Bennett's sober reflection: "'Secret diplomacy' may have its faults, 'open diplomacy' its drawbacks, but diplomacy conducted to the deafening chorus of the newspaper clamour over most of a continent is almost impossible."[56]

---

did so." *The Origins of the Second World War* (London, 1961), p. 36.

But Soviet suspicion of a four-power alignment persisted until it was reconfirmed through Moscow's exclusion from the Munich Conference in 1938. Assistant Commissar for Foreign Affairs Vladimir Potemkine denounced the meeting as a rebirth of the Four Power Pact to Schulenburg on September 29. Cf. J. W. Wheeler-Bennett, *Munich: Prologue to Tragedy* (New York, 1948), pp. 235-237, 275, 366; Andrew Rothstein, *The Munich Conspiracy* (London, 1958), pp. 23-24; Boris Celovsky, *Das Münchener Abkommen, 1938* (Stuttgart, 1958), p. 42; Keith Eubank, *Munich* (Norman, 1963), p. 204; Irshi Gaek, *Miunchen* (Moscow, 1960), p. 22.

[56]John W. Wheeler-Bennett, *The Pipe Dream of Peace* (New York, 1935), p. 130.

Chapter V

FINAL NEGOTIATIONS

THE NEGOTIATIONS for the Four Power Pact were dominated by the conflicts between national diplomacies and the struggles between the political leaders and the permanent diplomatic services within each country. This double contest shaped the final instrument as markedly as the outcry of international opinion. The contradictory tendencies tugging and tearing at Mussolini's proposal were so strong that the signing of the pact was more than once in doubt: "Amended versions and documents dealing with the pact became as thick as leaves in Vallombrosa."[1] Without much exaggeration Vansittart could describe the discussions in his memoirs as "a diplomatic orgy of niggling metamorphoses."[2] The countless proposals, counter-proposals, crises, deadlocks, and compromises, though only transitory stages on the road to the pact's consummation, revealed distinctly the basic diplomatic realignment during the spring and summer of 1933.

---

[1]John W. Wheeler-Bennett, *Pipe Dream of Peace* (New York, 1935), p. 130.

[2]Robert Vansittart, *The Mist Procession* (London, 1958), p. 454.

Undeterred by the chilling welcome of world opinion, the diplomats continued to talk informally during
the last week of March.   But before any substantial
progress could be made, a definite procedure for the
negotiations had to be established. Mussolini's special relationship to Hitler formed the basis of the evolving pattern.   In order to maintain the Führer's confidence, the Duce kept in close touch with Berlin, repeated his acceptance of the German reservations when
questioned, and even withheld the publication of the
text on Hassell's insistence.   But since the international atmosphere had not brightened as much as he
had hoped, Mussolini continued to fear French aggressive designs and seemed at times doubtful of the eventual adoption of his scheme.[3]

The second step in the development of a negotiating procedure was taken by MacDonald, who was profoundly anxious over the future of the pact. In his
unorthodox style the British Prime Minister sent a personal letter to Mussolini to thank him for the pleasant
reception in Rome and to alert him to the criticism
which the pact had encountered in other countries.
"There are difficulties, of course, and you, as a realist, no doubt see them clearly."   MacDonald's chief
concern was the French press. "If we were to assume

---

[3]The Italian assurances can be found in GFP, I,
120, 122, 123, 125. Cf. also GMF, D 675802, D 675804,
D 675844, D 675866. A typical exchange was Hassell's
interview with Suvich on March 27:   "To my question
if Italy were still counting on the possibility of success of the Pact proposal he [Suvich] answered that
the hopes were not high."   World opinion had taken
the offensive against the pact, while "the state of mind
in Paris evidently bordered on paroxysm, and people
were more and more toying with preventive war." Graham also stressed Mussolini's skepticism. BFP, V, 52.

that it reflects definite French opinion accurately, we should give up all hope of being able to create co-operation between the four powers. . . . The French have the impression that Italy has been hostile in intent and policy for some time and they approach this proposal for agreement somewhat suspicious of what it may really mean." But there was no reason to despair. Only, "the ground must be prepared beforehand, not merely between ourselves . . . but also with the various Governments in Central and South Eastern Europe who at present feel uncertain as to the methods and objectives of the Great Powers." In this, MacDonald's conception of his role in the negotiations became apparent: the British Prime Minister saw himself as mediator between France and her satellites and the revisionist powers led by Italy and Germany.[4]

Mussolini's reply on April 10 tended to reinforce Britain's role as intermediary. After the customary courtesies and congratulations for MacDonald's "great and truly courageous speech" in the House, the Duce attempted to defend his original intentions. "If, as I believe is indispensable, the document which we shall sign is to act on the public opinion of the various countries and operate in the sense which we desire, it is essential that it shall remain the expression of an act of policy and not be transformed by means of tireless elaboration into an act which is merely judicial

---

[4]BFP, V, 51, 62, 63, 64, 67; GMF, D 675944. Mac-Donald also suggested a rewording of Articles Two and Three to reassure the Little Entente and to exclude mention of the probable failure of the Disarmament Conference. He further thanked the Italians for accepting the MacDonald Plan *in toto*, and concluded his epistle of March 30 with the ominous phrase: "I am convinced that this is the first step towards appeasement in Europe."

and inoperative." Mussolini was rather sensitive about the possibility of weakening his proposal and suggested a number of counter—amendments to the British draft, which directly supported the German position. From the outset of the negotiations the two Locarno guarantors were less than neutral, each one advocating the views of his ideological ally.[5]

It was more difficult for France to find her place in the evolving pattern of negotiations. On March 25 Paris informed Berlin of a formidable list of objections,[6] but five days later de Jouvenel was more confident in a conversation with Graham, because he had just received an encouraging letter from Herriot.[7] The French government insisted on dealing with security and dis-

---

[5]It is ironical to consider how well Mussolini was aware of the dangers of watering down the pact and how little he succeeded in averting the inevitable. In vain he pleaded with MacDonald: "I must, however, state in all candour that I would view with great regret the disappearance of the final paragraph of Article One, since it appears necessary to me that it should remain reaffirmed that all the states shall participate in the policy of co-operation and peace..." BFP, V, 71.

[6]Paul—Boncour raised five specific points with Koester: First, the French government rejected any agreement which would give the impression of replacing the League. Second, Paris repealed the idea of using force to make the small powers conform. Third, the government had not yet defined its position and was still toying with the Briand idea. And lastly, he suggested bilateral exchanges. GFP, I, 117.

[7]Herriot, *Jadis* (Paris, 1952), p. 362. On March 20 Jouvenel wrote Herriot, assuring him of Mussolini's good-will and defending the pact. Herriot's answer attributed the detente to de Jouvenel's skill. GFM, D 675877.

armament before entering discussions on the Mussolini pact. The Quai d'Orsay, therefore, opposed the
postponement of the Disarmament Conference, which
was decided in early April over French objections. De
Jouvenel, on the other hand, urged that both sets of
discussions should proceed *pari passu*. His advice
was so completely adopted that Eden later complained
that this procedure ruined any chance for the adoption
of the MacDonald Plan.[8]

The conversations in the European capitals during
the end of March and the first days of April produced,
if not immediate progress, at least a clarification of
further procedure. Collective discussions were abandoned because of the delicacy of the subject and bilateral exchanges of views were agreed upon. Great
Britain would serve as spokesman for France and Italy
would represent Germany. Such a pattern would re-
duce friction to a minimum, since the two more moderate powers would deal with each other. It did, however, unnecessarily prolong the process, since every
compromise had to be made twice and all the proposals
had to pass through the hands of two middlemen.

The actual negotiations reopened with Sir Ronald
Graham's presentation of a revised British draft to
Mussolini on April 1.[9] The changes suggested were
extensive and went a long way towards allaying French
suspicions of the pact. The previous English text
which had been worked out in the Rome conversations
of MacDonald and Mussolini was adopted as a basis,
but Articles One to Three were amended substantially.
The concluding sentence of Article One which had
aroused fear of great power coercion was dropped en-

---

[8]BFP, V, 60. Anthony Eden, *Facing the Dictators*,
p. 40.

[9]BFP, V, 64. For a synoptic comparison with other
drafts, see Appendix, col. ii.

tirely to placate the French.   The second Article retained the reference to the observance of existing
treaties already introduced in the first British redraft.
The dangerous principle of revision was "denicotin-
ized" by making the operation of Article XIX of the
Covenant contingent upon "agreements to be reached
on equal footing between the four powers and the governments directly concerned." Such negotiations would
have to take into account the interests of all powers
concerned and should take place "within the framework
of the League." The British counter-draft in effect
rendered the ominous reference of revision harmless.[10]

The third Article was revised to avoid mention of
the failure of the Disarmament Conference and to limit
German equality to the Five Power Declaration of December 11, 1932. The wording was changed from "effective bearing" to "practical value," which amounted
to a weakening of Mussolini's intention. MacDonald's
desires were incorporated by the declaration that his
plan "constituted in a satisfactory manner the first
step to general disarmament" and that it should be
recommended to the Conference in Geneva.   Finally,
all reference to Austria, Hungary, and Bulgaria was
omitted, and "Germany, for her part agrees that the
principle of equality of rights shall be put into practice by degrees under agreements to which each of the
four powers must be a party."

----

[10]The British counterproposal was the fruit of ten
days of intensive discussion in Whitehall. The impact
of the change in British public opinion was clearly evident since the April 1 version corresponded more to
French desires than MacDonald's original objections
in Rome. The reasoning behind the changes was substantially that of Sargent's memorandum of March 23,
BFP, V, 49.   For an evaluation of the British position
see GMF, D 675893, D 675903 and for a defense of
the amendments by Vansittart *v.* GFP, I, 132, 133.

These British changes eviscerated the Four Power Pact for all intents and purposes. Mussolini was shocked by London's response when speaking his mind to Hassell three days later. It was apparent that he no longer had great hopes for the success of his proposal. He had expected French opposition, but no such English modifications: "His proposal had been a boy at first, the English now wanted to make a hermaphrodite out of it and in the hands of the French it would become a girl. . . . He would not play that game for he wanted it to stay a boy." Even if one must discount some of this language, since the Duce was talking to the German ambassador whom such an outburst could only please, Mussolini could hardly accept the changes if he wanted to preserve the original spirit of his pact. First, "equal footing" was unacceptable, because it subverted the hierarchical idea of a Great Power directorate; second, the inclusion of the MacDonald Plan was inadmissible, since the fate of the pact should not be tied to the moribund Disarmament Conference; and third, the expression "practical value" was inaccurate. Hence he encouraged German opposition to the British redraft.[11]

Already in the closing days of March the Wilhelmstrasse had protested in London against the first British amendments and had proposed a new version for Articles Two and Three. The second British version was decidedly a change for the worse as far as the Germans were concerned, and Neurath quickly sent new instructions to Hassell and Hoesch to counteract the English move. The German rebuttal pointed out that the proposals converted the pact into its very opposite

---

[11]GFP, I, 135. "Mussolini seemed to me [Hassell] not to have very great hopes of success any longer," especially since the British modifications represented a Cabinet decision.

by limiting German freedom of action rather than increasing it. Article One was seriously weakened, but
could be tolerated if necessary. Article Two actually
represented a deterioration of the existing situation,
because the four powers would no longer be explicitly
committed to revision. Article Three was the worst,
since it recognized German equality only in terms of
the December 11 declaration. Obviously, it was impossible to accept the MacDonald Plan *in toto*, because it would bind Germany for ten more years. Neurath now saw as the principle task of German diplomacy
the prevention of a united front against revision of
England, France and Italy.[12]

As a step in this direction the German Ambassador
to the Court of St. James, Leopold von Hoesch, went to
see Simon and Vansittart in Whitehall on April 7. The
British hosts apologized for not having incorporated
the German amendments of March 30, which had been
mislaid in the Foreign Office and had therefore failed
to reach them in time. This apology put Hoesch on the
defensive and he listened passively to a lengthy exposition of the British attitude. According to Vansittart, the modifications were only designed to facilitate
French acceptance of the four-power arrangement. Eu-

_____

[12]GFP, I, 115, 138. GMF, D 675809, D 675893,
D 675923, D 675926, D 675933, D 675936, D 675946,
D 675969, D 675976 and D 675980. Hoesch had been
urging German participation in the discussions even
during the elaboration of the second British draft, but
Whitehall politely refused these advances. Neurath
was bitterly critical of the British amendments to Sir
Horace Rumbold: "These proposals could only be regarded as a general deterioration of the Mussolini plan,
the acceptance of which would be impossible for us
[the Germans], if they would not be changed again."
D 675986.

rope could not be pacified without Paris. Hence references to the League, assurances to the small powers, and a gradual approach to German equality had to be included. If the Germans persisted in their stubborn wishes, Vansittart threatened that "there would be no prospect of the conclusion of the pact." The German ambassador was discouraged, although he concluded from Simon's more conciliatory demeanor that the British had no categorical objections to the German demands, but merely considered them unrealizable at present from their knowledge of the French position.[13]

Nothing more could be done until Paris had spoken officially. The French reply took considerable time, since the difficulties created by public opinion in Paris and in the capitals of the Little Entente made acceptance of the pact a moot question. The project had been discussed in government circles, but only after Titulescu's visit and Jouvenel's abrupt return from Rome was a cabinet decision reached on April 3 to draft a French counter-memorandum. Anatole de Monzie, Minister of Education, was the warmest champion of the pact in the cabinet. Henry Berenger, chairman of the Senate Foreign Affairs Commission, advocated it in the Upper House, while Joseph Caillaux lent his voice to

---

[13]GFP, I, 138, 146. GMF, D 676010, D 676012ff. According to Hoesch, "Vansittart who had just finished a long conversation with Titulescu declared point blank that there would be no chance for the conclusion of the pact if the Germans were to maintain their desires." The British Foreign Office on the whole vehemently opposed the Four Power Pact, since it smacked of appeasement. Martin Gilbert and Richard Gott, *The Appeasers*, p. 8f. The misplacement of the German objections throws an interesting sidelight on the position of the permanent officials, regarding MacDonald's and Simon's policy. BFP, V, 69.

it in the Chamber. As in Great Britain and in Germany, the permanent service under Alexis Saint-Léger Léger was skeptical, if not openly hostile.   A considerable struggle behind the scenes developed in Paris before a French counterdraft could be composed.[14]

Fortunately Paul-Boncour's and de Jouvenel's conceptions of the French reservations were almost literally identical. Their meeting of minds greatly facilitated the wording of the memorandum, once the decision had been reached to send it. By April 10 de Jouvenel had returned to the Eternal City where the next morning he submitted the draft, together with a covering letter to the Duce.   It represented the ultimate in French concessions, since it had been more than doubtful if the cabinet would even approve this much. The memorandum was based on the British proposal of April 1, but weakened it still further.   It was a masterpiece of

---

[14]Reporting on April 1, Koester defined the line-up: "Paul-Boncour under the influence of de Monzie, Cot and especially of de Jouvenel, is reputed to be relatively favorable towards the proposal, whereas Daladier under the influence of the rest of the ministers and of the high officials of the Foreign Ministry ... is supposed to be opposed." GMF, D 675907. Despite the denial of Paul-Boncour in *Entre deux guerres*, p. 359, that the Quai d'Orsay was italophobe, George Bonnet, *Le Quai d'Orsay sous trois Républiques* (Paris, 1961), pp. 123-126, and Elizabeth Cameron, "Alexis Saint-Léger Léger" in *The Diplomats*, p. 384ff., seem more nearly correct in concluding that in the dilemma of rejection or acceptance "the permanent services of the Foreign Office played a restraining part."

In the GMF there is a handwritten instruction of Neurath to an unidentified "Vertrauensmann" to enter the behind-the-scenes maneuvering against Herriot. D 675925.

French diplomatic finesse, since, while officially accepting the Four Power Pact, it widened the breach created by the British modifications and succeeded in completely subverting its original purpose.[15]

The covering letter only restated previous French reservations, but a lengthy preamble, which had been missing from the first three versions of the pact, preceded the text proper. In this preface Paris included all its objections, before enumerating the actual provisions. The draft rationalized four-power co-operation by a general reference to the Locarno Pacts, defining its purpose as the strengthening of peace. Its form was to be determined by the Covenant, the Locarno Treaties, the Kellogg-Briand Pact and the No-Resort-to-Force-Declaration, which had been finally adopted by the Geneva Conference on March 2. By repeated references to the Covenant of the League, the small states were reassured that their interests would not be decided without their consent. These reservations made the rest of the text superfluous.[16]

The clauses themselves were riddled with modifications. Article One was shortened, since the other pacts had already been mentioned in the preamble. Article Two excluded all reference to revision and substituted a phrase invoking Articles X, XVI and XIX of the Covenant. The High Contracting Parties "decide

---

[15]The origin of the French draft is discussed in BFP, V, 216; GFP, I, 79; and in Paul-Boncour, *Entre deux guerres*, pp. 339ff. Although both Paul-Boncour, and Jouvenel supported the pact as prelude for closer relations with Italy, it is evident from the sweeping changes which they suggested, that even they were not willing to sacrifice French national interests lightly. Cf. BFP, V, 76; FRUS, p. 404.

[16]For the text see GFP, I, 151 and Appendix, col. iii.

to examine among themselves without prejudice to the
decisions which can only be taken by the regular organs of the League of Nations, any proposal tending
to give full efficacy to the methods and procedures
provided for by these articles." In this manner revision was bound to the procedure of the League, where
French influence would predominate.[17]

The question of German arms parity was tackled
in a fashion closely resembling the British drafts. After
a reference to the No-Force-Declaration and a polite
reaffirmation of the MacDonald Plan, the French demanded that "Germany for her part recognized that
equality of rights in a system affording security for all
nations cannot be realized except by stages in accordance with Article XIII of the Covenant." Equality was
again limited by security. The remaining Articles,
which had been left untouched by British revisions,
were also changed by the French counter-draft. Article
Four of the first three versions was dropped entirely,
and the former Article Five which took its place was
made to include economic co-operation. The Quai
d'Orsay even attempted to revive the ghost of Briand's
abortive Study Commission for European Unity.

London responded favorably to the French counter-
proposals. Although Whitehall considered the changes

---

[17]These modifications corresponded closely to
Roger Nathan's and Andre Tardieu's suggestions in
L'Europe Nouvelle and *L'Illustration*, taking the sting
out of their acid critique. On April 15 an unsigned
article in *La Revue des Deux Mondes* (Maurice Pernot?) pointed to the basic French dilemma: "Either
one does not have to harbor any afterthoughts regarding the project, and then one is forced to admit that
it contains nothing new ...; or one can discern certain
ominous implications, and then it must be dangerous."
(P. 954.)

too sweeping, it could let others bear the brunt of opposition. It was hardly necessary for de Jouvenel to emphasize the explosive international atmosphere and the dangers of an Italo-German front to Sir Ronald Graham in order to make Graham receptive to the French version of the Four Power Pact. The British ambassador proved most agreeable and hoped that the remaining German objections could be quickly overcome.[18]

Mussolini's reaction to the French counterdraft was surprising. Against all expectations he did not balk, but admitted cynically that the French draft was considerably better than he had hoped, since it was so much clearer and more logical than the British one. The Duce did, however, provoke a minor incident by refusing to accept the covering memorandum from de Jouvenel, ostensibly because of some unfriendly references to the new Germany. Aside from this temporary feint, Mussolini accepted the revision as a basis for future discussions, telling Hassell that the fate of the proposal now rested in German hands. If Berlin was willing to continue the negotiations on this basis, he would be only too happy; but if not, he was willing to bury the project. After all, as Aloisi pointed out to Hassell, the original idea of four-power collaboration remained intact, despite all changes. Berlin should, therefore, swallow the draft with as little haggling as possible and entrust the fate of revision and equality to future four-power meetings.[19]

Such tactics could only provoke renewed German

---

[18]Although Jouvenel's optimism about the pact had almost become proverbial and had caused him to be called "Mussolini's ambassador" in the Paris press, he was visibly shaken by the strength of the opposition in the French capital. BFP, V, 79.

[19]BFP, V, 78; GFP, I, 154, 159; GMF, D 676021, D 676050; FRUS, p. 409.

stubbornness.   Criticism from Berlin was swift and
sweeping. On the day after the delivery of the French
memorandum, Neurath instructed Hassell to lodge a
protest with the Palazzo Chigi.   German objections
were as numerous as French revisions had been ingenious. They began with the preamble, which in Neurath's opinion gave the pact a false note from the outset
by referring to political activity within the League only.
Such excessive emphasis on already existing agreements made the pact superfluous. Similar criticism
was levelled against Article One. In the French text
of the Second Article nothing remained of the positive
recognition of the idea of treaty revision. Strictly interpreted, it might be constructed to exclude territorial
questions altogether. The Third Article was little better, since it froze German military equality in terms of
the December 11 agreement. The Wilhelmstrasse took
the revival of the European Study Commission in Article
Four as a joke in dubious taste.[20]

The strong German objections brought the negotiations to the brink of collapse. The press had already
pronounced them dead repeatedly, but Mussolini once
again made their continuation possible.[21] The Duce per-

---

[20]GFP, I, 165.

[21]*Vossische Zeitung*, April 6, editorial: "Four Power Pact Shipwrecked?" London *Daily Herald*, April 8:
"Four Power Pact Doomed" and an editorial: "The Dead
Plan"; London *Times*, April 20, quoting Herriot: "We
can breathe again. The Four Power Pact, which I have
opposed for my part in the name of the self-determination of the peoples, has been thrown overboard and the
vigorous British democracy had understood what was
hidden under the sophism of the revision of treaties."
From the second week in April the Four Power Pact
disappeared from the headlines, not to reappear until
its imminent conclusion almost two months later.

suaded Hassell to use the French counterdraft as a starting point for future criticism and to puncture it with amendments rather than reject it out of hand. The German Foreign Office should draw up a new proposal which the Italians would present as their own in London and Paris after making some minor modifications.[22]

During the Easter holidays a number of prominent political visitors arrived in Rome. German Vice-Chancellor von Papen and Hitler's right hand Goering came from Berlin, while Austrian Chancellor Dollfuss made the pilgrimage from Vienna. These travellers were only secondarily concerned with the Four Power Pact, since Papen was negotiating for a Concordat with the Holy See,[23] while Goering and Dollfuss were struggling over the independence of Austria.[24] Mussolini was sorely irritated by the unconcealed German pressure for *Anschluss* and decided to back Dollfuss. Goering's brusque manners backfired and dampened Mussolini's enthusiasm for friendship with Hitler's Germany. The Austrian Chancellor was more successful, obtaining a guarantee for his country's independence and a promise of economic and diplomatic support in return for the creation of Austro-fascism at home. The suave and

---

[22]GFP, I, 154, 159; GMF, D 676039. In preparing a set of instructions for Papen's forthcoming visit, Hassell recommended to use the French draft as basis and to stress a return to Mussolini's original ideas.

[23]Caesare Ottenga, "Il concordato fra la Santa Sede e la Germania del 20 Luglio 1933," in *Nouva Rivista Storica* (1960), pp. 181-205, 382-457; George O. Kent, "Pope Pius XII and Germany: Some Aspects of German-Vatican Relations, 1933-1943," in the *American Historical Review*, 1964, pp. 59-78. For t. documents see GFP I (1933), *passim*.

[24]GFP, I, 173; BFP, V, 74, 75, 77, 80, 81, 82, 85, 90, 101.

worldly Papen was well received by Mussolini, but Goering's visit, in the words of a British diplomat, was "hardly an unqualified success."[25]

Only the German Vice-Chancellor von Papen briefly participated in the negotiations for the Four Power Pact. Summarizing Germany's attitude to the press, he declared that the policy which Mussolini's proposal embodied was fully and unreservedly supported by Hitler's government. He sincerely hoped and trusted that the negotiations would return to the original spirit of the pact. But the victory of the "national rising" in Germany had shown to those who were willing to see that "The revisionist idea is on the march and no futile bulwark of protocol can arrest it." Baron Aloisi tried to impress on the visitor from Berlin the importance of an accord signed at the present state of international tension and handed him the latest Italian revisions of the French draft to take them home and to present them to Hitler.[26]

---

[25]The tangle of negotiations during the Easter Days in Rome cannot be expected to be fully unravelled until the publication of the *Documenti Diplomatici* reaches 1933. In the meantime see Francesco Jacomini, "Il Patto a quattro," pp. 44-50; Pompeo Aloisi, *Journal*, p. 107ff. For Mussolini's dealings with Austria, cf. also Ernst Rüdiger von Starhemberg, *Between Hitler and Mussolini: Memoirs of Ernst Rüdiger Prince Starhemberg* (New York, 1942) and the equally unreliable Anton Rintelen, *Erinnerungen an Österreichs Weg: Versailles Berchtesgaden, Grossdeutschland* (Munich, 1941). BFP, V, 77, 85.

[26]Francesco Salata, *Il Patto Mussolini*, p. 60. GFP, I, 164. P. Aloisi, *Journal*, p. 111f. Victor Arnold, *The Little Entente and the Revisionists*, p. 459. Mussolini counted heavily on the possibility that Papen, because of his independent position, could better re-

The Wilhelmstrasse meanwhile had recognized that Germany "must not lose any more time, if it wants to participate effectively" in the negotiations. During Neurath's absence, Bülow and Gauss, the head of the legal section of the Foreign Office, elaborated a new version based on the reports of Papen's interview with Mussolini on April 19. After Hitler's approval two days later, this memorandum became the official German counterdraft. Berlin's suggestions were less radical than expected, and clearly reflected Mussolini's moderating influence on Papen. In the main they were directed towards restoring the British line of compromise: The preamble was shortened, but its tenor was retained. The Second Article was more balanced: "The Four Powers confirm that the obligations of the Covenant demand scrupulous respect for all treaty obligations as a means of ensuring peace and security, but they also recognize the possibility of revision of the Peace Treaties in circumstances that might lead to a conflict among nations." The reference to the sanction clause of the Covenant was dropped. The question of equality of rights was approached by circumventing mention of the MacDonald Plan in a general pledge to "collaborate as quickly as possible . . . in a convention ensuring a substantial reduction and limitation of armaments." If the Disarmament Conference failed, the Western powers should guarantee that German parity in armament would have an "effective bearing"——a

---

strain Hitler's impulsive stubbornness and overcome the objections of the Wilhelmstrasse to the acceptance of the pact. Fr. Jacomini, "Il Patto a quattro," p. 50. Cf. also GMF, D 676085, D 676088. Papen and Hassell attempted to work out a minimum programme which could serve as a basis for the German counterdraft. Their suggestions were considerably more conciliatory than those of the Foreign Office.

return to the original Italian formula. The restrictions
of the first Disarmament Convention would last only
five years.   In Article Four, the reference to Briand's
ill-fated commission was deleted.[27]

Since the German demands were less extensive
than he had feared, Mussolini promised his support; if
the Four Power Pact was to become a viable instrument
at all, he felt that this text represented the minimum
required to ensure its usefulness. Yet he continued to
press the Germans with his stock argument that at
present any agreement was better than none and that
speed was imperative, since the Daladier cabinet was
once again on the verge of being overthrown.[28]

---

[27]Since both Hitler and Neurath were spending the
Easter holidays in Bavaria, confusion reigned in the
Wilhelmstrasse.   Secretary of State Otto Meissner
finally reached Hitler at his vacation hideout by telephone and procured his approval of the German counter
proposals with only minor modifications.   The main
stumbling block for the Germans was the question of
mentioning the Articles X, XVI and XIX of the Covenant
in Article Two. The new draft put the emphasis not on
"methods and procedures" but on the "material principles embodied in them," a more direct reference to
revision. The question of the time limit to Germany's
obligations under a Disarmament Convention also continued to trouble the negotiations, because it involved
the extension of legal restrictions on German rearmament and was stubbornly opposed by the Bendlerstrasse.
GMF, D 676088, D 676090, D 676091, D 676093, D
676153, D 676154, D 676164, D 676169.   For the text
of the German draft see Appendix, col. iv.
[28]The threat was by no means empty, since the
S.F.I.O. split on the issue of retrenchments in the budget (which meant cut-backs in the salaries for small
government employees, part of the Socialist voting

With the German memorandum of April 20, all governments concerned had stated their positions. A more difficult phase of the negotiations began. The different proposals had to be brought together and a common text agreed upon if the treaty were ever to be signed. Now the procedure of discussions was altered radically. In response to the German draft, Sir Ronald Graham took the initiative by suggesting a series of conversations *à trois* between Signor Suvich, M. de Jouvenel, and himself, because agreement between Britain, France, and Italy might be reached more speedily. Mussolini was willing to agree to this arrangement, since he had gained the impression that Neurath and the Wilhelmstrasse were dragging their feet. A series of meetings therefore took place in the Palazzo Chigi, from which a common text gradually emerged.[29]

The difficulties concerning Article One were settled by a formula which corresponded closely to the French draft. The disagreement over Article Two was more protracted, since Berlin resolutely refused to budge on the principle of including treaty revision. Also, the reference to the sanction clause of the Covenant remained a bone of contention until the very last minute. But the greatest problem arose from the German reluctance to be tied down for longer than five years by a Disarmament Convention in which parity of arms would only be recognized in stages and in complete agreement with the other signatories. De Jouvenel succeeded in expunging any mention of Austria, Hungary, and Bulgaria on the grounds that it

---

strength) and Herriot's enigmatic attitude towards Daladier's foreign policy made the fall of the cabinet only a matter of time. Ed. Bonnefous, *Histoire politique de la IIIe République*, vol. V, p. 145f.

[29] BFP, V, 216; P. Aloisi, *Journal*, p. 113.

would unnecessarily infuriate the Little Entente.[30]

Conversations continued throughout the last week of April, primarily in Rome, but also in Berlin and London. On April 19 the French Ambassador Andre Francois-Poncet was entertained by Bülow at the Wilhelmstrasse. An ironic scene developed in which the French envoy reprimanded the Secretary of State for his unwillingness to accept the Four Power Pact because of narrow criticism of the French draft. In the course of this remarkable interview Francois-Poncet even suggested a pact of mutual assistance between the two countries, but he allowed the suggestion to lapse, when Bülow was somewhat less than enthusiastic about the proposal.[31] On the same day Hoesch restated the well-known German complaints to Simon in

---

[30]GFP, I, 178, 190; GMF, D 676154. The German obstinacy in rejecting any legal obligation which might bind Berlin in matters of armament is probably a result of General Blomberg's pressure. There is some evidence that the War Minister participated in the deliberations beyond the cabinet decisions on the pact, but unfortunately the Foreign Office files contain nothing more than several notices of telephone conversations and letters between Neurath and Blomberg, without specifying their content. GMF, D 676315, E 447131, E 447136.

[31]Franco—German conversations continued *pari passu* with the negotiations in Rome and London. On April 15 the French chargé Arnal transmitted the official text of the French counterdraft and "emphasized that his government was as before firmly resolved to keep negotiating. The statement which had appeared in the French press to the effect that the pact was as good as dead corresponded in no way to reality." GMF, D 676048.

French Ambassador Francois-Poncet had spent the holidays at the Seine to receive new instructions. When he returned full of good will and proposed a

London. He succeeded in obtaining British assent in two minor points, the deletion of Article XVI and in Briand's Study Commission, but the larger questions of revision and German equality remained unresolved.[32]

During the first two weeks of May negotiations in Paris and London were virtually at a standstill. Ramsay MacDonald and Edouard Herriot travelled to Washington to meet Roosevelt and to discuss the forthcoming World Economic Conference, the ticklish problem of war debts and reparations, and the French Premier's favorite idea of a united front of the Western democracies against Fascism.[33] Except for one lively ses-

---

Franco-German rapprochement, he ran into solid granite with Bülow. D 676080. A week later, on April 27 he complained to Neurath about the rudeness of his reception, but the German Foreign Minister countered sarcastically that he would well explain Paris' reluctance to sign the pact if Francois-Poncet had been reporting in a similar vein all along. A conversation between Koester and Daladier in Léger's presence was little more productive, since the French insisted on the whole Covenant, whereas the German envoy demanded greater military equality. GMF, D 676166, D 676163.

[32]BFP, V, 97. The inevitable colonial question cropped up a last time in the shape of a German proposal for a gentleman's agreement, but it was effectively buried by Mussolini's insistence on its inclusion in a broader settlement. GFP, I, 172. GMF, D 676151, D 676152, D 676158.

[33]FRUS, pp. 494-501. Herriot, *Jadis*, pp. 363-366. Michel Soulie considers Herriot's "constant desire to build the peace on the triangle of the democracies one of the dominant lines of his policy." (P. 588.) He judges Herriot's mission a success, since the French statesman believed to have won President Roosevelt for his scheme. *La Vie politique*, pp. 426-428.

sion in the French Senate on May 4, when Berenger
and Paul-Boncour defended the Four Power Pact; and
several parliamentary questions on the progress of
negotiations in London, there was little public or diplomatic discussion of Mussolini's proposal in the two
Western capitals.[34]

Only conversations between Berlin and Rome continued apace. In the early days of May the Italians
developed a summary of the existing suggestions which
bore witness to their genius for compromise and equivocation. Incorporating the major French and German
demands, regardless of the difference in intention,
into the same document, the Palazzo Chigi produced
a draft which still possessed more elegance and internal logic than all previous creations. In a brief and
clear preamble, the Italian draft paid due respect to
the permanent seats of the League Council, the Locarno
Pacts, the current European malaise, the fidelity to
previous treaties, and the respect for the rights of
other states as well as the pact's intention to give
full effect to the Covenant. The First Article established the principle of four-power co-operation, while
the second paragraph included a reference to the Articles X, XVI, and XIX of the Covenant and the phrase
"methods and procedures" side by side with the German stress on the "re-examination of the Peace Treaties" and on "the principles" embodied in the Covenant. Article Three was the longest, the most obscure,
and the most unsatisfactory. While emphasizing the
"practical value" to be given to the principle of German equality, it stipulated that this right could "be
realized only by stages and by virtue of accords to

---

[34]Annales du Sénat, *Débats Parlementaires*, vol.
CXVIII, pp. 785-799. House of Commons, *Debates*, vol.
CCLXXVI, cols. 1579f., 2176; vol. CCLXXVII, cols. 23f.,
368, 1859f., 2069. Cf. GMF, D 676196.

which each of the contracting powers must be a party."
The concluding paragraphs contained the familiar
clauses on economic co-operation, ratification, and
deposition of the document.[35]

The Italian attempt at mediation was a remarkable
tour de force. The new text was almost wholly unacceptable to the French, while still not satisfying
German demands. In a detailed critique, the disillu-
sioned Neurath stated: "Even if our present amendments will be accepted the pact will no longer bring
us any real progress. We had only decided on these
[the German] modifications with the approval of the
Reich chåncellor in the first place, since we hoped for
a relaxation of international tension as a result of the
pact." In a series of long and trying conversations
with Mussolini, Hassell tried to put forward the criti-
cisms of the Wilhelmstrasse. The German Ambassador
pushed for exclusion of the sanction clause and for
elimination of the phrase "methods and procedures."
But Mussolini was weary of diplomatic haggling and
returned to the larger argument: "It was of decisive
importance for Germany to achieve a breathing spell
for which three things were crucial: first, the conclusion of the pact...second, the influencing...of
British public opinion, and third, propaganda...in the
United States." Hassell returned from the interview
in low spirits and reported to Berlin that "a strong deterioration of the political importance of the pact as a
consequence of the watering down" had taken place,

------

[35]For the text, see GMF D 676278ff. and Appendix,
col. v. Dino Grandi's explanation of the intention of
the draft to the American chargé in London stressed
the nuisance value of the German objections and the
merely tactical inclusion of concessions to Berlin in
the Italian proposal. FRUS, pp. 409-411. GMF, D
676274.

and resignedly counseled continued negotiation only "for dilatory reasons."[36]

Hitler's obstinate refusal to have the paramilitary organizations of the SS, SA, the Stahlhelm, and part of the police counted among the number of effectives in the disarmament negotiations at Geneva produced a diplomatic crisis of threatening proportions in May, 1933. After even Mussolini had agreed to have his Fascist blackshirts considered as combat troops for the purpose of limiting the size of the armed forces of each country, Germany was alone in her stubbornness, facing a united front of the other powers who favored disarmament.[37] Tension was aggravated by a rash ar-

---

[36]GMF, D 676177, D 676181, D 676268, D 676269 and Serial 8903 H / E 621666 and Serial 8904 H / E 621680.   Mussolini again harped on the moral importance of the conclusion of an agreement and thought that the French position was weaker now than even a short time before, since Herriot's trip to Washington had not been a success. There were also serious differences between Herriot and Daladier and the financial position of the French state was a cause of worry. There was an all-pervasive flavor of pessimism in the Italo-German talks during the beginning of May. It seemed as if negotiations continued merely by default, since neither side believed in the positive effect of the pact any longer.

[37]See John Davis, *Hitler and the Versailles Settlement*, pp. 99-203.   On May 10 Brigadier A. C. Temperley submitted a memorandum to the British Foreign Office on "Germany and Disarmament," giving details of German violations of the Treaty of Versailles. BFP, V, 127.   On May 11 the Committee on Effectives at Geneva voted that the SA, SS, the Stahlhelm, and the part of the police which was quartered in barracks, be counted as effectives. Again the impasse seemed complete.

ticle by the German Minister of War, General von Blomberg, of May 10, in which he proclaimed willingness
to continue the talks, but refused categorically to accept anything like an ultimatum. An interview of Neurath the next day, in which he called for disarmament
of the other powers and threatened rearmament in case
of failure of the Conference, lessened the gloom as
little as a belligerent speech of von Papen in Münster,
extolling the manly virtues of Prussia. In response,
the English Minister of War, Viscount Hailsham threatened sanctions for the violation of the Treaty of Versailles (nobody knew what they were to be, since they
were not spelled out in the Treaty) and French chau-
vinists began to talk of a march on the Rhine. An ex-
plosion seemed imminent.[38]

---

[38] The headlines of the international press faith-
fully mirrored the mounting tension. May 13, London
Daily Herald: "HITLER DRAGGING GERMANY TO RUIN:
Arms Race and Money Crisis Threatened: FRENCH
TALKING OF MARCH TO RHINE"; May 14, *New York
Times*: "EUROPE ANXIOUSLY AWAITS HITLER ARMS
DECLARATION: Isolation Disturbs Reich"; May 15,
"NAZI LEADERS NOW UNEASY OVER HOSTILITY OF
WORLD"; May 16, London *Times*: "THE TENSION IN
EUROPE: Preventive War Talk in France"; *Völkischer
Beobachter* (s.d.): "HEAVY TENSION IN ENGLAND:
Feverish Anxiety: One can say that the international
atmosphere has never been as tense since the war
today"; May 17, *Le Temps*: "A WARNING TO GER-
MANY!"
    German Ambassador Hoesch reported that the
excitement had reached a fever pitch in the British
capital and that "all plans and proposals...are held
in suspense at the moment and the whole world is
awaiting tomorrow's speech of the Chancellor, which
is expected to furnish the key to the coming deci-

The showdown came on the evening of May 16, but it belied all expectations. President Roosevelt saved the situation with a typically American gesture. Anxious to prevent the crisis from boiling over, he appealed directly to the heads of fifty-four states to preserve the peace. The United States President suggested that all states accept the MacDonald Plan; that they agree on a procedure for disarmament and prepare the next concrete step; that they declare a holiday on arms construction and conclude a solemn pact of non—aggression including the whole world. The practical value of the proposal was even less than that of the Kellogg-Briand Pact, but Hitler understood the implicit warning and followed with a second, even more surprising gesture.[39]

---

sions." GFP, I, 242.

Although interrupted by momentary upturns, the international crisis generated by Hitler's accession to power had steadily worsened until mid-May. World opinion had almost solidly turned against Germany, and Hitler faced his first real test as a statesman.

[39]German Ambassador Luther in Washington saw the purpose of Roosevelt's declaration correctly: "Even if there is a desire to keep up the appearance of neutrality, this step is directed primarily towards us considering its factual circumstances." A clue to Berlin's understanding of the demarche is given by an internal press directive to criticize the appeal positively, to emphasize the points of similarity with the German position, and to stress its noble motivation. GMF, H 17669-176705.

Although Hitler had given an interview on May 6 to Sir Foster Fraser of the *Daily Telegraph* in which he stressed his desire for peace, the motives for the May 17 speech are still not quite clear. Domarus, *Hitler*,

On the next morning, May 17, the Führer addressed the crowded Reichstag, which he had hurriedly convoked in the Kroll Opera House. In a low and moderate voice he read a speech which left his audience in utter astonishment. It was a masterpiece of ambiguity. For home consumption it was a biting attack on the shackles of Versailles, but abroad it could be interpreted as a call for peace and understanding.[40] One of the least-noted sections of this "peace speech" dealt with the Four Power Pact: "I again welcome on behalf of the German government the farsighted plan of the head of the Italian government to create, by means of a special

---

p. 269, surmises "Hitler rather wanted to procure an alibi for the exit from the League of Nations, which he had already planned at that time." But such an interpretation telescopes events too much. Davis, *Hitler and the Versailles Settlement*, pp. 129-136, stresses the disarmament deadlock and the general political isolation of Germany. Probably the remonstrances of the chief German delegate to the Disarmament Conference, Nadolny, helped to sway Hitler away from a belligerent pronouncement. *Mein Beitrag*, p. 133f. One may further suppose that Hitler knew his military weakness too well to engage in premature adventures, especially after Mussolini and the British had also counselled caution. BFP, V, 127; GFP, I, 220, 230, 247.

[40]It is instructive to compare the comments of the London *Times* of May 18: "HITLER'S SPEECH: Behind Herr Hitler, demagogue and showman, the world caught a first glimpse yesterday of Herr Hitler the statesman," with the headlines of the *Völkischer Beobachter*: "THE WHOLE NATION STANDS BEHIND ADOLF HITLER: Versailles! The Beginning of the Ruin of All States: We Have Fulfilled [the treaty]: We Now Demand Fulfillment from the Other States!"

pact, close relations of confidence and cooperation between the four great European powers, the United Kingdom, France, Italy and Germany. The German government is in wholehearted agreement, and will show the greatest good will, provided that the other nations are prepared really to overcome any difficulties which may arise."[41]

With this stroke Hitler turned the tables on the French. By accepting the MacDonald Plan as a definite outline of a future disarmament convention, he suddenly made France appear as the sole obstacle to peace.[42] The speech created a momentary detente and gave both the Geneva Conference and the Roman negotiations a new lease on life. Mussolini quickly grasped the chance to salvage his proposal, and the discussions over the Four Power Pact entered their decisive phase. The British and French resumed the debate where the German-Italian exchanges of early May had left off. Although Berlin had yielded much ground, the problem of a time limit to German inequality had hitherto prevented any substantial progress. Roosevelt's

---

[41]*Verhandlungen des Reichstags* (VIII Wahlperiode, 1933), vol. 457, p. 52. Even such a critical observer as F. P. Walters commented upon the effect of Hitler's speech: "He defined the Nazi attitude towards the problems of treaty revision and disarmament, in terms which were firm, clear and reassuring.... Even now it is impossible to read it without feeling that the speaker was sincerely anxious for disarmament and peace." *A History of the League of Nations* (London, 1952), p. 547.

[42]GMF, H 176450. According to Nadolny's observations at Geneva, "the speech of the Chancellor... has to a considerable degree lessened the tension and has put the French into a difficult position."

message and Hitler's speech suddenly thrust open again the door to negotiations.[43]

The pace of conversations quickened perceptibly from the leisurely speed which had prevailed, and the conclusion of the pact seemed for the first time to lie within reach. After the weeks of painstaking discussions only two stumbling blocks remained. All except the Germans were agreed to have the Disarmament Convention last for ten years. All except the French had accepted the omission from the pact of Article XVI of the Covenant. The Duce kept pressing for speed, since an early signing would be a psychological boost for the World Economic Conference which was scheduled to begin on June 12 in London.[44]

The British government was equally anxious to take advantage of the detente, and on the day of Hitler's peace speech Simon instructed Graham to push harder for some accord which would ease international tension.[45] On May 18 Goering flew to Rome with a new German proposal for Article Three, which was, however, rejected by Mussolini.[46] The next day the Quai d'Orsay

---

[43]BFP, V, 160; P. Aloisi, *Journal*, p. 123. On May 22, Mussolini "underlined that the general European atmosphere had notably improved as a consequence of the Roosevelt message and of Hitler's discourse," when reporting the results of the recent negotiations to the Grand Council of Corporations. *Opera Omnia*, vol. XXV, p. 230. See also Suvich's reference in a speech before the Italian parliament on May 22. Atti Parlamentari, *Camera dei Deputati, Discussioni*, pp. 8865, 8858.

[44]BFP, V, 158, 167.

[45]BFP, V, 149.

[46]GMF, D 676309, D 676316, D 676319, D 676334. This latest version of Article Three had been hammered

produced a draft of the first four articles, including the sanction clause and Article Three as it had evolved in the tripartite conversations at Rome.[47]

On the afternoon of May 20 another discussion took place in the Palazzo Venetia between Mussolini, Graham, Jouvenel, and Goering. Hitler's special envoy was more conciliatory than the hardboiled professionals of the Wilhelmstrasse, agreeing to the studiously vague formula suggested by Graham to break the deadlock. "Germany, Italy, France and Great Britain shall concert on the modalities which have to be applied in order to realize this principle [of equality] by stages." Goering was even willing to accept a ten-year limitation on German rearmament, but after consultation with Neurath had to withdraw the concession.[48]

---

out in discussions between Neurath and Blomberg, and was handed to Goering with a set of instructions emphasizing the impossibility of further German concessions in arms parity.

[47] BFP, V, 216; FRUS, p. 411.

[48] In an exciting long distance call to the Wilhelmstrasse Goering pleaded for a change of instructions, but Neurath remained adamant in his refusal. GFP, I, 254; P. Aloisi, *Journal*, p. 124; GMF, D 676321f. In a stormy interview with Neurath in Berlin, Goering defended his concessions. He had obtained the "most determined assurances by Mussolini" of Italian support, but Neurath stubbornly pointed out that the pact had "not only become useless for us now, but it moreover contained obligations which at a later date could yet become very uncomfortable for the Germans." Goering saw the "advantage in the fact that through the pact, they had to deal only with a small circle of four, in which Mussolini had pledged his support at all times." Goering also brought with him a draft protocol of procedure, suggested by Mussolini, which created another minor crisis at a later stage of the negotiations. GMF, D 676329, D 676332, D 676225f., D 676238.

The next day the British once more took the initiative and proposed dropping Article Four entirely.
This change eliminated the reference to Briand's Study
Commission, and economic co-operation was instead
tacked onto Article One. Negotiations finally seemed
on the verge of success, except for the continued dispute over the inclusion of the sanction clause. Goering's conciliatory attitude had contributed no small
amount to the unexpected progress. The Nazi leader
viewed the conclusion of the pact in a broader context,
realizing that it would be to Germany's advantage to
deal only with a small group of powers among which
Mussolini's support was assured at all times. But
Neurath saw the negotiations in a more narrowly legalistic light, and dreaded every concession to the other
powers. To him the pact was no longer attractive and
should only be signed to do Mussolini a favor.[49]

The decision now lay in Hitler's hands. On May
24 he called a conference in the Reich Chancellery to
listen to the arguments between Goering, Neurath, and
Blomberg and to make up his mind. More agile and
better versed in international politics, Neurath succeeded in persuading the rump cabinet to postpone
a decision until the response of the British and the
French governments to the Roman draft of May 20 would
be known. Hitler agreed to consent to the Four Power
Pact only if the Disarmament Conference had either
broken down or its result had become totally inadequate for Germany. In order virtually to exclude German signature of the pact, Neurath suddenly jumped at
Mussolini's proposal of a protocol of procedure, which

---

[49]BFP, V, 165; GFP, I, 258. In his opposition Neurath was supported by conservative newspapers like
the *Deutsche Allgemeine Zeitung*, April 7: "It is completely impossible for Germany to accept a denatured
Four Power Pact," or one day later: "The work of demo-
lition of the pact in Rome is in full swing."

should be appended to the Four Power Pact to spell out
the forms of co-operation in detail: one responsible
minister from each country should attend the conferences on the basis of the pact. The initial meeting
should take place within four weeks after the signature, while, once in operation, the conferences should
be held every six months or upon special request. And
last, as a matter of pride, if the MacDonald Plan were
mentioned, the Roosevelt message and the Hitler speech
should also be included in the document. At last the
Wilhelmstrasse was catching on, and attempting to
beat the French at their own game.[50]

The reaction of the other governments to the Rome
draft of May 20 was less critical than the German response. On May 26, Sir John Simon authorized Graham to concede the inclusion of Article XVI since this
seemed to be the last major point of dispute. H.M.
Government was more interested in the conclusion of
the accord than in its precise form. The next day de
Jouvenel presented a new draft of Article Four, now
pertaining only to economic co-operation. This version
was approved by Mussolini and, together with another
slight revision of Article Three, it was cabled to Berlin
on May 27. Although the internal situation in Paris remained far from clear, the sole obstacle to success
once again appeared to lie in the German capital.[51]

That very day Cerruti pressed for German acceptance in an interview with Neurath at the Wilhelm-

----

[50]GFP, I, 260. (Memorandum by Neurath) The internal struggle within Germany paralleled that in England, France, and Italy, where the politicians favored
the Four Power Pact and the diplomats tried every ruse
to postpone its adoption.

[51]Although the areas of substantive disagreement
were no longer large, de Jouvenel seemed unusually
downcast in a conversation with Hassell. GMF, D
676352. The British text of the modifications is in
GFP, I, 268 and BFP, V, 171. The Italians directed a

strasse. On May 29 he was finally received by Hitler in the presence of Goering, Neurath, and Blomberg to accept two new German requests to be transmitted to the Duce. Hitler asked for an authentic statement of Mussolini's interpretation of the phrase "such as was recognized" in Article Two, and he demanded that the Duce, after the initialling and not later than the signature, define the exact details of procedure for practical implementation of Germany's equality of rights. The Führer further complained about the rumors of imment signature which were circulating in the Western capitals, and declared that he refused to be rushed by public pressure.[52]

Faced with these unexpected demands, Mussolini resorted to his favorite diplomatic expedient and sent a personal message to Hitler. Rather than making a rebuttal of the specific points at issue, the Duce urged Hitler to accept the pact with his customary general reasons. He deplored German stubbornness, especially in the light of the turbulent situation in Paris, where Daladier might not last another day. It was entirely out of the question that Germany be outvoted in the Four Power Pact. Mussolini even feigned hurt innocence, reprimanding Hitler for his lack of confidence in his friend and protesting that "during the entire

---

veritable barrage at the Wilhelmstrasse to pressure Berlin into signing. Already on May 27, Suvich was officiously optimistic about the prospects for conclusion. GMF, D 676335. By phone call, letter and interview Cerruti urged his German opposites to speed up the agreement, especially since "one cannot comprehend in Rome the attitude of the Reich government during the last days; an attitude which constitutes at the present stage of negotiations the only obstacle to the initialling of the text." GMF, D 676351, D 676354f., D 676358, D 676360f., D 676371, D 676391.

[52]GFP, I, 269, 270; GMF D 676390, D 676402, D 676433.

three months of negotiations he had never lost sight of the German interests." Moreover, it would be most inopportune to approach the other powers *now* with the request for a protocol of procedure. The matter should be dropped entirely. The Duce concluded with the optimistic assurance that first of all the Four Power Pact had to be concluded, and then the rest would take care of itself.[53]

On May 30, Hitler succumbed to Mussolini's pressure. After Cerruti had delivered the Duce's letter to Hitler in person, a conference was held between the Führer, Neurath, and Blomberg to arrive at a final decision about the Four Power Pact. Finally the massive Italian pressure began to tell. The German ministers agreed to initial the pact in its latest version after they had approved the editing of the text, which was then going on at Geneva.[54] Berlin's numerous objections had been overcome. Germany was ready to initial the Four Power Pact.[55]

---

[53]GFP, I, 276 (Bülow minute). Ironically the Duce sought to deny what seemed in many people's minds the main motive for his initiative of a Four Power Pact: "In urging immediate conclusion Mussolini was in no way motivated by vanity as father of the idea or by concern for the prestige of Italy." Hardly a convincing disclaimer.

[54]GMF, D 676356, D 676363, D 676395, D 676419.

[55]GFP, I, 274 (Völkers minute). The evidence for the reasons for Hitler's change of mind is very scant. The minutes give nothing beyond the announcement of the decision. One has to surmise that Hitler, who had all through the negotiations been more favorable to the project than Neurath, finally overrode the advice of the experts for his friendship with Mussolini and for the ideological solidarity with Fascism, rather then because of any hope in its diplomatic effect.

In Paris the fate of the Daladier cabinet hung in the balance. Foreign Minister Paul-Boncour had left for Geneva to take a stand on the British disarmament plan and to reassure Beneš, Titulescu, and Yevtitch in private conversations. At the same time the situation of the government became critical when the Chamber reassembled after a month's recess to discuss the budget. The growing industrial depression required stringent measures of retrenchment, including a 5 per cent cut in public expenditures. Since the S.F.I.O. drew a large share of its support from petty government employees who were to suffer the loss in salary, the party was divided in key votes in the Chamber. On one occasion Daladier escaped defeat on a technicality by the narrow margin of 289-285. To make matters worse, the French Premier had in earlier debate pledged his word of honour that he would not enter any new commitment without consulting the assembly, and Herriot's ambivalent role boded ill for the passage of the pact.[56]

---

[56]London *Times*, May 26, *passim*. As the difficulties of the Daladier cabinet increased, Herriot became more openly hostile to the pact. On May 25 he wrote in *L'Ère Nouvelle*: "Either the Four Power Pact has no significance or Poland and the Little Entente will be worried. It is difficult to escape the brutal dilemma: either the pact is useless or it is dangerous." More than anybody else Herriot exemplified the ambivalence of the political center in the Third Republic: "In retrospect the history of the Radical Party from 1932 to 1934 strikes one as a perfect stalemate between the unthinking Left and the outmoded right. The conservatives knew what they wanted, but they were not strong enough to get it. The Left, on the other hand, had the necessary strength, but was simply too confused to pursue a coherent policy." Peter Larmour, *The Radical Party*, p. 136.

Despite these danger signals, French public opinion rallied behind the Daladier government. The press
clamour over the Four Power Pact had never penetrated
very deeply and the threat of National Socialist Germany caused Frenchmen to subordinate their differences
to the national interest. And one other factor must be
added. Lord Tyrell, the keenest and perhaps also the
kindest judge of French mentality, explained the support for Daladier's moderate policy by a newly won
feeling of strength: "Now for the first time in twelve
years perhaps, France finds that her feelings and fears
are shared by Great Britain and the United States. She
is no longer isolated. . . . The effect of this change in
world opinion has a soothing effect." And then, in a
flash of irony, he added: "If Hitler had been paid by
the nationalists to do their propaganda for them he
could not have served them more thoroughly. . . . French
opinion, in the face of the new menace, instead of ad-
vancing specious reasons for active measures against
Germany, has confined itself, in fact, to pointing out
the necessity of maintaining France's existing superiority in armaments."[57]

The test of the Four Power Pact came in a violent
debate in the Chamber on May 30. The nationalist
spokesman Louis Marin viciously attacked the cabinet,
demanding information on the negotiations, which the
government consistently refused to divulge as long as
the discussions had not yet been concluded. "It is
even more inadmissible, gentlemen, that, as you know

---

[57] BFP, V, 186. According to Koester the press was
still divided along its previous lines and "in general
the negative voices are more numerous, since the sheets
which advocate the initialling are in a defensive position." The Left, in particular, assailed Paul-Boncour
as a weak Foreign Minister and dared him to find enough
courage for a clear "No!"

very well, the chief of your majority, M. Herriot, is himself strictly opposed to the Four Power Pact. Thus in voting against our demand for discussion, you will be voting against your own chief!" charged Franklin-Bouillon. But the majority was little impressed, and endorsed Daladier with a smashing vote of 434-135.[58] Nevertheless, the issue was far from settled, since the cabinet preferred to await Paul-Boncour's return from Geneva before making the final decision. In an equally stormy session of the Foreign Affairs Commission, Maurice Thorez and Ybergarnay assailed the project forcefully: "The Four Power Pact equals revision; revision equals war; hence the Four Power Pact leads to war!" Only the little-known Vienot and Poit defended the pact, while Herriot as chairman once more avoided a commitment, and the bill was reported out of committee without recommendation.[59]

Finally, on May 31, the French cabinet decided in favor of the initialling, provided that France's allies would acquiesce. The French signature now depended upon the Little Entente. In the last days of May large anti-revisionist demonstrations took place in Prague, Bucharest, and Belgrade, in which over 100,000 people protested against the "overturning of the peace treaties."[60] The prospect of Little Entente agreement, therefore, seemed doubtful. But French diplomacy accomplished the near impossible. Calmed by further

---

[58] Chambre des Députés, *Débats Parlementaires*, vol. 150, cols. 2721-3, 2725-7. The skillful defense of Daladier with its emphasis on the satisfaction of all major French objections made it more difficult for the hostile papers to attack the government. Only the extremes on either side continued to vote against the pact. GMF D 676409.

[59] *Journal des Débats*, May 26.

[60] *Le Temps*, May 30.

British and Italian assurances, the Council of the Little Entente decided during their May 31 meeting in Prague to accept the Four Power Pact, subject to these reservations: "The first version, whose spirit was contrary to international law, has definitely been abandoned. ... The new text establishes the principle that the Four Power Pact can only touch questions which concern the signatories of that accord....Thereby the two principal objections have been met: the inviolability of the League [is assured] and finally the rule of unanimity applied to Article XIX." The Council had only agreed because "with these guarantees the Four Power Pact cannot become an accord which directly or indirectly has for its purpose the revision of the frontiers of our countries." Although this interpretation made the effective application of Mussolini's pact impossible— as long as the Great Powers considered themselves bound by them—it cleared the way for French approval of the scheme. After a tiring battle Paris had finally been pushed into initialling the Four Power Pact.[61]

At the end of May everything pointed to an early conclusion. The last obstacles in Berlin and Paris had been overcome. In Geneva the legal experts of France, England, Germany, and Italy were busy preparing the official draft. On questions of procedure it had been decided that the treaty was to be a "Heads of State" agreement, and that there were to be four texts with the French as the governing one. On May 31 a meeting took place in the Palazzo Chigi, but de Jouvenel and Hassell had not yet received their official instructions to initial. Even a bitter interlude between Neurath and

----

[61]FBB, No. 10. The Italian and the British diplomats also exerted constant pressure upon the Little Entente representatives at Geneva, and therefore deserve together with Paul-Boncour some credit for the reversal. Aloisi, *Journal*, pp. 103-137.

Rumbold over the use of the word "efficacy" rather than "due effect" could but momentarily delay the conclusion. In all countries the press expected the immediate initialling.[62]

At this moment a new hitch occurred in the negotiations which was at once annoying and ridiculous. At the eleventh hour de Jouvenel suddenly informed the other ambassadors that the French government had been discussing the proposed text completely at cross-purposes. While the French ambassador in Rome had been acting on the text which had been jointly elaborated there on May 20, the Paris government had treated its own draft of May 19 as a basis for the final agreement. Taken by itself the difference between the two versions was slight, but the matter assumed diplomatic significance because the Quai d'Orsay had based its communications to the Little Entente on its own version. This draft bound the Germans more explicitly than the Roman compromise, and Berlin, therefore, refused to concede the latest French caprice.[63]

The reasons for this contretemps are still not quite clear, but it is probable that the villain of the piece was the telephone. Since de Jouvenel was no career diplomat, his papers were not in as good order as might otherwise have been expected. The Roman draft of May 20 appears to have been telegraphed to

---

[62]BFP, V, 216. Rumbold interpreted the incident as evidence for the hostility of the Wilhelmstrasse against the pact and as proof for the strength of the Italian pressure which eventually made the Germans yield. GMF, D 676414-676418.

[63]BFP, V, 195; GFP, I, 282; FRUS, pp. 412-5, 421-4. Only a day before the unpleasant discovery Bülow had instructed Hassell that "he would not be allowed to permit even the slightest modification of the central articles." GMF, D 676406, D 676438.

Paris the same night that the Quai d'Orsay transmitted
its own version to the Palazzo Farnese. De Jouvenel
was under the impression that both texts were identical, and the error was not detected until the final wording was elaborated by the legal experts. Although this
was the official explanation given, there remains the
strong possibility that the French Foreign Office de-
liberately referred the false text to the French ministers. The permanent officials were certainly jealous
of the careless dilettante in Rome and might have given
him enough rope to hang himself.[64]

The muddle in the French files created a mild
storm. At the last possible moment negotiations were
once more deadlocked, and after the long weeks of
close bargaining and the large concessions which had
already been made to the French, none of the other
powers was willing to yield an inch. British exasperation was so strong that Simon instructed Tyrell to impress on Daladier in an official demarche: "It makes
all negotiations between governments impossible, if,
on the eve of the settlement, one government repudi-
ates the text agreed upon by its representatives ten
days before. I am astonished to be offered the explanation that owing to an oversight this agreed text

---

[64]This was at least Hassell's contention. GFP,
I, 281. See also Francesco Jacomini, "Il Patto a
quattro," p. 61. An editorial in the *Giornale d'Italia*
sharply rebuked the French press for blaming Berlin for
the delay. GMF, D 676439. The buoyant optimism
about the initialling turned into sudden gloom in Rome
and diplomatic circles openly admitted the failure of
the Four Power Pact. GMF, D 676443. A semi-official
article in the *Deutsche diplomatisch-politische Korrespondenz* (June 2) blamed the "egotistical demands
of a power-political interest group," i.e. France for the
impending breakdown. GMF, D 676440.

was unknown during all this time to the Ministry of Foreign Affairs in Paris. I must state that if, as a result of this oversight on the part of the French government, the pact now falls through, the fault will be due to the carelessness of the French Foreign Office and the French Government will solely be responsible for the international consequences of such a breakdown." Such language from the British ally had not been heard in Paris for a long time and was taken amiss because of Daladier's precarious parliamentary position, which had in part been created by his defense of the Four Power Pact.[65]

The familiar pattern of compromise was repeated, and on June 2 the translation of the disputed phrases in Article Two and Six was settled. De Jouvenel kept bombarding Paris with long-distance calls, arguing for a conciliatory attitude, since France was beginning to drift into diplomatic isolation. Another tripartite meeting was held, but the atmosphere had deteriorated markedly after the unfortunate incident. The French ambassador admitted sole responsibility for the delay, but he could propose no more enlightening solution than to drop the contested article entirely. In such an eventuality Signor Suvich threatened to abandon the pact. Despite the acrimonious exchanges, the French acceptance of blame paved the way for the eventual compromise.[66]

For the next two days Rome buzzed with attempts to break the stalemate. Makeshift corrections and all-too-ingenious solutions were discarded as quickly as they were proposed. Finally the British offered their services and proposed a text which altogether omitted the disputed reference to the December 11 Declaration and the other previous Great Power agreements. The

---

[65]BFP, V, 195.
[66]BFP, V, 216.

new wording circumvented both French and German objections by its vagueness: "The High Contracting Parties undertake to make every effort to ensure the success of the Disarmament Conference and, should questions which concern them remain in suspense on the conclusion of the Conference, they reserve the right to re-examine those questions among themselves in pursuance of the present agreement with a view to ensuring their solution through appropriate channels."[67]

The diplomatic struggle now centered around this version. De Jouvenel continued to send emphatic messages to Paris, imploring Daladier: "If you accept, you will be assuming great responsibility before parliament, but if you refuse, you will be assuming great responsibility before the world."[68]   More effective than such entreaties was de Jouvenel's threat of resignation. Only after he had pointed out again and again that virtually all French objections had been met, and that it would be morally impossible to desert the ranks *now*, did he receive authorization to initial the latest

---

[67]GFP, I, 265. Hassell thought this version "pretty much acceptable," but the French government posed the unpleasant alternative of either resuming the discussions on Article III from the beginning or of striking it entirely. Since the latter possibility appealed to no one, the British and the Italians elaborated a meaningless compromise, which avoided the problem by neither mentioning equality nor security. Graham pressed Hassell to agree to the new version of Article Three "since the pact was of the greatest psychological importance especially at the present moment, and its content in spite of everything was still useful for [Germany], and nobody could assume the responsibility for its failure." GMF, D 676448, D 676452. For the text of the final draft see Appendix, col. vi.

[68]*New York Times*, June 7.

version shortly before noon on June 6.[69]

All seemed well when another unexpected obstacle arose, this time from the German quarter. The eleventh-hour bickering had exasperated Hitler, and now he in turn withheld his approval. Foreign Minister Neurath was delighted that the eyes of the world rested on the Wilhelmstrasse for the first time since Versailles, and he invented another twenty-four-hour delay by inform-ing the Palazzo Chigi that neither Hitler nor Papen could be reached during the Pentecost holidays, and that a decision would have to be postponed until after the weekend.[70]

Bülow explained the reasons of the German hesi-tance to Cerruti in Berlin, complaining that the pact had become an entirely different instrument which had

---

[69]Hubert Lagardelle, *Mission à Rome*, p. 47; GFP, I, 287. The Havas version of the communique of the French Council of Ministers empowering Jouvenel to initial is in GMF, D 676461. For public opinion anal-yses of Paris at the eve of the initialling see GMF, D 676346, D 676511.

[70]Hassell, Cerruti, Rumbold and even Francois-Poncet bombarded the Wilhelmstrasse with messages and requests for a speedy conclusion, but Bülow was not to be budged; Hitler, Papen, and for a time even Neurath were absent, and he refused to assume the responsibility for such a potentially momentous de-cision. Hassell called repeatedly from Rome, but could not reach anyone but Bülow. Hence he had to justify the delay to Suvich with the legalistic argument that he had accepted the May 30 text only "as long as no new modifications will be made regarding Article Three." The Pallazo Chigi suspected rather that Hitler had left Berlin in order to avoid pressure for last-minute con-cessions. GMF, D 676454, D 676463. Fr. Jacomini, "Il Patto a quattro," p. 62.

lost all the advantages of Mussolini's original proposal.   Only an enfeebled version of Article One was
left. The word "revision" had been struck from Article
Two, and the last redeeming feature of the scheme, the
recognition of Germany's equality of rights, had been
deleted. But behind these technical arguments, Berlin
was only sulking and stalling in an attempt to force
some last-minute concessions, since even the German
press remained guardedly optimistic about the fate of
the pact.[71]

The Italians, on the other hand, were desperately
trying to obtain approval, since Mussolini was scheduled to speak before the Italian Senate on June 6 in an
address which would be broadcast throughout the country and also in the United States.   All during the day
Suvich kept urging Hassell to agree, but Berlin remained
silent and the Duce had to be content with the disap-
pointing declaration that "The negotiations for a pact
of collaboration and understanding among the four great
powers of Western Europe have reached a stage which
may shortly become conclusive in one way or another.

---

[71]This was at least the Italian explanation of Berlin's obstinacy. There remains, however, the alternative that the responsible ministers of the German government were thoroughly fed up with the Four Power
Pact. Their previous assent had only been conditional
and designed to do Mussolini a favor.   But the latest
British amendment to Article Three had made the pact
entirely useless from their point of view.   It seems
that General von Blomberg was strongly opposed to
any limitations on German rearmament and, therefore,
he disliked the pact heartily. Neurath was also highly
skeptical about its usefulness, and only Goering seems
to have championed it in the cabinet. GFP, I, 287; GMF,
D 676459 (on Blomberg's opposition).

I shall, therefore, if necessary, reserve the right to speak on this matter tomorrow."[72]

Finally, during the late afternoon of the next day, the message of consent which had been so anxiously awaited arrived from Berlin. It is difficult to see clearly what prompted Hitler to change his mind. According to Long, the American envoy to Paris: "It is generally understood here that in dealing with the Germans, Mussolini rarely had recourse to the regular diplomatic channels. . . . The chief of the Government spoke time and again directly with Herr Hitler or Captain Goering by telephone, and it appears to have been Herr Hitler's wish that both Baron von Neurath and the German For-

---

[72] Francesco Salata, *Il Patto Mussolini*, p. 125. Cerruti called three times on June 6 to hasten Berlin's decision. He even suggested a direct telephone conversation between Mussolini and Hitler, but the proposal was sidetracked in the Reich Chancellery. Bülow repeated the argument that "it would be entirely impossible for us to accept within such a short time a completely new version of the pact." But finally he consented to "attempt to reach a decision the next day." Suvich sent the Director of the Political Division of the Italian Foreign Office, Signor Buti, to Hassell, but he was no more successful than the Italian Ambassador Cerruti in Berlin. GMF, D 676456, D 676459-676462, D 676499, D 676515. For the Italian ambassador's description of the German obstinacy, see V. Cerruti, "Collaborazione internazionale e ragioni dell insuccesso della Societa della Nazioni," in *Rivista di studi storici internazionale* (January—June 1946), p. 59ff. Mussolini's speech is in Italy. Parlamento. *Atti Parlamentari della Camera dei Senatori, Discussioni* (Legislatura XXVIII, 1929-1933), p. 6524.

eign Office and Herr von Hassell...be excluded as far as possible from the negotiations."[73] The German Foreign Office files reveal only that Hitler instructed Hassell to initial the pact on Wednesday afternoon, June 7, 1933. In doing so the Führer spoiled the game of the French nationalists, who had exclaimed only a few hours before in the Chamber: "If he refuses, Hitler will render [France] a great service!"[74]

---

[73]FRUS, pp. 421-4. Unfortunately it is impossible to verify this rumor, since the Foreign Office files do not contain any material on it. Whenever Papen or Goering were involved in the negotiations some clear documentary trace can be found, but the personal telephone conversations—if they ever existed—naturally went unrecorded.

On June 7 François-Poncet called the Wilhelmstrasse at noon, but no decision had been reached at that time. Sir Horace Rumbold sent a personal letter to Neurath, stressing that the text had already been accepted by three of the four powers and Germany was the sole recalcitrant: "The conclusion of a pact between those four Great Powers must inevitably produce in itself a sensible detente in the present international atmosphere besides being the best send off for the Economic Conference." The British Ambassador could only "once again express the earnest hope that [the German] Government would see their way to accept the new draft." GMF, D 676515, E 447607.

[74]GFP, I, 290; GMF, D 676492ff. Fr. Jacomini, "Il Patto a quattro," p. 62. The Foreign Office files contain a series of handwritten notes scribbled on small pieces of scratch paper which were evidently taken by Neurath during the decisive cabinet meeting. After a piecemeal reconstruction the fragments only state Hitler's decision to initial. Neurath noted on the margin that he had called Hassell at 5:45 p.m. on June 7, about half an hour before Mussolini announced the decision in the Italian Senate.

Since Ronald Graham had already received the authorization to initial earlier the same day, the arduous negotiations for the Four Power Pact had finally achieved success.[75] The twofold diplomatic struggle had left deep scars on the final document. In the conflict of national points of view, the French triumphed, since they had proved the most unyielding and most resourceful. Faced with the Italo-British proposal of a Four Power Pact, openly challenging the French diplomatic system, the agile draftsmen of the Quai d'Orsay reduced Mussolini's pact to an innocuous affirmation of already existing alliances and commitments. "If then the voice might still be called the voice of Jacob, the hands were the hands of Esau. There was more of Paris and Prague than there was of Rome in the final draft."[76]

During the initial stages of the negotiations it had appeared that Paris might succumb to the united pressure of London, Rome, and Berlin. But the Quai d'Orsay adroitly exploited public revulsion against Hitler's rise to power to detach Whitehall from the revisionist front. The storm of international public opinion, the vociferous objections of the Little Entente, and the always precarious position of the French government were important assets in extracting concessions from the other partners. Since Mussolini had staked his prestige on the signing, but had lost almost all interest in the content of the pact, he was vulnerable to pressure from Paris, because he seemed in the last analysis determined to reach an agreement regardless of the price. French Foreign Minister Joseph Paul-Boncour could congratulate himself on the result: "In all cases ... the negotiations were conducted in such a manner that the final text gave full satisfaction

---

[75]BFP, V, 204.
[76]M. Macartney and P. Cremona, *Italy's Foreign and Colonial Policy, 1929-1938*, p. 134.

to the precautions demanded by France, whatever they were. "[77]

The internal struggle between the diplomats and the politicians within each country resulted in a stalemate. Although the political leaders appeared successful in achieving the initialling of the pact, it was a hollow triumph; the professionals of the foreign offices could claim victory in view of the substance of the final text. The Wilhelmstrasse had opposed the pact from the beginning, and only at the last moment and with great disappointment and ill-feeling towards Rome did it participate.[78] The Palazzo Chigi contributed only reluctantly to Mussolini's project, and the Duce often had to conduct negotiations alone.[79] The French

---

[77] Joseph Paul-Boncour, *Entre deux guerres*, p. 347. Cf. his testimony to the Commission chargée d'enquêter sur les *Evènements survenus en France de 1933 à 1945* (Paris, 1947), ed. by Ch. Serre, vol. III, p. 291ff.

[78] Although Neurath staunchly denied the charge, the conduct of the Wilhelmstrasse during the negotiations supported Alexis St. Léger's and Mussolini's opinion that the German Foreign Office was more than reluctant to agree to the Four Power Pact. FRUS, pp. 421-424. Cf. also GMF, D 676543; De Witt C. Poole, "Light on Nazi Foreign Policy," in *Foreign Affairs* (1946), pp. 130-151, stresses Hitler's dominance in policy decisions; Donald C. Watt, "The German Diplomats and the Nazi leaders, 1933-1939," in *Journal for Central European Affairs* (1955), pp. 148-160; and Paul Seabury, *The Wilhelmstrasse: A Study of German Diplomats Under the Nazi Regime* (Berkeley, 1954).

[79] Even Mussolini was aware that the Palazzi Chigi was less than enthusiastic about the pact. On May 10 he told Hassell that Germany "possessed an absolutely reliable friend in Mussolini. One should never be dis-

permanent services more than once drove de Jouvenel
to desperation, so that he exclaimed bitterly: "If the
Quai d'Orsay would only go to the trouble of reading
my dispatches."[80] Neither did Whitehall further Mac-
Donald's hazy designs. Vansittart admitted gleefully
that: "We had no intention of forming a governing
body, but the Germans and Italians had. We felt con-
tinually obliged to water down and explain away."[81]

And yet the negotiations had succeeded against
overwhelming odds. In 1933 the desire for peace and
reconciliation was still strong in Europe. Mussolini,
MacDonald, Daladier, and Hitler had overcome their
mutual suspicions and hostilities. It is ironical that
the traditionalist diplomats defended the ideals of the
League of Nations, while the upstart politicians saw
the solution to Europe's ills in a Great Power direc-
orate. At any rate, instead of erupting into open war,
the diplomatic crisis of the spring of 1933 had produced an extraordinary diplomatic instrument. After
three months of arduous negotiations the world awaited
the initialling of the Four Power Pact.

---

suaded from this belief, even if there existed trends
within the Italian Foreign Ministry, which opposed the
outlines of Mussolini's foreign policy." GMF, Serial
8904 H / E 621680. Cf. also Norman Kogan, *The Politics of Italian Foreign Policy* (New York, 1963), p.
35, which points out that the career diplomats did not
differ so much in basic philosophy from Mussolini as
in their choice of more peaceful means.

[80]Georges Bonnet, *Le Quai d'Orsay*, p. 125 and
supra, p. 120.

[81]Robert Vansittart, *The Mist Procession*, p. 454;
for the British Foreign Office see also M. Gilbert and
R. Gott, *The Appeasers*, pp. 15-20.

Chapter VI

THE SIGNING

IN THE LATE AFTERNOON of June 7, 1933, several hundred persons crammed into the visitors' gallery of the Italian Senate in Rome. Outside, the Piazza di Campidoglio was black with people tensely waiting for Mussolini's announcement of the successful conclusion of negotiations for the Four Power Pact. Like wind in a dense forest, rumors stirred the expectant crowds. The diplomatic gallery was packed; even the ambassadors of the Little Entente had made their appearance. On the floor of the Chamber the Senators conversed in anxious groups. Yet the seats for the other three Great Powers were conspicuously vacant.

Finally at 6 P.M. Henry de Jouvenel, Sir Ronald Graham, and Ulrich von Hassell entered and assumed their seats. Tension mounted, and twenty minutes later Mussolini himself strode into the Senate Chamber. The crowd hushed in respectful silence when the Duce raised his voice: "The war chapter is closed," he announced dramatically. It was clear that the Four Power Pact would be initialled. The Senate broke into prolonged enthusiastic applause, which spread outside and whipped through the waiting crowds. For more than an hour demonstrations of joy continued, and it seemed to one American journalist that "not since the armistice had Rome witnessed so much enthusiasm for the cause of peace. Mussolini, man of war, had dismounted his charger."[1]

Mussolini's oration lasted only half an hour, but it left an extraordinary impression upon his listeners. The Four Power Pact, he said, was to be the keystone of a structure which would guarantee the peace in Europe for ten years. After a lengthy exposition of the genesis of the pact, the Duce turned to its central theme: "There is no question of setting up by treaty a definite and immutable hierarchy of the powers. The existence of such a hierarchy in so far as the four States of Western Europe are concerned, is a matter of historical fact." Trying to reassure the smaller states, while at the same time stressing the ideological roots of four-power co-operation, the Duce resorted to an old argument: "The States which thus possess a permanent seat at the League are precisely the four States of the West——England, France, Germany and Italy. These States, therefore, permanently enjoy... the possibility of direct action, and thus possess greater responsibilities both as regards themselves and the world. Upon the more or less cordial state of their relations depend likewise the tranquility and peaceful progress of the other States."[2]

---

[1]*Newsweek*, June 17. Vivid descriptions of the Mussolini speech can be found in all major international papers. For an analysis of the event, see GFP, I, 295. The oration is in Italy. Parlamento. *Atti Parlamentari della Camera dei Senatori, Discussioni* (Legislatura XXVIII, 1929-1933), pp. 6689-6695.

[2]John Wheeler—Bennett, *Documents on International Affairs*, pp. 267-277, contains a smooth translation of the speech. Throughout the address Mussolini was engaged in the futile endeavor of pleasing everyone. Claiming that the pact was in full harmony

The Duce went on to deal with the objections to the scheme. He could not refrain from a vindictive reference to Beneš in passing, but in a very effective juxtaposition of the first draft and the final version, he emphasized that "the fundamental principles have remained unchanged." In harmony with the ideals of the League, he claimed, the Four Power Pact was directed against no one. All too well aware of the French success in emasculating the pact, Mussolini tried to make it more acceptable to Hitler by repeating the importance of German equality and treaty revision, even if they were no longer mentioned in the final version.

As a matter of course, Mussolini heaped praise upon the British. He uttered some friendly words about France, alluded ironically to Herriot's contribution, and expressed the hope of better co-operation on the basis of the pact. Belgium also received some of the credit. Finally, he spoke sympathetically of the "new Germany," reminding his audience that no truly European policy could be carried out without her, or still less against her. As a political realist the Duce confessed that all international difficulties would not disappear overnight. Nevertheless, the Four Power Pact would be an invaluable contribution to world peace. At the peroration Mussolini uttered the wish: "May the pact become operative, not so much in regard to its expressed clauses as in regard to the spirit which permeates it——a spirit which puts an end to a chapter of post war history and begins a new chapter which must guarantee ten years of peace to Europe, during which the harrassing and complex problems of national and international nature will be settled."

---

with the principles of Geneva, he at the same time stressed the Fascist concept of hierarchy and the Nazi desires for equality and revision. The result could only be self-contradictory and pathetic, no matter how much the public was impressed by Mussolini's delivery.

Thunderous applause marked the end of the speech. The crowds rushed out of the chamber and hastened to the Palazzo Venetia, where the initialling was to take place. The ceremony was simple. The ambassadors with their secretaries met in the Sala del Mappomondo, where the Duce had received MacDonald and Simon scarcely three months before. After ascertaining that all texts corresponded to the original, Mussolini affixed his signature to the document. The representatives of Britain, France, and Germany followed in alphabetical order. The Duce spoke a few informal words, and at 7:30 P.M. the ceremony was completed "while cherubs and angels smiled bland approval from the painted ceiling."[3]

During the first few weeks after the initialling it appeared as if the Four Power Pact would quickly outgrow the difficulties which had attended its birth and become a viable part of the fabric of international agreements. This illusion stemmed from the acclaim which greeted its conclusion. In Italy a wave of celebrations swept the country. The masses who had listened to Mussolini's oration over loudspeakers sang and danced in the streets and erected triumphal arches of flowers; half of Naples turned out for a gigantic parade. Never before had the Duce been as popular as at that moment. Since Hitler's advent fear and uncertainty had been mounting in Europe. Now the ominous clouds had been dispelled by one bold stroke of statesmanship. The nation praised Mussolini as the

---

[3]During the ceremony Mussolini approached Hassell and politely pointed out that the initialling was an important event for Germany in spite of all amendments: "Germany which had only been slandered in the past, had now for the first time been honoured and recognized by the head of a foreign government." GMF, D 676518.

angel of peace and the prophet of a better future. The
countless telegrams of congratulation glowed with
satisfaction: "Mussolini has succeeded in breaking
the ground, in laying the foundation, and in erecting
the structure of a new era in the history of Europe and
the world."[4]

No comparable celebration took place in Germany.
The pact's reception in the press was hardly enthusiastic. Conservative circles acknowledged its significance as a prestige victory for the Duce and intimated
the possibility of its usefulness in case of the failure
of the Disarmament Conference. But at best they were
willing to assign to it the value of a "European interim
solution."[5] Only the Nazi papers showed greater satisfaction, calling the Four Power Pact a "document created
for peace and the future." In an editorial in the *Völkischer Beobachter*, Rosenberg hailed the four-power
principle as a victory won by immense labors, including a mention of his own advocacy of the same idea

---

[4]*Nuova Antologia*, June 17, pp. 480-485, 602-604.
Cf. Salata's conclusion: "In the history of Europe
opened today, by common consent, a new era." *Il Patto
Mussolini*, p. 127. In Hassell's words the event was
celebrated in an "exuberant manner" in the Italian
press, while the content of the pact was neglected in
favor of stressing its moral importance. Extensive
coverage was given to the better relations with France
on the basis of the pact in order to assist Daladier in
the parliamentary battle for its approval. Only the
Popolo d'Italia dwelt on the possibility of revision.
GMF, D 676259ff.

[5]*Vossische Zeitung*, June 8, 9. "One will have to
regret all the same that more has not been achieved in
the pact. . . . It is proof of the German desire for peace."
The nationalists had hoped for large gains in revision
and equality and were, therefore, the most disappointed.

at the Volta Congress. The Nazi theoretician saw the
initialling as a triumph for Fascism on the international
scale. "The Four Power Pact represents perhaps the
most important treaty of the last fourteen years....
Europe owes this success especially to the two *Führer*
who have fought most energetically for the cause of
peace: Mussolini and Hitler." Yet even Rosenberg's
welcome sounded forced and artificial.[6]

The British public received the news of the initialling with no greater emotion. The old champions of
the pact, such as the *Daily Telegraph*, lauded its conclusion vociferously. But the Labour press revived its
attack, warning that even in its diluted state Mussolini's formula had proved to have an unsettling influence
on Europe.[7] The London *Times* had come a long way
from its original advocacy of revision, and reflected
the cautious appraisal of most influential Englishmen:
The Four Power Pact "is instinct with calm and good
will...but in [itself] does not bring peace, because

---

[6] *Völkischer Beobachter*, June 9: "On the Four
Power Pact." Although aware that "the pact in its present version does not fulfill all wishes," Neurath in a
circular nevertheless hailed it as "political progress."
The Wilhelmstrasse looked upon the final draft as a
defensive victory, since the four power principle had
remained untouched. "The conclusion is primarily due
to the moderate stand of the Government of the Reich,"
claimed Neurath, which was "unchallengeable proof of
Germany's peaceful policy," while in no way restricting
German freedom of action. GMF, E 44769, E 447221-
447228.

[7] London *Daily Herald*, June 8: "Assuming Failure
...: The peace machinery must be strengthened, but
that will not be done by deserting the League at such
a moment for the antiquated seductiveness of a Four-
Power junta."

[it] does not remove the causes of unrest. . . . [The pact] will be honest and useful, too, if the signatories are determined to translate its few constructive ideas into action. In itself it is a jejune document."[8]

To present the government's case for the initialling, Sir John Simon had a *White Paper* published on June 8, which Major Attlee attacked four days later in the Committee of Supply without too much vigor and yet with some skill: "It strikes me as a very peculiar White Paper. There is a dispatch from the British Ambassador in Rome which is almost entirely made up of excuses and apologies for what the pact does not do." Unable to refute the charge, the government defended its actions in a manner strikingly different from Mac-Donald's open call for revision only four months earlier. Anthony Eden's answer reflected the change: "I think the House will agree that an agreement is more than worthwhile which brings about that closer understanding between the Latin sisters referred to by M. Daladier, which no government would be so happy to see as His Majesty's Government in the United Kingdom."[9]

On July 5, Foreign Secretary John Simon once more stated the British cabinet's position. Complimenting "that most remarkable man, head of the Italian government" on his initiative and expressing the hope for

---

[8] London *Times*, June 9, "LOCARNO CONTINUED? "

[9] *British White Paper* (Cmd. 4342); House of Commons, *Debates*, vol. 279, cols. 35-36, 38-39, 81-86, 107-108, 124-125, 137-139. Analyzing the *White Paper*, Bernstorff of the German Embassy in London came to the conclusion that it first contained a remarkable stress on the inviolability of the Covenant, and second, that it repeatedly asserted that the British government did not assume any new, far reaching obligations on the Continent. GMF, E 447212, E 447219.

a quick signature, Simon declared: "I believe the
making of the Four Power Pact is a matter on which we
are entitled not as a Government, but as the British
People, to find some satisfaction and grounds for hope.
... The true position was this, that there was a real
danger that you would get developing in Western Europe two opposing blocs of powers, with special relations or special associations binding one set to one
view and another set to another view." A remarkable
analysis, even if the remedy proved inadequate![10]

In Paris a surprising change of public opinion took
place regarding the Four Power Pact. Ably led by the
always dissatisfied Pertinax, the journalists of the
Right continued their vehement hostility, even after
their failure to halt the initialling."[11] But circles closer
to center reversed their position and accepted the pact
in its revised form. In an editorial which aroused
much comment, *Le Temps* signalled the shift, calling
the pact "a new fact in international relations. . . . In
its definitive form it is a work of good faith and of
considerable importance for the collective order, if
interpreted and applied in a true spirit of collaboration." Moderate opinion in France had come to favor

---

[10]House of Commons, *Debates*, vol. 280, cols.
361ff.

[11]*Journal des Débats*, June 1 *et seq.* called the
pact "a criminal act . . . one of the most mistaken dates
of our history . . . the most dangerous operation per-
petrated since 1919" and concluded "we rest firmly
opposed to the Four Power Pact." But the initialling
found, except in the Right press, a favorable reception,
since French desires had been fulfilled almost entirely.
The possibility of closer co-operation with Italy received most coverage, and the ten years' truce was
hailed as a major achievement. GMF, E 447080.

the acceptance of the Four Power Pact.[12]

The French cabinet, especially Daladier, Paul-Boncour, de Monzie, and Léger, was very well satisfied with the initialling. The Ministers viewed the final draft as a victory for their diplomatic skill and were quite surprised that it had come so easily.[13] But one hurdle remained. The agreement had to be piloted safely through the Chamber, in which the government's position was most delicate. Some last minute maneuvering by Herriot to stall debate and delay passage was wrecked by the Socialists, whose internationalism triumphed over their fear of Hitler. Two days after the ceremony in Rome the Chamber was packed for the crucial debate on the Four Power Pact.[14]

---

[12]*Le Temps*, June 9: "The Pact and Mussolini's discourse." *L'Europe Nouvelle* and *L'Illustration* also swung around in the end. The French Action Committee for the League of Nations, to which the veteran organizations belonged, even sent a congratulatory resolution to Foreign Minister Paul-Boncour. GMF, E 447263.

[13]GFP, I, 320. Paul-Boncour explained the ease of the success by Mussolini's disinterest in the content of the pact. Koester reported perceptively: "As far as the pact is concerned they seem here to want to use it only as a basis for an improvement in Franco-Italian relations."

[14]According to Léger, the backstage maneuvering was serious enough to throw a real scare into the Daladier government. Since the Right and the Communists were clearly opposed and the S.F.I.O. wavered between hostility against Nazism and the desire for peace, there had been a strong possibility for the success of the plot: "The consequences would probably have been the rejection of the pact in an extraordinary session and the fall of the government." Hence Paul-Boncour was not allowed to defend the pact, and Daladier hid the passages relating to the pact in a more general speech on internal policy. GMF, D 676543.

Premier Daladier opened the discussion with a cautious discourse warmly thanking Mussolini for the "moving words" which he had addressed to France in the Roman Senate. Thanking England and the other participants in the negotiations, and reassuring those whose fears had almost prevented the conclusion of the treaty, Daladier defended the pact by showing how each of the major objections of public opinion had been met. All rights were safeguarded; no directorate had been established; the League had not been violated; France's friends welcomed the pact; the principal benefit would be closer co-operation with Italy.

The "little bull," as he was nicknamed by the American correspondents, ended with the exhortation: "It is our duty, gentlemen, to appreciate the result of the negotiations and to compare the advantages and inconveniences of the new pact with those of a rupture."[15]

Sensing defeat, the opposition hastily introduced a motion to "bar French signature from any pact in which the Little Entente, Belgium, and Poland would not participate on par with the Great Powers, and which would not leave the right of immediate accession to the other European powers." Sponsored by the Communist Henry Torres, the move was also supported by the leading Nationalists Marin, Doumerge, Fabry, and Lerolle. The debate grew heated and charges and coun-

---

[15]Chambre, *Débats Parlementaires*, vol.150, cols. 2825-2844. GFP, I, 303. Not all were pleased with Daladier's overly cautious defense. Since he had hoped for a more radical change in French policy away from the League, Anatole de Monzie sarcastically wrote in his memoirs: "But on June 9 our parliament repudiated in effect the instrument which was adopted that very night and chose to maintain, cost it what it might, the illusions by which our dreams of universal disarmament were protected." *Ci-devant* (Paris, 1941), p. 49.

ter-charges flew through the air. Waving the bloody
shirt, the Right warned France not to let "the fruits of
victory" be sacrificed. The Four Power Pact was "one
of the gravest errors committed in a long time." Aware
of the split in the cabinet's forces, Franklin-Bouillon
charged: "Even the President of the Commission of
Foreign Affairs is in his private thoughts against the
pact; he has declared that what you are about to do is
almost a crime against the nation!" This acrimonious
allegation finally forced Herriot into the open. He accepted the challenge, declaring that his original apprehensions had been quieted by the modified text, and
openly endorsed the Four Power Pact. The opposition
was bitterly disappointed by his declaration, since
until the very last minute Herriot's stand had been in
doubt. They had forced the issue, gambled, and lost.
The vote in favor was 405-169.[16]

Reaction in the rest of the world was predominantly
favorable. The United States welcomed the pact. The
attitude of the State Department was expressed in a

---

[16]The impressive margin of victory was primarily
due to the support of the S.F.I.O., although the size of
the negative vote had grown by some fifty ballots over
earlier votes. It still did not reach, however, the 212
adverse ballots in the first test of the pact. Since Herriot's maneuvering failed to weld a coalition together
to topple Daladier he finally came out to support the
scheme. Moreover, the financial difficulties of the
cabinet were a more rewarding domestic issue for an
overthrow of the government, especially since moderate
opinion by now favored the Four Power Pact. There
were, however, some irreconcilables like *Le Journal
des Débats*, who grew even more bitter over this "CA-
PITULATION OF THE CHAMBER" (June 11), and predicted gloomily that France was "preparing her down-
fall as a great power."

congratulatory telegram signed by Roosevelt: "The initialling at Rome of the Four Power Pact between France, Germany, Great Britain and Italy is a good augury. The United States welcomes any effort toward replacing the conflicting national aims by international cooperation for the greater advantage of all. This agreement of the principal European powers to work closely together for the preservation of peace should give renewed courage to all who are striving for the success of the Geneva and London Conferences."[17] The *New York Times* followed suit. "To many the transformation will seem like that of a fire brand into an olive branch." But the paper was more generous in its final evaluation: "What is left bids fair to be of highest value. . . .It embraces and most keenly interests the whole world in its scope and effect."[18]

Even the Secretary General of the League of Nations, Sir Eric Drummond, joined the chorus of acclaim: "The Four Power Pact should be very favorable for the future work of the League. I have often thought that consultations among the powers occupying a permanent seat in the Council about the questions in which

---

[17]U.S. Department of State, *Press Releases* (Washington, 1933), pp. 432-3.

[18]*New York Times*, June 9: "More than four powers." According to Ambassador Luther, political circles in Washington welcomed the initialling as the first step towards a political detente in Europe. The press was divided, since the isolationist papers especially charged the treaty with complete uselessness. GMF, D 676548, D 676570, E 447439. In a conversation with the Italian Minister of Economics, Jung, Roosevelt called the pact "the only means to Europe and the world, to assure the political peace which is the only foundation of economic stability." Cited in V. Gayda, *Was Will Italien*, pp. 134-150.

they carry in the final analysis the greatest responsibility, should be very useful."[19] In an address to the Spanish pilgrims who had gathered to celebrate the Holy Year, Pope Pius XI paid tribute to Mussolini's sincere desire for peace: "The world is again in search of peace, of spiritual pacification. ... Finally there emerged, what had been doubtful and insecure for a long time, something which today all call the Four Power Pact; that pact of the Great European Powers which assures not only to themselves, but to the entire world—what precious assurance—a period of ten years of peace, of better understanding, of more complete harmony of interests, be they ever so contrasting and difficult to reconcile."[20]

But one discordant voice was heard in the chorus of the Great Powers—that of Soviet Russia. Despite numerous German and Italian assurances, the Soviet Union remained hostile to the pact. A rebuff from the Quai d'Orsay to an inquiry of Dogalevsky, Soviet ambassador to Paris, to determine the French obligations under the treaty did not add to Moscow's love of the proposal. *Pravda*, therefore, carried a hostile editorial at its initialling, in which Radek resumed his criticism, denouncing the pact as an attempt of British imperialism to weld a common capitalist front together against the USSR. Soviet pride was hurt by the exclusion: "To attempt to regulate the affairs of 165 million inhabitants, possessing a great industry and being full of sympathy for all the 'better things in man,' is

---

[19]*Ibid.*, pp. 145-149.

[20]GMF, E 447151, E 447167. On June 9, the *Osservatore Romano* greeted the conclusion "with the satisfaction of a man, who sees in peace the highest treasure of mankind, [since it provides] the holy atmosphere in which Christian faith and progress prosper." Fr. Jacomini, "Il Patto a quattro," p. 64.

an effort which is doomed to ridicule. The European powers overestimate their own forces and underestimate those of the Soviet Union. Russian opinion takes note of this effort to move the boundary posts of Europe from the Urals to the shores of the Beresina and judges it accordingly. "[21]

The ideological consequences of this evaluation of the Four Power Pact did not become apparent until January, 1934, when Radek penned another article on Soviet policy for *Foreign Affairs.* Here the two ideological steps away from the German alliance towards collective security were clearly outlined: "The Soviet Union is confronted both in Europe and in the Far East with hostile camps which are preparing war against one another. It holds toward them a position of neutrality." But then Radek returned to advice given earlier by Lenin: "A situation might arise when the Soviet Union would carry on action parallel with the enemy of its own enemy, or would even co-operate with him in a joint action. This solution remains today one of the guiding principles of Soviet policy." Although the roots of this development go back as far as 1929 with Litvinov's takeover in the Narkomindel, the Four Power Pact was a contributary factor in the reversal.[22]

The reaction of the smaller powers varied little from their initial response. In Stockholm the *Svenska Dabgladet* and *Dagens Nyheter* ridiculed the pact and

---

[21]The Soviet press continued to suspect ulterior motives behind the pact. *Pravda*, June 9, "The Four Power Pact and the Anti-Soviet Plans of the Irreconcilables" was a pointed attack by Radek. GMF, E 447101, E 447259. Moscow papers also suddenly grew fond of quoting editorials from the Polish press, notably from the *Gazeta Polska*. GMF, E 447385.

[22]K. Radek, "The Bases of Soviet Foreign Policy," in *Foreign Affairs* (January, 1934), pp. 193-206.

called it entirely superfluous.[23]   In Madrid the *Sol*
could hardly conceal its displeasure with the untimely
French concessions to Nazi Germany.[24]   But Athens
refused to be drawn into the chorus of criticism and
continued to favor the scheme.[25] Ankara's earlier fears
had been dispelled not so much by the diminution of
Mussolini's proposal as by the signature of the Litvinov Protocol defining aggression in early July.[26] The
tremors of the initialling penetrated as far as Beirut,
where the French High Commissioner seized on the
event to disabuse Syrian nationalists of their hopes of
Italian or German support for their aspirations.[27]

The Italian satellites enthusiastically celebrated
the success of Mussolini's initiative.   In Vienna the
Reichspost paid tribute to the initialling as a European event, while only the Socialist *Arbeiter Zeitung*

---

[23]GMF, E 447171, E 447209.   The Swedish press
dwelt especially on the timidity of Hitler's first steps
in the international arena, which belied his truculent
vows to tear up the Versailles Treaty.

[24]GMF, E 447244.

[25]GMF, D 676350.

[26]In Turkey the press stressed more the Soviet
rapprochement with France, expressed in the signature of a number of Litvinov Protocols with France's
Eastern allies on July 3-5, 1933.   The *Miliyet* of July
22 called "the rapprochement between Russia and
France the most significant phase of international
relations in the post—war era."   GMF, E 447434, E
447552.

A long range effect of the conclusion of the Four
Power Pact was its stimulation and acceleration of the
Turkish plans, which culminated in the Balkan Entente
early in 1934.   Cf. the conversation of Koester with
Massigli on January 9, 1934, GMF, E 447467.

[27]GMF, E 447243.

and some liberal organs continued their criticism.[28] In
Sofia the *Slowe* had no doubts that the front of the vic-
torious powers had been breached by the Four Power
Pact. "The day of revision is approaching with giant
strides. ... The decisive step towards revision has already been taken."[29] Budapest echoed the revisionist
acclaim.[30]

In Brussels, Foreign Minister Hysmans stressed
before the United Foreign Affairs Commissions of Senate and House that the Belgian desires had been taken
into account. Although right—wing papers like the
Nation Belge warned that "the pact condemns Europe
to war and Belgium to invasion," in general the politically important circles moderately favored the conclusion.[31] The response of the Little Entente followed
the Belgian example, because the exchange of notes
with France had calmed their fears. The French note
asserted that revision could only be undertaken under
the auspices of Article XIX of the Covenant, within the
framework of the League and under conditions of complete unanimity of all parties.[32] This assurance

---

[28]GMF, E 445173.

[29]GMF, E 447138. The Bulgarian pronouncements
on revision were the noisiest and the most futile in-
vocations of the Four Power Pact.

[30]See the conversations during Kanya's visit to
Rome during the closing days of July. GMF, E 447425ff.

[31]See Lerchenfeld's reports, GMF, E 447155, E
447261. As spokesman of the Second International,
Vandervelde blasted the pact on June 23: "While the
National Socialists in Germany act like 'mad dogs,'
Hitler is being made socially acceptable through the
appeasement of the other powers!"

[32]FBB, Nos. 12-14. In Prague the reception of the
pact was moderately favorable, but there existed considerable disquiet over Poland's continued intransi-

amounted to a one-sided interpretation of the pact, making it utterly ineffective as a tool for revision. Beneš, Titulescu, and Yevtitch gladly accepted the guarantee from Paris, and their respective ambassadors expressed deepest gratitude at the Quai d'Orsay.[33]

Similar assurances were extended to Poland, but here they were given in vain. Despite Paul-Boncour's and Laroche's pleading, Pilsudski remained hostile, and expressions "of the concern of the French Government that nothing may affect the policy which both Governments follow on the basis of the treaties which unite them," found no echo.[34] For Poland it had become a question of wounded *amour propre* rather than

---

gence and its effect on the united front of the Central European states against revision. Edouard Beneš welcomed the French assurances in an interview with *Le Petit Parisien* on June 7: "If the proclamation of territorial intangibility of the three [Little Entente] states was made in such a solemn fashion, one must consider it absolute, definitive, irrevocable and unanimous." GMF, E 447075, E 447200, E 447204.

[33]FBB, Nos. 15-17. In Bucharest the government stressed Hitler's recognition of the previous treaties implied in the Four Power Pact, while in Belgrade Yevtitch answered an interpellation in the Yugoslav House: "The Signature of the Four Power Pact cannot constitute any danger for the countries of the Little Entente, nor for the common policy of the Little Entente and of France. The guarantees are of such a nature that the Four Power Pact cannot transform itself into an entente which has for its purpose, directly or indirectly . . . the revision of the frontiers." But beneath such professions of security there remained a considerable feeling of uneasiness in the capitals of the Little Entente countries. GMF, D 676524, E 447106, E 447168.

[34]FBB, No. 18.

of practical fear of the consequences of the pact. To underline his country's independence, Foreign Minister Beck issued a communique through PAT on June 8, sensibly discriminating between the first and the final draft, but proudly refusing any co-operation with the new instrument: "In case the powers agree to modify the treaties to which Poland is a partner and which do not exclusively concern these powers, the Polish government reserves the right to do the same." For a brief moment Polish and Soviet policies were in accord. Both rejected the Four Power Pact, and their common resentment facilitated the signing of the Litvinov Protocol between them on July 3.[35]

The publication of the French *Blue Book* on June 9 brought into glaring relief the deep chasm which existed between the partners of the Four Power Pact before it

---

[35]Jules Laroche, *La Pologne de Pilsudski*, p. 131. The text of the communique is in Josef Beck, *Beiträge zur Europäischen Politik*, p. 57f. According to Moltke the pact "had found the sharpest rejection," and ironically enough, "France and Poland seemed to have played with exchanged roles in the last weeks." An editorial in the *Gazete Polska* described the impact of the pact: "Concerning the French Polish relations, there are two circumstances to be noted: on the one hand the factor of will and purpose, on the other hand that of possibility. We do not doubt the good will of France for one moment. . . . But what concerns the possibilities, we fear that they can only decrease from the moment at which France binds herself to the Four Power Pact." GMF, E 447090, E 447196. For the Litvinov Protocol with a series of Central European States on June 3-5, see Robert J. Kerner, *The Balkan Conferences and the Balkan Entente, 1930-1935* (Berkeley, 1936), pp. 118-119, who also stresses the Four Power Pact as antecedent to the Balkan Entente of 1934.

had even been signed. The French assurances to the
Little Entente, which had been necessary to make
Prague, Belgrade and Bucharest acquiesce in Mussolini's proposal, infuriated Hitler, since they not only
further invalidated the pact, but also (in his eyes)
broke a previous promise of the French government.
On May 28 *Le Matin* had published what purported to
be the substance of a French note to the Little Entente,
containing four points: The pact in no way enfringed
upon existing agreements; Paris would not admit any
territorial revision; the Quai d'Orsay would insist on
the Covenant; and the French would demand unanimity,
i.e. a small-power veto, in all important decisions.[36]
Questioned about the accuracy of the disclosure, Alexis
St. Léger categorically denied its truth and implied
that the canard originated with Henri de Korab, a Polish
exile journalist.[37]   Although the Wilhelmstrasse put
little stock in the *démenti*, it could do nothing but
wait, especially since Mussolini also minimized the
importance of the incident, because some such assurance would have to be given at any rate.[38] Hitler ranted
about the "French duplicity," and only a prolonged

---

[36]Wolff release, May 28. GMF, D 676380f. GFP,
I, 272, 275. Neurath called the French note "a com-
plete devaluation . . . and a political contradiction."
GMF, D 676393.

[37]GMF, D 676412. Léger stated that the French
government had only the intention of publishing its
own interpretation of the pact, which centered around
the assertion that the four powers had every right to
discuss all matters which concerned them alone and
debate all means to ensure European peace.

[38]GMF, D 676400. Mussolini tried to gloss over
the incident and it was not until Hassell's protest two
weeks later that the Palazzo Chigi realized the gravity
of the German objections.

series of negotiations could placate his wrath sufficiently to allow Germany to sign the pact.

On June 13, Hassell lodged with Mussolini a
strongly worded protest against the unilateral action
of the Quai d'Orsay. The ambassador raised three
specific objections against the French interpretation.
The assertion that the "pact precluded any consideration of the principle of revision and of concrete cases
of application" was untenable. The contention that
"there can be no question of raising a question of revision outside the provision laid down in Article XIX
was factually incorrect. And the stipulation that revision "requires in each case the unanimous agreement
of the League members who are present" was clearly a
violation of the spirit of the pact. Without consulting
the other partners, France had committed herself to a
certain interpretation of the pact to outsiders. Such
action was contrary to the spirit if not the letter of the
treaty and Hassell repeated in a firm but friendly tone
that Germany would only be too happy to sign *after* the
little incident had been cleared up.[39]

The demarche placed Mussolini once more in an
awkward position. Any open Italian disavowal would
endanger the budding rapprochement with France; any
action short of protest would make Hitler leave the
pact. Hassell added to his difficulties by threatening to appeal to the public, and by reading a harsh
draft memorandum to be presented to the French. The

---

[39]GFP, I, 300, 304. GMF, D 676537, D 676541, D
676549, E 447118, serial 8910 H / E 621744. Neurath
was "extremely disgusted" because the note excluded
revision by limiting it to Article XIX of the Covenant
and eliminated certain questions beforehand from common deliberation. When Koester delivered a similar
protest to Léger, he found the French diplomat ada-
mantly repeating his previous assurances.

Duce could only stall for time and propose nothing
more ingenious than Anglo-Italian mediation.[40] Several
suggested solutions were quickly discarded.[41] Approached directly from Berlin, Paris stuck to its guns
and replied philosophically that a general "devaluation" of all established boundaries might be the answer.[42]

Although the whole crisis bore the unreal features
of a *coup de théâtre*, it produced a flurry of diplomatic
activity during the last weeks of June. Finally the ver-
satile Suvich hit upon the suggestion that it might suffice for Germany to express her objections in a note to
Mussolini, the father of the pact, who would then orally
inform the French and the British of its contents.[43] To

---

[40]GFP, I, 308. The problem for the Italians was to
give satisfaction to the protest of the Wilhelmstrasse
without endangering the signing by the French. GMF,
D 676557, D 676573.

[41]The Palazzo Chigi for instance proposed to have
the Germans publish their own interpretation through
Wolff. But the Wilhelmstrasse rejected the offer, since
it believed that a declaration of equal weight should
confront the French notes.

[42]GFP, I, 315, 402. Paul-Boncour was even more
stubborn than Léger and denied any need for a *démenti*
from Paris. GMF, D 676568, D 676559, E 447213, D
676578.

[43]GFP, I, 317. In a series of conversations at the
World Economic Conference from June 12 to 17, Neurath
pressed for some kind of satisfaction with Suvich. The
Italian finally came up with his complicated plan,
mainly to forestall answers to the German protest by
Paris and London which could then develop into an
open controversy. Bülow and Neurath slowly warmed
up to the idea and elaborated the text of the German
note. GMF, Serial 6058 H / E 447035; D 676567, D
676571, D 676576, D 676578.

forestall an open break, Mussolini sent another personal message to Hitler, emphasizing that the French
interpretation concerned only the Covenant and not the
Four Power Pact.[44] In consecutive conferences in the
Palazzo Chigi the text of the German protest was wa-
tered down sufficiently to be acceptable to the Italians.[45] Hassell was to present the note to Mussolini,
who would then be at complete liberty to "convey the
contents of the note, in whatever form he may deem
suitable, to the other governments." Germany would
refrain from making its objections public to avoid an
open rift between the signatories.[46] The salient passages read: "It is impossible for the German government to accept this unparalleled action of the French
government in silence.... Should we fail to [protest]
now, it might be justly argued against us later that by
our signature of the pact ... we had acquiesced in the
interpretation and application of the pact therein."[47]
The German protest was transmitted to Paris and London in the early days of July together with a few lines
of Mussolini, stressing that such differences of interpretation were in the future to be settled at meetings of the member powers. Neurath considered the
incident closed and instructed Hassell to sign.[48]

---

[44]GFP, I, 318.

[45]GFP, I, 321. At the same time the Wilhelmstrasse
buzzed with attempts to produce an acceptable draft
in Berlin. For the three versions elaborated see GMF,
D 676585, D 676583, D 676591. This latest text was
handed to Suvich on June 19, who declared himself
satisfied. GMF, D 676593. The directives to Hassell
were issued after a consultation between Neurath and
Bülow on June 23. GMF, D 676595.

[46]GFP, I, 332 and GMF, D 676598-701 contain the
instructions to Hassell.

[47]GFP, I, 337.

[48]GFP, I, 358. Although the oral representations
were considerably stronger than the note, Hassell in-

The last obstacle to the signing of the Four Power Pact was the unstable parliamentary situation in Paris, which necessitated the postponement of the ceremony until after July 14, when Senate and Chamber would be in recess.[49] Originally Mussolini had hoped to have the three other heads of government present to crown his work by a great public display of reconciliation. But Hitler's reluctance to travel and Daladier's change of mind destroyed these plans and the Duce had to be content with a meeting of the foreign ministers, to be followed by a conference of the heads of state at some later date.[50]   This scheme also failed to materialize; the World Economic Conference absorbed all attention in June and early July.[51] It is typical of the decline of importance of the Four Power Pact in the eyes of the

---

cluded in them an assurance of the inviolability of Austria's independence which made Mussolini receive the German protest in good humor. GMF, D 676612. The Italian *note-verbale* to Paris and London was sheer equivocation, since it refuted the German protest as unjustified, while reprimanding the French for their unilateral interpretation.   GMF, serial 6958 H / E 44729. In a circular of July 28 Neurath celebrated the incident as a diplomatic victory for Berlin. GMF, E 447328.

[49]GFP, I, 323.

[50]GFP, I, 340. All along Neurath preferred to have it signed merely by the ambassadors. GMF, E 447141, D 676611.

[51]GFP, I, 301.   Rome was confident despite the formal snags: "Nobody had any doubts about the ratification either, even if it could drag out until fall." GMF, E 447291. A proposal to have the pact signed at the World Economic Conference in London was also quickly dismissed.

Great Powers that instead the Duce had to be content
with the mere signing by the ambassadors.[52]

At 11:50 A.M. on July 15, 1933, the Four Power
Pact was formally signed in Rome. In the great hall of
the Palace of St. Marc about two hundred dignitaries
had assembled beneath the ringing bells of the ca-
thedral to watch Mussolini slowly print his name with
a gold pen on gold-embossed paper. "At noon [wrote
Baron Aloisi] the signing of the Four Power Pact took
place. The ceremony unfolded with great gravity and
precision. The three Ambassadors Jouvenel, Hassell
and Graham affixed their signatures. Mussolini followed. I was present with Suvich and the high per-
sonnel of the ministry. Mussolini was calm and
satisfied and chatted with the three Ambassadors.
Many photographs were taken of the spectacle." By
12:30 P.M. everything was over. The Four Power Pact
had finally been concluded.[53]

In order, perhaps, to ease their consciences because of their absence, the heads of the other Great
Powers sent glowing telegrams of congratulation. De
Jouvenel was the first to present Daladier's "confidence
in the happy results which the pact of Rome cannot fail
to have for the friendship of our countries and for the
good of all nations." The British statesmen followed

---

[52]GFP, I, 343. The press began to report the imminent conclusion on June 9, and Hassell asked for
pleins pouvoirs on June 11. GMF, D 67662, D 676623.
The technicalities can be found in GMF, D 676628-33,
E 447298-371ff.

[53]Baron Aloisi's description, *Journal*, p. 139. According to Hassell there was only a small crowd of
diplomats and journalists present, while Mussolini
conversed amiably with the diplomatic corps. GMF,
E 447365.

suit, but Hitler outdid them all. In his inimitable style
he wrote: "Especially in view of the present situation
of the world this commitment of the four powers to co-
operation and mutual understanding is a beacon of
light in the life of the peoples of Europe." In most
countries the press was full of hope, and only a few
irreconcilables continued their gloomy prophecies for
the future. For a fleeting moment a new era of peace
and good will seemed to have dawned.[54]

----

[54]Max Domarus, *Hitler*, p. 290. *Nuova Antologia*
(vol. 368, 1933), pp. 452-457. For Daladier's telegram,
see GMF, E 447333. Neurath, Hitler, Hindenburg, and
Hassell also congratulated each other. GMF, E 447304,
E 447334, E 447337, E 447381. For Mussolini's replies
see GMF, E 447383, E 447395. Even *Le Temps* shared
in the euphoria: "Through this ceremony one of the
most important negotiations of the history of post-war
diplomacy has been brought to a good end. . . . The
opinion is unanimous: the Four Power Pact is a corner-
stone of the edifice of peace." July 16. Cf. also Robert Lambel in *L'Illustration*: "The so-called Four Power
Pact is the most important fact in international relations since the Locarno Treaties, which it reinforces
and completes." July 22. Celebrating with the French
colony in Rome, de Jouvenel expressed the high hopes
universally held: "With the help of Great Britain and
Italy, [the Four Power Pact] has built a bridge spanning
the abyss between the French and the German people
over which one can pass to new negotiations." *Journal*,
July 15.

Chapter VII

THE FAILURE

CONTRARY TO THE ebullient predictions of a brilliant future which accompanied the signing of the
Four Power Pact, its life was short and inglorious.
Mussolini's creation did not even last long enough to
be ratified by all signatories. It had been concocted
to resolve the international crisis after Hitler's advent,
but when test situations arose, it failed to meet them.
Some of the forces which were to end its precarious
existence had already become apparent during the arduous negotiations and in the interval between initialling and signing. Others emerged during the uneasy
summer and troubled fall of 1933. Sir Robert Vansittart had been only too correct when he sarcastically
admitted his hostility to the proposal: *"En foi de quoi*
we initialled in June, and signed in July, an elaborate
nullity."[1]

After the conclusion of the pact, three sets of
problems dominated the international scene: the world
economic crisis, the Central European question, and
German rearmament. The first was to have been over-

---

[1] Sir Robert Vansittart, *The Mist Procession*, p.454.

come by the World Economic Conference which began
with much fanfare on June 12 in London, but Soviet
Ambassador Maisky had no illusions about its result:
"The universal crisis of capitalism aggravated by the
world economic crisis 1929-1933 did its destructive
work and undermined the ground under the feet of the
Conference beforehand." For once Marxism provided
a correct prophecy, the meeting disbanded after weeks
of futile talks because Roosevelt's unorthodox methods
of recovery made international cooperation to stem the
tide of devaluation impossible. But although a psychological boost had been expected from the initialling of the Four Power Pact so shortly before the opening, the breakdown of the World Economic Conference
had no detrimental effect on the future of the pact.[2]

---

[2]FRUS, pp. 452-762. The former Soviet Ambassador to the Court of St. James linked the failures of the
Disarmament Conference, the World Economic Conference, and the Four Power Pact to the Great Depression:
"If one adds,... that in June 1933 the Geneva Conference of Disarmament has been fruitlessly in session
for one and a half years and was near total collapse,
and that in March [*sic!*] 1933 the anti—Soviet Four
Power Pact...was signed, which could not go into
effect or be ratified because of the deep contradictions
between its signatories (it was never really ratified),
then the picture of the condition of the capitalist world
at the moment of the opening of the London Conference
becomes quite clear." *Vospominania Sovetskogo Posla*
(Moscow, 1964), vol. II, p. 216.

In an article entitled "After London," Mussolini
used the failure of the World Economic Conference to
emphasize that there remained no other way of dealing
with Europe's economic problems than the Four Power
Pact: "The pact has in fact envisaged the failure of
the Conference... and has bound the four powers to

A second complex of problems proved to be more crucial for Mussolini's pact. The perennial question of Danubia, or more precisely the political and economic reorganization of the area of the former Austro-Hungarian empire, provided the first diplomatic test for the Four Power Pact. Here the national interests of three member states, France, Germany, and Italy, clashed openly, since all three sought to control the succession states. A French journalist wrote perceptively in July: "Concluded on the banks of the Tiber, it is on the shores of the Danube that the pact will be proven. The period of oratorial optimism is past; the time of practical difficulties has begun."[3]

The Franco-Italian discussions which opened immediately after the initialling centered upon the restoration of political and economic co—operation in Central Europe. Since the antagonism between the Little Entente and the Revisionist bloc had in the past prevented a constructive approach to the area's problems, the British urged the newly reconciled "Latin

---

collaborate in the matter of disarmament as well as in economic questions." *Opera Omnia*, vol. XXVI, pp. 36-38. The article was released on July 28 by *Universal Service*.

[3]Albert Musset in *Journal des Débats*, July 19. For the Danubian problem in the inter-war period, see Gerhard Schacher, *Central Europe and the Western World* (London, 1936); Robert J. Kerner, *The Balkan Conferences and the Balkan Entente, 1930—1935* (Berkeley, 1936); Robert Machray, *The Struggle for the Little Entente* (London, 1938); Antonin Basch, *The Danube Basin and the German Economic Sphere* (New York, 1943); Frederick Hertz, *The Economic Problem of the Danubian States: A Study in Economic Nationalism* (London, 1947); and Victor Arnold, *The Little Entente and the Revisionists*, pp. 439-443.

sisters" to harmonize their interests before Hitler seized the initiative. Time and again Vansittart stressed in his instructions to Graham: "The Franco-Italian rapprochement is a question in which the future of everybody, including ourselves, is now obviously involved; indeed the chief value of the pact in my eyes was from the beginning that it must conduce to this specific end." De Jouvenel's imminent retirement also made speedy agreement mandatory.[4]

The discussions between Paris and Rome dealt mainly with two sets of problems. Those exclusively concerning both countries, such as naval parity, Tunisia, Italian refugees, and colonial possessions, were postponed for the time being. A second, more urgent category comprised the defense of the independence of Austria, the maintenance of political stability in South Eastern Europe, and "the policy of encouraging the states of Central and South Eastern Europe to seek among themselves economic arrangements such as would help them to become collectively self-sufficing."[5] The debates made good headway even before the signing, but eventually foundered on the Italian refusal to give some general assurance regarding those points which would placate the Little Entente and make it easier for Daladier to defend himself in the Chamber. Mussolini hedged because he was afraid of losing his satellites by endorsing too much reconciliation. Although professing to be unable to comprehend the subtleties of the Latin mind, the British pressed Mussolini for the desired statement. A very vague assurance from the Duce was eventually obtained on the eve of the signing by de Jouvenel. Insignificant by

---

[4] BFP, V, 224, 228.

[5] BFP, V, 209, 235. These negotiations ran parallel to the squabbles over the French note to the Little Entente and over the modalities of the signing.

itself, the episode merely showed that the conflicting interests of France and Italy were not to be reconciled easily, "unless the fear of Germany meanwhile makes very great strides in the Italian mind."[6]

But there were also powerful interests within the two countries which pushed for a common solution of the Danubian problem. In France a considerable body of opinion, led by Foreign Minister Paul-Boncour and ably seconded by Maurice Pernot in *L'Europe Nouvelle* as well as by a number of other papers, advocated some kind of reorganization of Central Europe partly to prop up the French alliance system and partly to reverse the process of balkanization. In an interview on June 19 Paul-Boncour stated that "the Four Power Pact seemed to provide the possibility for preparing two big solutions: first the removal of the existing difficulties between France and Italy and second, co-operation of Italy in creating an economic federation of the Danube which alone would make the restoration of the whole area possible."[7]

---

[6]BFP, V, 223-250 *passim*. A semi-official article in the *Deutsche diplomatisch-politische Korrespondenz* of July 22 on "France, the Little Entente and the Four Power Pact" stated that the main importance of the treaty in French eyes was its use for the reorganization of Central Europe with the consent of Italy. GMF, D 676641. For a time there was even considerable talk of a Daladier visit to Rome, but the plan quickly evaporated. GMF, D 676594, D 676618. Hassell was skeptical about any substantial agreement, since Mussolini did not seem overly eager to come to terms with Paris. GMF, E 447281.

[7]The French conception of a solution was most clearly expressed in the abortive Tardieu plan for a customs union between the five Danubian states, which the Little Entente would dominate economically. The

For Mussolini the Danubian area had always been of cardinal importance. "For us a pan-German solution of the Danubian question is as little acceptable as a pan-Slav one," he had said. "The Danube basin is our European hinterland. That is why we seek a firm position there. Without it we shall be forced to play the insignificant role of a peninsula on the periphery of Europe. We might even be pushed into Africa."[8] Hitherto border quarrels with Jugoslavia had prevented the establishments of close ties with the Little Entente, and Mussolini chose the three other remaining states— Hungary, Austria, and Bulgaria—as revisionist satellites. The Duce, therefore, saw the Danubian problem through the eyes of the revisionist bloc, while France championed the claims of the Little Entente. The detente produced by the Four Power Pact created the possibility of the fusion of both conceptions into a higher, economically viable and politically independent unit,

---

project was checkmated by Italian and German resistance at the Stresa Conference of 1932. Victor Arnold, *The Little Entente*, p. 339f. The Paul-Boncour interview is in GMF, E 447189. In talks with representatives of *Le Matin*, *Le Journal des Débats*, and of *Havas*, de Jouvenel on his return from Rome stressed the renewed intimacy with Mussolini and the chance for solving the Danubian question. GMF, D 676638, D 676639, E 447392, E 4474515. Cf. also Maurice Pernot, "The Four Power Pact and the Danubian problem," in *L'Europe Nouvelle*, July 22, p. 687ff.

[8] A remark to Heimwehr leader Starhemberg who was seeking support against the Austrian Nazis in Rome. Mussolini added in characteristic fashion: "I may tell you that my friendship for Austria is dictated by the interests of Italy. For the same reason I want to strengthen the friendship with Hungary." *Between Hitler and Mussolini*, p. 105.

before the resurgence of Germany would render any Franco-Italian solution obsolete.[9] The prospects for the success of such a scheme looked so bright that Hassell repeatedly urged the Wilhelmstrasse to antici-pate a Franco—Italian deal by using Hitler's "inner front" with Mussolini to divide the spoils of Central Europe on the basis of close co-operation between Na-tional Socialism and Fascism.[10]

---

[9]The Four Power Pact even prompted a book by Freiherr von Sarkotic, in a pun on Spengler called, *Aufbau des Abendlandes: Ein Arbeitsplan auf Grund des Viermächtepaktes* (Vienna, 1933). The author, an Austrian official of the League and Secretary General of the "Mitteleuropa Institut," attempted to "find a synthesis between the necessary collaboration of the small central European powers and the policy of the Great Powers on the basis of the Four Power Pact." Ideologically related to Coudenhove-Kalergi, Lucien Coquet and Elmer Hantos, this programme suggested acceptance of the Roman pact as interim solution and the creation of an economic union of the five Central European powers to reap the benefits of the economies of scale. "For the duration of the Four Power Pact the Danubian states have only the possibility of continu-ing to starve alone or to follow the path of economic progress together." Sarkotic was very optimistic, since for him the Four Power Pact represented the first real chance of reconciling the conflicting interests of France, Italy and Germany and of reversing the bal-kanization of Central Europe.

[10]This suggestion was Hassell's pet project, but it found little response in the Wilhelmstrasse. More than one question or exclamation mark adorned the margins of his reports. In a private letter in April, he had already asked for instructions on Danubian co-operation, but received no answer. GMF, D 676596ff. Again in reports of June 15, July 14, 17, he reiterated

But Mussolini was not about to share with anyone. Concurrently with the negotiations with Paris
and Berlin, he initiated a series of unilateral moves
to ensure Italian predominance in Danubia under the
cover of the Four Power Pact. In the closing days of
June Hungarian Premier Gömbös and his Foreign Minister Kanya visited Rome. As charming host, the Duce
had little difficulty in eliciting warm praise for his
pact. More substantially, he coaxed his guests into
signing a *procès-verbal* setting forth their common
aims in the Danube basin: First, a close Austro-
Hungarian rapprochement, but without Hapsburg restoration or personal union; second, a customs union
between Rome, Vienna and Budapest; third, collaboration with Germany, as long as Austrian independence
were respected; fourth, unconditional opposition to the
Tardieu plan, since it would obviate revision, and last,
the Four Power Pact should serve as a common platform for a policy of rearmament and revision.[11]

---

the demand "that the internal German—Italian front
must be strengthened through an understanding of the
basic lines of policy and economic policy, especially
in the Danubian area, and through collaboration with
Hungary." Hassell also mentioned the improbability
of a Franco-Italian entente, pointing to the contradictory interpretations of the Four Power Pact in Paris
and Rome, where each side was out to use the treaty
for its particular national advantage. GMF, E 447221-
30, E 447360, E 447402f.

[11]FRUS, pp. 203-204. GFP, I, 344. P. Aloisi, *Journal*, p. 141. Kanya reassured Hassell that Mussolini
valued the German tie over friendship with France, and
that the ground would have to be prepared better before
the first Four Power Pact meeting would be called. GMF,
E 447425f. C. A. Macartney, *October Fifteenth: A
History of Modern Hungary, 1929-1945*(2nd ed., Edin-
burgh, 1961), vol. I, pp. 307ff.

The second step towards consolidating Italian
hegemony over Central Europe under the auspices of
the Four Power Pact was Mussolini's support of Austria, making Vienna subservient to Italy not only in
foreign but also in domestic policy. "We must summon up courage to conform this ideal of a Greater
Germany with the ideal of an absolutely independent
Austria," he told Heimwehr leader Prince Starhemberg
during the latter's visit in April, while promising two
million schilling and diplomatic support for the creation of Austro-fascism.[12] On June 6, and on August 19
Chancellor Dollfuss reported to Mussolini to discuss
Italian aid against the encroachments of National Socialism. Under the condition of an accelerated transformation of Austria into a clerical-fascist regime, the
Duce assured his intention to help and sketched the
plans for a tripartite customs union and some larger
solution under the Four Power Pact, which he had already discussed with Gömbös. The official *Stefani*
communique only mentioned that "the head of the Italian government confirmed the principles of Italian
policy regarding the future and existence of Austria,
the Danubian problem, and the wider issues, the solution of which is bound up with the workings of the
Four Power Pact." Austria was falling under Mussolini's sway; Italy had won the first round of the struggle on the Danube at the expense of both Germany and
France.[13]

---

[12]Ernst R. Starhemberg, *Between Hitler and Mussolini*, pp. 103-113. When Prince Starhemberg paid
another visit to the Duce in September, Mussolini
showed himself pleased with the results of the counter-
terror and exhorted the Heimwehr leader: "Don't give
in!"

[13]For the text of the communique see John Wheeler-
Bennett, *Documents on International Affairs*, pp. 391-
392. Documentation in this phase of Austro-Italian

Under these circumstances the agreement reached between Paris and Rome, expressed in an Italian memorandum of September 29 "On the Position in Central Europe," could be little more than a pious reaffirmation of shop-worn principles. After a long and laborious introduction which invoked the Stresa Conference, the note suggested these guidelines for a solution: Bilateral accords; preferential treatment for cereals; advantageous handling of Austrian industrial production; amelioration of the trade balances; facilitation of traffic; and measures to equalize the balance-of-payment difficulties. The proposals seemed plausible enough, but the political difficulties involved were only tangentially mentioned in the concluding sentence: "More precise propositions will be formulated only after an exchange of views between the signatories of the Four Power Pact, the Danubian states and others."[14]

---

relations is still rather spotty. One has to use such doubtful sources as Rintelen's and Starhemberg's memoirs and such collections as Karl H. Sailer, ed., *Geheimer Briefwechsel Mussolini-Dollfuss* (Wien,1949). Cf. also Maurice Pernot, "Italy and the Question of Danubia," in *L'Europe Nouvelle*, August 26, p. 806f., and Paul-Boncour's commemorative address for Briand in Trébeurden, September 3, reprinted in *Europäische Gespräche* (1933), pp. 262-268.

[14]J. Wheeler-Bennett, *Documents on International Affairs*, pp. 410-414. Cf. also *Journal des Débats*, October 9, for substantially the same text. The agreement marked the high point of the Franco-Italian rapprochement caused by Hitler's appearance on the European scene. It never became operative, although de Jouvenel, once again Senator, campaigned tirelessly for a similar program. Following the content of a cabinet decision, he called for bilateral trade accords, a

If one can regard the first trial of the Four Power Pact in the strengthening of Mussolini's hold over Central Europe and in the Franco-Italian agreement as modestly successful, the second application was a complete fiasco which in turn jeopardized even the meager fruits of the first. The problem of Austrian independence had been smoldering since the day of Hitler's takeover and was on the verge of bursting into a conflagration throughout the summer of 1933. Austria was the blind spot of Hitler's otherwise perceptive manipulation of German foreign policy. The Führer could be reasonable, when the occasion seemed to demand it, as on May 17, but he was inflexibly determined upon the *Anschluss* of his native Austria. As early as March 23 he declared to Cerruti that "elections would have to take place in Austria which would create clear cut conditions, and in particular give the National Socialist movement in Austria the place to

---

common policy on cereals and a common currency. Neither France nor Italy should pursue any territorial ambitions; Austrian independence should be guaranteed; and the Little Entente and Austria, Hungary should be treated on the basis of perfect equality. Italy continued its unilateral drive for hegemony under the cover of the Four Power Pact, which culminated in the Rome Protocols of March 17, 1934, between Italy, Hungary and Austria. G. Schacher, *Central Europe and the Western World*, p. 110f. A. Basch, *The Danube Basin and the German Economic Sphere*, p. 159f. C. A. Macartney, *October Fifteenth*, pp. 144-148. In his defense to the Commission chargée d'enquêter sur les *Evènements survenus en France de 1933 à 1945*, vol. III, p. 792, however, Paul-Boncour claimed that the negotiations had been a success and that Franco-Italian relations had never been as cordial as after the French acceptance of the Four Power Pact.

which it was entitled." Although he instructed Hassell
to reassure Mussolini that he harboured no sinister
designs, the wave of brutal incidents and the state of
near civil war in Austria belied his professions of
peace.[15]

---

[15]GFP, I, 219, 234 *et seq.* The *Anschluss* has been
interpreted as the prime example of Hitler's technique
of "indirect aggression," of working from the inside
with a fifth column and of preparing the diplomatic
situation from the outside by using the vocabulary of
self-determination to isolate the prospective victim.
Hans Booms, "Der Ursprung 2. Weltkriegs—Revision
oder Expansion?" in *Geschichte in Wissenschaft und
Unterricht* (June, 1965), pp. 329-352.

In 1933, however, the later so successful tactics misfired. A series of incidents such as the near-
expulsion of Bavarian Minister of Justice, Frank, the
expulsion of the inspector of the Austrian Nazi Party,
Habicht, the counter-expulsion of the Austrian press-
attaché, Wasserbäck, and the attempted assassination
of the Heimwehr leader Steidle increased in frequency
and severity all through the summer. Dollfuss finally
forbade the Nazi Party in June and drove it underground,
but bomb terrorism continued. Hitler retaliated by
creating an "Austrian legion" of volunteers and refugees in Bavaria across the border and by imposing a
1,000-mark tourist fee for an Austrian visa.

But the threats and extortions were ineffective
and only served to arouse international sympathy for
little heroic Austria fighting the big bully Nazi Germany. In mid-June Hoesch reported from London "the
further deterioration of the German-Austrian relations
... has deepened the already bad feeling towards Germany even more. . . . The demonstrative applause for
the speech of Chancellor Dollfuss at the World Economic Conference was meant to express the sympathy
towards Austria, which reigns in wide circles of dele-
gates." GMF, Serial 8665 H / E 600646.

Vansittart intuitively grasped the reason for Hitler's stubborn defiance of all rules of diplomacy: "A
glance at Hitler's past will show that Austria is for
him the psychological possession of the renegade. . . .
It is his first trial of strength with the forces of a de-
tested stability, and on the success or failure of his
will to domination the success or failure of his regime
may in large measure hinge. . . . It is, moreover, a question of prestige." If one adds the special position of
the Nazi party, which, because it was organizationally
a branch of the Reich organization, made Hitler look
at the matter as an internal party affair; and if one
also admits of the possibility of a simple miscalcu-
lation, then Hitler's single-minded fixation on the
Anschluss becomes intelligible.[16]

As early as one week after the initialling of the
Four Power Pact there had been discussions about the
advisability of a protest on the basis of the pact in
the British Foreign Office.[17]   Towards the end of June
Lord Tyrell discussed the subject with Alexis St. Léger
and found full understanding and encouragement.[18]   On

---

[16]BFP, V, 371.   There is a considerable body of
literature on the *Anschluss*, but most of it is rather
impressionistic and of scant value for the historian.
For general treatments see Charles A. Gulick, *Austria
from Hapsburg to Hitler* (Berkeley, 1948), vol. II; H.
Benedikt, ed., *Geschichte der Republik Österreich*
(Wien, 1954); Ulrich Eichstädt, *Von Dollfuss zu Hitler* (Wiesbaden, 1955); Margaret M. Ball, *Post-War
German-Austrian Relations: The Anschluss Movement, 1918-1936* (Stanford, 1937); Walter Goldinger,
Geschichte der Republik Österreich (München, 1962)
to supercede the older volume by Benedikt; and Jürgen
Gehl, *Austria, Germany and the Anschluss, 1921-
1938* (London, 1963).
   [17]BFP, V, 210, 211, 213, 214, 215, 222.
   [18]BFP, V, 228.

July 4, the League financial advisor to the Austrian
government, Rost, arrived at London to convey Dollfuss' fears to Sargent at Whitehall. The Austrian Chancellor was reluctant to appeal to the League directly,
since such defiance of the German government would
cost him all nationalist support at home. He rather
suggested a joint Anglo-French-Italian demarche, or if
that were of no avail, direct four-power negotiations
under the auspices of Mussolini's pact.[19] But Paris
preferred League action, since the Quai d'Orsay was
skeptical regarding the invocation of a treaty yet un-
ratified, and Mussolini refused out of resentment
against the Austrian attempt to escape his tutelage.[20]

Incidents at the Austro-German border multiplied
at the end of July, and the open outbreak of the crisis
seemed imminent. On the 24th Dollfuss, against Mussolini's expressed advice, requested the intervention
of the three Western signatories of the Four Power
Pact. The Austrian Chancellor complained of extensive terrorism, the dropping of seditious leaflets from
unidentified planes over Austrian territory, and of per-
sistently subversive broadcasting, especially from
Munich.[21] Vansittart, therefore, urged Paris and Rome

---

[19]BFP, V, 233.

[20]BFP, V, 237, 246.

[21]BFP, V, 270; GFP, I, 385. After his expulsion
from Vienna Herr Habicht, the inspector general of the
Nazi Party in Austria, made inflammatory speeches
over the Munich radio: "The whole of Austria, the
whole world shall see and understand that National
Socialism is a living force in Austria and that no power
on earth can remove it. . . . Let us now take up the struggle, which the Dollfuss government has thrust upon us,
and carry it through, ruthlessly, relentlessly to victory.
With us are a thousand years of German history, behind us stands the whole German people, but before

to consult about a joint representation in Berlin.[22] Agreement with the French was quickly reached and a note was drafted protesting German violations of Article LXXX of the Treaty of Versailles and of the spirit of the Four Power Pact. Only Mussolini hesitated, because he clung to his role of "honest broker" between Germany and the Western powers. "If [Italy] made common front with France and Great Britain against Germany, she would not only lose the [special] influence, but she would also drive the Germans into open defiance."[23]

The Wilhelmstrasse had in the meantime gotten wind of the impending demarche and tried to urge restraint on Hitler. Since his assumption of power a struggle over policy towards Austria had developed between the diplomats and the party officials, with Hitler in his favorite position as arbiter.[24] The representations of the Foreign Office had little effect, and subversive propaganda continued to be broadcast across the border. On the last day of July, the Italians attempted to forestall a common Western protest by communicating the essence of the Anglo-French note to Berlin. Secretary of State Bülow was in a quandary, for he realized Germany's delicate position and feared that "intervention by the three powers with whom we had just concluded this pact would of necessity destroy the pact."[25]

---

us lie, as our goal, the liberation of Austria and the establishment of the German nation. Long Live Adolf Hitler, long live the greater Germany!" John Wheeler-Bennett, *Documents on International Affairs*, pp. 387-388.

[22]BFP, V, 271.

[23]BFP, V, 257.

[24]GFP, I, 107, 219, 249, 156; GMF, E 447424, serial 8665 H / E 600646.

[25]GFP, I, 383.

Three courses of action lay open to Hitler at this point. He could flatly reject any outside interference in the matter; he could have the incidents stop; or he could compromise.[26] Typically enough, he chose a combination of the first two. Neurath was recalled from his vacation, and Hitler promised him on August 4 that he would order Habicht to observe greater moderation in radio propaganda. The mysterious flights would cease, but economic warfare would continue and any intervention by the other powers would be rejected.[27] The next day Cerruti protested to Bülow in Berlin without waiting for the British and French steps. The German Secretary of State denied all charges, but promised to have the provocation stop. The tone of the interview was amiable, and the incident seemed closed.[28]

The real test of the Four Power Pact, however, came on August 7. Due to Simon's vacation Vansittart was left in charge of the Foreign Office during the early days of August. Profoundly anxious about the future of peace in Europe, he was bent on teaching Hitler a lesson: "Austria has only been chosen for the first breakthrough of the renewed will to power, because it is the easiest and weakest point. The next move will be upon the Polish corridor. . . . The seriousness of the challenge can only be realized if it is seen not as an isolated case, in which the country has no

---

[26]GFP, I, 385.

[27]GFP, I, 390.

[28]GFP, I, 391. In many ways Austria was a perfect test case for the Western response to Hitler. The interests of London, Paris, and Rome coincided in the defense of Austrian independence. World opinion was solidly in favor of "democratic Austria." It was all the more remarkable that the Western powers delivered a protest only after much soul-searching and that Mussolini preferred not to associate himself with their step.

direct interest, but as the first of a series of chal-
lenges, each of which will carry with it a nearer threat
to this country, culminating in the demand for a navy
and a colonial empire."[29] Despite the positive results
of the Italian demarche, he did not reverse his original
instructions to the British chargé in Berlin, who was
left in the unenviable position of having to protest
against a violation for which satisfaction had already
been obtained.[30] A few hours earlier the French had delivered a nearly identical note at the Wilhelmstrasse.[31]

Bernhard von Bülow was indignant over the invocation of the Four Power Pact. He stolidly denied the
correctness of its application in the Austrian question,
ironically defending himself with the very French thesis

---

[29]BFP, V, 371. "Memorandum by Vansittart on the
Present and Future Position in Europe." Vansittart was
acutely aware of the importance of Hitler's intentions
in Austria. He even claimed: "The future of Europe
turns largely on the fashion of our facing the German
challenge over Austria, in which we are at present
likely to lose." Cf. also the memorandum "on the circumstances under which measures may be taken to
compel Germany to her observance of her obligations
under Part V of the Treaty of Versailles." BFP, V, 185.

[30]BFP, V, 301. The newly appointed Ambassador
to Vienna, Sir Walford Selby, criticized Vansittart's
high-handed action bitterly: "Sir Robert Vansittart had
despatched his protest to Berlin without consulting
me, in total ignorance of my two political despatches
from Vienna." His counsel had been ignored, although
he was on leave in London and his first two political
reports had been mislaid in the Foreign Office for ten
days. *Diplomatic Twilight, 1930-1940* (London, 1953),
pp. 15-17. Cf. BFP, V, 302, 303, 304, 305, 308, 309,
310, 312ff.

[31]GFP, I, 392; BFP, V, 314.

which he had shortly before assailed so zealously.
The pact could only deal with matters which affected
the signatories alone. "This was the first application
of the Four Power Pact. It was incomprehensible...
that it should be invoked in justification of the demarche," he said, adding that he felt constrained to
point out that "such a misuse of the pact," which had
not even been ratified yet, seemed to him "dangerous
for the future of the pact, even for its existence."[32]

The second attempt to apply the Four Power Pact
had thus ended in dismal failure. Mussolini's conception of his "special position" had ruined the united
stand against Hitler. Discontent was universal. The
British resented that "the Italians had stolen a march
on us in order to avoid a step with us."[33] The French,
who had wisely left the leadership in the protest to
London, were keenly disappointed and more than ever
determined to stand firm against Nazi Germany.[34] Hit-

---

[32]GFP, I, 393.

[33]BFP, V, 371.

[34]The French press had launched a vigorous campaign for intervention and had been predicting a diplomatic defeat for Hitler in the last week of July. The
rude rebuff of the Wilhelmstrasse, therefore, came as
a particular shock to public opinion and raised severe
doubts about the value of the Italian friendship and
the usefulness of the Four Power Pact. "The response
has not satisfied French opinion and this morning
nearly all the newspapers expressed their discontent.
The majority among them used the opportunity to underline once more the uselessness of the Four Power
Pact." *Journal des Débats*, August 10. Cf. *L'Europe
Nouvelle*, August 12: "The Austrian dilemma."

The British Labour papers at the same time called
to "ARRAIGN HITLER BEFORE THE LEAGUE: Summon
the Council at once.... Austria must be given better

ler was "very indignant over the manner of Mussolini's intervention and declared that he would not stand for that sort of tutelage."[35] And Mussolini was unusually agitated over the continued provocations, fearing that the further development of the German-Austrian conflict might become a serious threat to the policy of peace in Europe which he had inaugurated with the Four Power Pact."[36]

The third and decisive test for the Four Power Pact came in the question of German rearmament, another major problem besetting European statesmen during summer and fall of 1933. At the signing, the president of the Disarmament Conference, Sir Arthur Henderson, hailed the pact as "an important factor in providing a solution to the disarmament problem." Yet these sanguine hopes proved unfounded and the treaty did little to assist the work of the Disarmament Conference. Ironically enough, the same sequence of events which broke up the Geneva Conference and enfeebled the

---

protection than the secret pressure of Signor Mussolini." London *Daily Herald*, August 23, editorial by Hugh Dalton.

[35]GFP, I, 402.

[36]GFP, I, 401. For the continued violations see GFP, I, 402, 407, 414, 416, 427 *et seq.* The Western powers realized that diplomatic protests alone would not impress Hitler. Hence they extended a new loan to Austria and authorized the creation of an auxiliary military force, enlarging the total strength of the Austrian army to 30,000 men. It is ironical that Vienna achieved this "revision" of the disarmament clauses of the St. Germain treaty in order to defend herself better against Hitler's "revisionism." Cf. the Austrian note to the signatories of the Treaty of St. Germain, August 30, 1933. J. Wheeler-Bennett, *Documents on International Affairs*, p. 388f.

League of Nations also doomed Mussolini's creation.
The Four Power Pact was shipwrecked on the very reef
which it had been designed to avoid.[37]

The explanation for this paradox lies in the drastic
change of international atmosphere since the conclu-

---

[37]The public records of the Disarmament Conference were printed by the League of Nations, *Records
of the Conference for the Reduction and Limitation
of Armaments* (Geneva, 1933). The memoirs of Baron
Pompeo Aloisi, *Journal*; Rodolf Nadolny, *Mein Beitrag*
(Wiesbaden, 1955); Paul Schmidt, *Statist auf diplo-
matischer Bühne, 1923-1945* (Bonn, 1949); Hugh R.
Wilson, *Diplomat Between Wars* (Toronto, 1941); Wer-
ner Freiherr von Rheinbaben, *Viermal Deutschland*
(Berlin, 1954); and A. C. Temperley, *The Whispering
Gallery of Europe* picture the atmosphere at Geneva
vividly. General accounts are by John W. Wheeler-
Bennett, *The Pipe Dream of Peace* (New York, 1935);
William E. Rappard, *The Quest for Peace Since the
World War* (Cambridge, 1940); Francis P. Walters, *A
History of the League of Nations* (London, 1952);
Colonel Jaques Minart, *Le Drame du désarmement
français: la revanche allemande, 1918-1939* (Paris,
1959); and John Davis, *Hitler and the Versailles Set-
tlement*, pp. 140ff.

In his speech on June 7 before the Italian Senate
to celebrate the initialling, Mussolini had still been
optimistic: "It is clear that if the Conference does
not succeed, a situation may result, which is as serious as it is intolerable. Such a suggestion can only
be made to be dismissed immediately; but since in
spite of everything this eventuality may take place,
the Pact allows and makes provision for it." But this
confidence was to be shattered quickly. John W.
Wheeler-Bennett, *Documents on International Affairs*,
p. 270.

sion of the pact in July. Slowly the full impact of Hitler's assumption of power in Germany began to tell.
The pivotal change had taken place in Great Britain:
"It still seems like a fairy tale when one recalls how
MacDonald in his speech of March 23 said in the House
of Commons — incidentally to the greatest horror of the
French — that the chief aim of the Four Power Pact was
to open the way for an approach to revision of the
peace treaties. . . . In its present attitude toward Germany public opinion, of which the government is watch-
ful, does not really want to hear anything of improvement or adjustment of the German armament level and
pays an increasing attention to the familiar argument
of Winston Churchill that a strong French army is still
at the moment the best guarantee of peace." The diplomatic constellations had completely reversed themselves since the beginning of the year. Britain no
longer was pro-German; she had defected from the
ranks of the revisionists into the open arms of France.
Now Hitler had to face an increasingly united front of
the Western powers.[38]

To check this tendency Mussolini twice took the

----

[38]GFP, I, 406. (Political report by Hoesch.) This
change of atmosphere was also noted by Paul Schmidt,
the chief translator for the Foreign Office: "It was
especially painful for me how the formerly good repu-
tation of Germany in Great Britain sank lower and lower
from day to day," and commenting on the Wilhelmstrasse: "Nothing had changed in Berlin. The new
time had passed without leaving its marks. But the
anxiety about the international repercussions of the
change in regime was great, since the reports, which
daily arrived from Europe and from overseas, showed
that within a few months Germany had once again become completely isolated." *Statist auf diplomatischer
Bühne*, p. 277. Cf. also *New York Times*, September 4.

initiative in the early fall.   On September 16 he proposed a compromise plan for disarmament in the form
of ten points, spelling out the minimum acceptable for
all sides.[39]   But Berlin decided to treat the suggestion
dilatorily, because the Wilhelmstrasse was not yet
convinced of the gravity of the situation.[40]   Paris accepted it only as evidence that Italy had moved closer
to its own position and hailed the approximation as
one of the first fruits of the Four Power Pact.[41] Mussolini's second initiative was meant more seriously. En-
visaging "the prospect of the more or less elegantly
concealed breakdown of the Disarmament Conference,"
he warned: "On that day the League of Nations will
practically have ceased to exist. Realignments of the
powers will take place.   The [national] antagonisms
will immediately become acute and a time of destruction of order and stability will commence in the history of Europe and the world."   Nevertheless, he still
professed to believe: "This is why, despite everything, an accord will be concluded."[42]

To save the Geneva conference from imminent
disaster, Mussolini proposed to transfer disarmament
discussions to the framework of the Four Power Pact.
Perhaps the collapse could be averted if a meeting of

---

[39]GFP, I, 431; BFP, 385, 386.
[40]GFP, I, 441.
[41]BFP, V, 399.
[42]*Universal Service* release, October 5. *Scritti
e Discorsi*, VIII, pp. 246-7. Noting the spreading gloom
at the League Mussolini wrote: "The first orators spoke
like inspired prophets, and great was the response from
among the peoples. But all this has evaporated during
the useless passage of twenty months. The orators no
longer speak. Nothing of striking significance of the
oratory of the League has been put into practice in
these days at Geneva." Cf. BFP, V, 395-6.

the signatories could be held at Stresa before the General Assembly reconvened in Geneva on October 16. Neurath announced his willingness to accept, gambling on a British or a French refusal.[43] He guessed correctly: Simon obliged by insisting on the prior conclusion of the Anglo-French talks in Paris before any four-power conference could be held.[44] The French maintained that disarmament discussions could only prosper in the congenial atmosphere of Geneva, and Norman Davis, Roosevelt's special envoy to the Conference, concurred. Mussolini's attempt to save the disarmament talks by shifting them into the framework of the Four Power Pact had foundered on the stiffening diplomatic fronts.[45]

During the first few days of October events took a rapid turn for the worse in Geneva. The Franco-British conversations, which had been progressing slowly during summer and early fall, suddenly produced substantial agreement. A list of common disarmament proposals was developed in Paris to be presented at the reopening of the Conference. At the Congress of the Radical Socialists at Vichy, Daladier marked the Western stand: "We do not think of menacing or humiliating any people, whatever regime they give themselves . . . therefore, we are resolved not to admit any new reduction of our forces outside of a sincere and loyal international agreement, which organizes progressive disarmament, assured by the establishment of permanent and automatic controls and safeguarded by effective guarantees of its execution." Despite

---

[43]GFP, I, 446.
[44]GFP, I, 447.
[45]BFP, V, 406; FRUS, 211-224, 232-235, 258-259 *et seq.* Cf. also Hugh R. Wilson, *Diplomat Between Wars*, pp. 267-301, and A. C. Temperley, *The Whispering Gallery of Europe*, pp. 254-258.

their realization that Germany could only reject these modifications of the MacDonald plan and had already done so repeatedly, the British agreed to the French demand for a trial period of four years, during which the system of automatic supervision could be tested. The probationary period would perpetuate the present French superiority and would serve as psychological preparation for effective disarmament.[46]

When the outlines of the Anglo-French proposals reached Berlin, Hitler called the new draft "in the final analysis unacceptable." Speaking with Blomberg and

---

[46]BFP, V, 382-419 *passim*; GFP, I, 478, 486ff. Colonel Minart summarized the Anglo-French demands as: "A period of four years is required, during which the control will be organized and will begin to work, while the different types of armies will transform themselves progressively into a short service army, excluding all paramilitary formations, and during which the free states will submit to the prohibition of the production of new matériel which is forbidden to all states." *Le Drame du désarmement français*, p. 55. These requirements would definitely perpetuate French military superiority and nip any German rearmament plans in the bud. The British were fully aware of the political implications of these demands and their support for such a programme expressed the magnitude of their shift away from revisionism back to an alliance with France. The French reasoning behind the French position was logical and convincing: "It would have been easy for them to offer disarmament to German Liberals like Stresemann and Brüning; it was a more difficult thing to carry the country into offering it to Hitler and Papen." BFP, V, 386. Cf. also Daladier's defense in Charles Serre, ed. Commission chargée d'enquêter sur les *évènements survenus en France de 1933 à 1945* (Paris, 1947), vol. I, p. 12f.

Bülow on October 4, he categorically refused to negotiate on the British suggestions, lest Mussolini act
again as "biased mediator" as during the negotiations
for the Four Power Pact. Germany had no choice but
to revert to the "previous question"—the MacDonald
Plan pure and simple—or to leave the Conference and
the League if the other powers would not comply with
her demands. On the same day Nadolny received a
new set of instructions, revised on October 6, which
left no doubt that Hitler was determined to risk the
break. Even the tolerant Italians characterized the
German counterdemands as "a remarkable step back-
wards."[47] Hitler met the Western proposal for a probationary period by suggesting that Germany be allowed to possess substantial samples of the forbidden
weapons during these four years, a device which clearly
subverted the military usefulness of the trial period for
the French.[48]

Technically speaking, the gap between the German
and French positions was rather small, but the diplo-

---

[47] BFP, V, 435.

[48] GFP, I, 479, 480, 484. The change of tone between the instructions of October 4 and 6 is striking.
While on the earlier date Nadolny was told to be "ac-
commodating" and allowed to grant certain concessions, such as the transformation of the Reichswehr,
the second document breathed a different spirit. Negotiations on the British demands were rejected uncon-
ditionally and a return to the original idea of the conference—the disarmament of the highly armed powers—to be requested. "It is to be intimated in this
connection that the failure to consider this demand is
apt to result in German withdrawal from the Conference
and therewith also in her leaving the League. The
Chancellor reserves to himself the decision concerning the carrying out of this intimation."

matic fronts had hardened gradually and consistently
until fall 1933, and the common ground from which a
compromise could have been drafted had largely disappeared.[49] The situation became critical when Neurath informed Nadolny laconically on October 11: "If,
as the statements of Simon to Ambassador Hoesch lead
us to assume ... the English proposals for amending
the MacDonald Plan are irreconcilable with German
equality ... we shall withdraw from the Disarmament
Conference."[50] A flurry of last minute compromise attempts was launched by the Italians, and everyone publicly professed certainty that the negotiations would
continue.   Desperately Nadolny tried to brighten the
mood in Berlin by emphasizing the hopeful aspects of
the situation in his dispatches.[51] But behind the scenes
tension was mounting, causing Mussolini to explode
in front of Sir Ronald Graham: "German policy at the
moment was in the hands of two men, Hitler and Goering, one a dreamer, the other an ex-inmate of a luna-
tic asylum, neither of them conspicuous for reasons of
logic and both suffering from a bitter sense of injus-
tice.   They would not be intimidated by a consensus
of opinion against them and if the four powers would
simply refuse to entertain their communications, they

---

[49]It is amusing to note that on September 25 it was
still possible for the President of the Council of the
League, M. Mowinckel of Norway, to speak from the
rostrum of this institution: "Great hopes were placed
in the Four Power Pact as a means of appeasing differences and bringing about mutual understanding and
cooperation not only between the signatories themselves, but also between other countries." *Monthly
Summary of the League of Nations* (Geneva, 1933).
    [50]GFP, I, 489.
    [51]GFP, I, 493-5 and Nadolny, *Mein Beitrag*, pp.
140-141.

would break off negotiation and would continue to re-
arm Germany without any control being possible."[52]

On October 13, Hitler announced to his ministers
the decision to withdraw from the Disarmament Conference and the League of Nations. In a long exposition of the reasons for the break and of his plans for
the future, the Führer stressed that any subsequent
discussions would have to take place outside Geneva,
and that "it was certain that Italy would use the Four
Power Pact for that purpose."[53] On the evening of the
same day Neurath instructed Hassell to inform Mussolini of Germany's withdrawal from the Disarmament
Conference.[54]

Despite these definite statements, some doubt
seems to have remained until the very last minute.
Nadolny was recalled to Berlin, and for a moment he

---

[52]BFP, V, 444. According to Rheinbaben, *Viermal
Deutschland*, the British did not heed the warning because they thought that Hitler was only bluffing. Hence
the German delegate at Geneva felt unable to reverse
the tide and later "could only write that this event was
the saddest one in my whole long life in Germany's
service." p. 278.

[53]GFP, I, 499. No attempt has been made in the
present study to sketch anything beyond the bare outlines of Germany's withdrawal from the League and
the Disarmament Conference. Hitler's decision to
abandon Geneva is treated only in as far as it is relevant to the simultaneous failure of the Four Power Pact.
For a detailed analysis of the German motives, see
J. Davis, *Hitler and the Versailles Settlement*, pp.
140-162, and Tyler Deierhoi, *The Conduct of German
Policy at the Disarmament Conference* (unpublished
Ph.D. dissertation at Duke University, 1963), especially pp. 340-400 *passim*.

[54]GFP, I, 489.

believed that he had been successful in stemming the
tide.[55]   Hitler withheld the official withdrawal notice
until Simon had publicly stated the Anglo-French conditions before the reassembled Disarmament Commission. On the morning of October 14, the British Foreign
Secretary endorsed the French thesis of a probationary
period from the rostrum of Geneva, thus, in effect,
abandoning the MacDonald Plan. Minutes later, Hitler
issued the fateful order to Baron Rheinbaben, the remaining senior German diplomat at Geneva.[56] Instead
of succumbing to the united pressure of Great Britain
and France, "Hitler—in an irrational reflex action—
loudly slammed the two doors of the Disarmament Conference and the League."[57]

Hitler had gambled skilfully and calculated his

---

[55]Nadolny, *Mein Beitrag*, p. 141.

[56]The telegram to Arthur Henderson, the Chairman
of the Disarmament Conference read: "In light of the
course which recent discussions of the powers concerned have taken in the matter of disarmament, it is
now clear that the Disarmament Conference will not
fulfill what is its sole object—namely, general disarmament. It is also clear that the failure of the Conference is due solely to the unwillingness of the highly
armed states to carry out their contractual obligations
and disarm. This renders impossible the satisfaction
of Germany's recognized claim to equality of rights,
and the condition on which the German Government
agreed at the beginning of this year again to take part
in the work of the Conference no longer exists. The
German Government is accordingly compelled to leave
the Disarmament Conference. See BFP, V, 454 for the
text. Cf. also Rheinbaben, *Viermal Deutschland*, pp.
277-281.

[57]Paul Schmidt, *Statist auf diplomatischer Bühne*,
p. 282.

odds correctly. Despite the furor which the walkout
created in the international press, despite the unanimous moral condemnation which it occasioned, the
Western powers took no military action. In Rome Hassell sought to soften the blow by proposing action under
the Four Power Pact as the only solution for the crisis,
and Mussolini showed little surprise at first about
Germany's withdrawal and promised to mediate under
the auspices of the pact, if Hitler would mention it in
his radio address to the German people.[58]   A comedy
of errors now developed around this last attempt to
employ the Four Power Pact.   Informed by newspaper
accounts only, Hassell believed that Germany had
merely left the Disarmament Conference and not the
League also, and he therefore urged application of the
Roman pact.[59] Assured by the German ambassador that
Hitler would grasp at this straw, Mussolini intimated
to the British and French envoys and to the press the
feasibility of resuming the disarmament discussions
in the framework of the Four Power Pact.[60]

---

[58]GFP, I, 500, 502; BFP, V, 457f. Sir Ronald Graham found Mussolini taking this "action seriously but
not tragically. . . . He thought it unnecessary and fool-
ish. . . . The Germans were apparently 'burning their
house down in order to cook an egg.'"

[59]GFP, II, 2, 4. GMF, E 447463, E 447464. Hassell quickly retracted his assurance by private letter
to Mussolini, but on October 17, Suvich still "thought
that the Italian government would employ any means,
and especially also the Four Power Pact." The initiative now had to come from England, least compromised
by Germany's exit, because the "British press championed the Four Power Pact energetically."

[60]BFP, V, 457; FRUS, pp. 269, 270f. These intima-
tions added only to the general confusion, because
they were vociferously debated by the press, while

But Paris categorically refused any such move on
"juridical grounds" in order not to annoy the Duce unnecessarily.[61] On October 17, Daladier denounced the
pact in the French Chamber as having been vitiated by
Germany's exit from the League. Hitler had violated
both the spirit and the letter of the agreement, especially the phrase: "Anxious to give full effect to all
provisions of the Covenant of the League of Nations,
while conforming to the methods and procedures laid
down therein, from which they have no intentions of
departing."[62] In a dramatic transatlantic telephone
conversation with Norman Davis, President Roosevelt
also refused to be drawn into four-power discussions.[63]
Moreover, the president of the Disarmament Conference, Arthur Henderson, publicly denounced any appeal
to the Four Power Pact, warning that "any attempt to

---

the Italian government disclaimed any responsibility
for them.

In a survey of European opinion on Germany's
walk-out conducted by the *Europäische Revue* (1933),
pp. 641-659, six out of the questioned prominent figures favored a recourse to the Four Power Pact, four
were indifferent and five opposed. Among those advocating an appeal to the pact were Sir Ch. Petrie, F.
Yeats-Brown, R. Forinacci, W. Wassilino, Herm. Neu-
bauer, and Fr. Orestano.

[61]FRUS, pp. 279, 297. BFP, V, 465; GMF,E 447464.
Strictly speaking, the legal case was not quite so
sound, since the German withdrawal would not go into
effect for another two years. Pertinax launched a rumor
about an official French government demarche, but it
was quickly disavowed by the Palazzo Chigi. GMF,
E 447471.

[62]Chambre des Députés, *Débats Parlementaires*,
vol. 151, p. 2757.

[63]FRUS, pp. 213-16.

substitute the pact for the Disarmament Conference would have a disturbing effect on the delegations, increase suspicion and create considerable damage to both the Conference and the pact."[64]

These disavowals, coupled with the reluctance of any of the signatories to take the initiative, sealed the fate of the Four Power Pact. Only a widespread and spontaneous action could have succeeded in making it the framework for negotiations, but none was forthcoming from any quarter. Even Mussolini, the once proud creator of the scheme, realized that the opportunity had passed, and he remained inactive.[65] There was some discussion in diplomatic and political circles about using the pact as escape hatch, but the gravity of the crisis made such action impossible. From the beginning Whitehall was openly skeptical. In the French capital Daladier decided over Paul-Boncour's and de Jouvenel's opposition to resort to regular diplomatic channels.[66] In Berlin Hitler seems to have made no effort to use the Four Power Pact, but Goering and Papen attempted to revive it. The German Vice-Chancellor remarked to Sir Eric Phipps, former British ambassador to the Hofburg, that he intended to invoke the pact, but Mussolini, sick with anger and disgust

---

[64]*New York Times*, October 20.

[65]BFP, V, 476, GFP, II, 10, 18. According to Hassell, Mussolini "was very upset over our step and deplored it extremely." The Duce gradually realized the full implications of the German withdrawal, especially after *Le Matin* hinted sarcastically that Germany's action had been the heaviest blow to his prestige since the Matteoti affair.

[66]FRUS, 273-6; BFP, V, 465; *Vossische Zeitung*, October 21. Cf. also Paul-Boncour's statement in Ch. Serre, ed., *Les Evènements survenus en France de 1933 à 1939*, vol. III, p. 792.

over German diplomatic blundering, refused to respond
to Papen's promptings.[67]

At the end of October the pact seemed irrevocably
doomed, but in early November, it cropped up once
more in the headlines. *Le Journal de Gèneve* rumored
that Hitler intended to convoke a conference of the
signatories of the pact immediately after the German
plebiscite, which was to prepare the ground for his
return to the League. The Four Power Pact would be
ratified and the Disarmament Conference would resume.
But the report that Goering had been sent with a personal message to Mussolini to initiate this negotiation
proved unfounded.[68] The same pro—League journals
which had so vehemently combatted the original proposal now clung to it as the remaining hope to pull
Europe out of the morass.[69] An even later sign of life

---

[67]In a memorandum on October 16, Bülow stated
the German reasons for not appealing to the Four Power
Pact. The document was too much permeated with references to the League and had not been ratified by all
members. Further, any rebuff to a German demarche
would be a signal diplomatic defeat. At best "it ought
to be buried quietly, without our accepting it explicitly."
Mussolini complained to Graham that the "Germans by their precipitate and ill-conceived action had
broken three windows, those of the Conference, the
League of Nations and the Four Power Pact. They now
expected him to pick up the pieces, but he would do
nothing of the kind." BFP, V, 476, 490.

[68]GMF, E 447680. Hitler's letter of November 2
to Mussolini contained no mention of the Four Power
Pact, although on October 27 Hassell still seemed to
hanker after the idea. GFP, II, 28, 32.

[69]The rumors were especially prevalent in the confusion of the first days after Germany's withdrawal.
Cf. London *Times*, October 16; *Vossische Zeitung*,

was a conversation between Sir Eric Drummond and Baron Aloisi, exploring the possibility of a four-power solution to the deadlock.[70] But on November 8 Sir John Simon quelled all further rumors when he answered an interpellation in the Commons on the government's intention to appeal to the pact: "In due course it may be so. At present the Four Power Pact has been ratified only by two of its signatories, but has not yet been ratified by the other two."[71]

The Four Power Pact received its well-deserved "first-class funeral" on November 13 before the Council of Corporations. In a solemn oration Mussolini paid tribute to his shattered hopes and parted only reluctantly with what had merely four months before ap-

---

October 19; "Four Power Negotiations Discontinued?"; *Journal de Genève*, November 9. The last mention of the pact in the press is probably a note in the *New York Times* of November 21: "London and Paris stand by League: Say ratification of Four Power Pact must await return of Reich to Geneva."

[70]Fr. Jacomini, "Il Patto a quattro," p. 66.

[71]House of Commons, *Debates*, vol. 281, p. 164. The Four Power Pact had only been ratified by Italy (on August 31) and Great Britain (September 16). GMF, E 447438, E 447462; FRUS, pp. 297-8. This point is missed by most students, such as Kirkpatrick, *Mussolini*, p. 288 and Salvatorelli, *Il Fascismo*, p. 129, whose admirable ideological hostility against the concept misleads them to assume ratification by the revisionists Germany and Italy only. The misjudgement is of some significance, because it underestimates the British involvement in the pact as well as the German opposition against the project. Similarly J. Wheeler-Bennett in Munich, p. 237, mixed up the ratification, maintaining that Great Britain and Germany had not ratified the pact.

peared to be his greatest political triumph. His voice
had a hollow ring when he spoke: "Europe is no longer
the continent which directs human civilization. . . . But
Europe can once again seize the helm of humanity's
destiny, if she only finds a 'minimum' of political unity."
The admirable enterprise of the League of Nations had
clearly failed. "As for the Four Power Pact, it has of
late been enveloped in silence. Nobody talks about
it, but everybody thinks about it. (Noisy and very vivid
applause.) And for this very reason we do not intend
to take any initiative to accelerate the development of
a situation, which must logically and inevitably mature
by itself."[72]

---

[72]*Scritti e Discorsi*, vol. VIII, pp. 265-266. The
ghost of the Four Power Pact reappeared for the last
time in the fall of 1934 in the form of a rumor about
Germany's accession to the Roman Protocols and about
a new Mussolini initiative towards a Great Power
grouping, this time also including Poland and the Soviet Union. See GMF, E 447478-447501.

CONCLUSION

THE FOUR POWER PACT was stillborn. It may have been "the most prodigious stunt of conciliation in diplomatic history," but Mussolini was never wider from the mark than when he predicted at the initialling: "Its conclusion will provoke more or less interesting discussions in professional political circles, but it will be welcomed with satisfaction by the multitude, who, farther from artifice and closer to the realities of life, feel and perceive the moral import of events which may be called historical." The illusion faded so quickly that nine months later a crestfallen Duce could only claim pathetically: "During the last two years Italy has tried to bridge the abyss of historical hostility between Germany and France; first with the Four Power Pact and then with the disarmament memorandum. One could not have done more."

Measured against its expressed goals, the failure of the Four Power Pact was so complete that one wonders not so much that it never became effective, but that it was signed at all. It failed to stem the division of Europe into two opposing camps. It failed to revise the peace treaties. It failed to secure Germany equality and to channel her rearmament. It failed to prevent the breakdown of the World Economic Conference. It failed to solve the perennial Danubian problem. But most of all, it failed to halt Hitler's withdrawal from

the Disarmament Conference and from the League. And
yet the reasons for its very failure may go far to explain its continuing significance.

The Four Power Pact was the capricious child of
the precarious balance of diplomatic forces in Europe
at the halfway mark between the two world wars.
Surprisingly enough——and even Bullock misses this
point——the constellation of power which brought the
pact into existence in the early spring of 1933 was
still fundamentally that of the 1920's. Great Britain
and Italy favored moderate revision of the treaty of
Versailles and were not opposed to granting Germany
greater military equality, while France, entrenched in
her alliances, insisted upon the sanctity of treaties
and upon the collective security of the League. Only
after Hitler's arrival on the European scene did this
alignment gradually begin to shift, since the Nazi victory acted upon world opinion as what British Ambassador Lord Tyrell was fond of calling facetiously "our
German ally." Whenever the opponents of Berlin found
themselves in a quandary, the Germans themselves
would come to their help by committing a colossal
blunder. With Hitler's establishment of a dictatorship
and his baiting of the Jews, the "German ally" turned
out in force. Although public revulsion at the one-
time "victim of Versailles" was a more prolonged process than hindsight may let it appear, the excesses of
the "brown revolution" penetrated deeply into European consciousness. The revisionist coalition which
had originally fathered Mussolini's pact dissolved
into its component countries: Great Britain began to
return to an entente with France, while Italy attempted
to steer an uneasy middle course between Hitler and
the Western powers.

The initialling and signing of the Four Power Pact
in the summer of 1933 marked the midpoint of the diplomatic revolution sparked by Hitler's rise to power.
London and Rome were still close enough to each other

to mediate between Paris and Berlin. Only the temporary stalemate between the forces of revision and those of the status quo made the conclusion of the Roman pact possible. Diluted almost beyond recognition, revision and parity of armaments were still implicit in the scheme, although, with Whitehall's benevolent acquiescence, the Quai d'Orsay had succeeded in tying the Four Power Pact to the moribund Disarmament Conference. The resulting document was a hybrid, neither fish nor fowl.

The Central European negotiations and the Austrian crisis in late summer and early fall further reversed the initial alignment. The formation of an Anglo-French-Italian group within the pact became possible, united by the common object of resisting Hitler's unreasonable and unjustified demands. Mussolini's creation displayed an amazing vitality by adapting itself to this perversion of its original purpose, but the London-Paris—Rome alliance could no more endure than the revisionist front. Instead of heeding Vansittart's and Paul-Boncour's advice to make the pact an effective instrument for combatting Nazi Germany, the Western powers preferred the enfeebled League as long as Mussolini was not yet willing to opt for London and Paris against Berlin. Both as instrument of treaty revision and as method of curbing German expansion, Mussolini's pact proved a signal failure. The balance of power was still too evenly divided in Europe to allow either side to use the Four Power Pact exclusively for its own designs. Unable to assume diplomatic life in its own right, the pact failed in its basic purpose. It was powerless to halt the deepening schism on the Continent.

And yet the Four Power Pact left its mark upon the 1930's by producing a number of specific results. In Italy the signing reinforced Mussolini's popularity and consolidated his dictatorial regime, while revealing in England and France a shift of public opinion regarding the defense against aggression. The non-communist, pacifist, and internationalist Left, to which both Daladier and MacDonald had belonged, began to put more faith into the methods of traditional diplomacy, easing away from advocating Germany's claims. The non-Fascist, nationalist Right, typified by Churchill, Tardieu, and the foreign offices, moved towards support of the League to stop the Fascist dictators. In Germany Hitler gained precious time to complete the "national revolution" and to take the first hazardous steps towards rearmament. By participating in the pact, Germany broke the ring of diplomatic isolation and National Socialism became respectable on the international scene. For a fleeting moment the signing of the treaty fulfilled the French desire for closer collaboration with Italy, although it severely strained Paris' relations with her Eastern allies, foreshadowing Daladier's decision at Munich to place the security of France above that of Prague. The ties between Czechoslovakia, Yugoslavia, and Rumania were strengthened by the common celebration of the diplomatic victory of the emasculation of the Roman pact. But the Four Power Pact also speeded Poland's alienation from France by slighting Pilsudski's pride, and made the Marshal more inclined to sign the non-aggression pact with Hitler. The dangerous overtones of revision in southeastern Europe produced the delayed effect of hastening the rapprochement between Greece, Yugoslavia, Rumania, and Turkey, the foundation for the Balkan Entente. On the other hand, it reinforced Mussolini's hold over Austria and Hungary which was to culminate in the Roman Protocols. And lastly, the Four Power Pact induced Moscow to speed the conclusion of a series of Litvinov Protocols with the states on her border, while heightening Soviet suspicions of a united front of the capitalist West, so crucial in the Munich crisis of September, 1938.

But the historical significance of Mussolini's pact

cannot be exhausted by listing its failures and its specific consequences. The lasting importance of the pact lay rather in its impact upon four aspects of European diplomacy in the 1930's. Most clearly, the Four Power Pact represented an attempt to restore the Great Power directorate which had ruled Europe during much of the nineteenth and the early twentieth centuries. The Nazi takeover threw the European system into a severe crisis, with which the new machinery of collective security was unable to grapple. Comparing the Locarno Pacts with Mussolini's creation, the former Italian Foreign Minister Dino Grandi wrote in *Foreign Affairs* (July, 1934): "Each of these great international treaties sought to establish a system of relations between the states which had been paralyzed by the vast and heavy mechanism of the League. They sought to remove the League from the world of prophecy to the world of hard facts, from purely theoretical and universal affirmations to the immediate guarantees necessary to satisfy the safety and protection . . . that animate the countries who were victims of the war of 1914-1918."

The cumbersome machinery of the League was unequal to Hitler's challenge. Could Mussolini, MacDonald and Daladier create another instrument, more effective, more flexible, and more just to press the warlike torrents of change into peaceful channels? For Mussolini, the solution was the Four Power Pact. But MacDonald and Daladier only wanted to reinvigorate the League, to remain faithful to its ideals while simplifying its procedures. Hence they denied the character of the Four Power Pact as Great Power directorate and chained it firmly to the ailing League. But was Europe really to be deceived so easily by cloaking four-power hegemony in the Wilsonian language of Geneva?

A second feature, intimately connected to the first, was the pact's importance as the principal expression of Europe's diplomatic response to Hitler's rise to power. Refusing to wage a preventive war, and yet unwilling to condone Hitler's disturbance of the equilibrium, the Western statesmen had to face the brutal choice, either to fight or to appease. The Four Power Pact could equally well have served for both. As de Jouvenel recommended, minor concessions could have been made to Hitler to soothe British pangs of conscience for Versailles. But as soon as German strength grew to dangerous proportions, the Western powers would hold Bismarck's famous position *à trois* in a group of four. In 1933 containment through the Four Power Pact was still a realistic possibility, since Germany was not yet prepared to challenge the three other powers at the same time. Hitler was primarily concerned with domestic policy, and his few excursions into foreign affairs revealed him as a cautious gambler, well aware of Germany's military weakness. Only where his innermost beliefs were touched would he suddenly balk and give the West a foretaste of the dazzling, somnambulistic self-assurance of his later diplomatic victories. As in the negotiations for the Four Power Pact, Hitler's central concern in the disarmament discussions was his striving for German equality. Complaining to Ward Price a few days after German withdrawal from Geneva, Hitler gave a glimpse of his motives: "If the League of Nations becomes more and more, as it has done lately, an interest group of certain states against the interests of other states, then I do no longer believe in its future. At any rate, Germany will never join an international organization or participate in it, unless it is recognized as a completely equal partner. We know that we have lost the war.... But we will not endure this eternal discrimination any longer!" The warning was plain enough. The negotiations for the Roman pact had disclosed Hitler's aims, his techniques, and his gambles. Would the West learn from the failure of its original response?

Another facet of continuing interest in the Four Power Pact concerned its exemplary character for Fascist foreign policy, since it reflected Mussolini's ideology and his diplomatic practice clearly. The central concept of the pact, *gerarchia*—from the Greek *gerontes* and *archia*: the rule of elders, wise men, aldermen—was rhetorically defined by Mussolini as: "Whoever speaks of hierarchy, speaks of the scale of human values; whoever speaks of the scale of human values, speaks of responsibility and duty; whoever speaks of hierarchy, speaks of discipline." In international affairs this idea meant the predominance of the Great Powers in decision-making and responsibility. The four Western European powers would no longer be hampered by the annoying criticism of the Little Entente and of Poland, but would rather be free to divide Europe into their national spheres of influence, within which each of them would reign supreme.

This mixture of mysticism and pragmatism was at the heart of Fascist ideology, but the Four Power Pact also revealed the dominant characteristic of Mussolini as diplomat in action: his complete opportunism. Dino Grandi clothed it in the dignified language of Italy's national tradition: "It is to be hoped that with the Four Power Pact . . . Europe may take a new turning, and that we may attain the proper balance . . . a positive, political and military equilibrium of the great powers." Only then would Mussolini's voice be decisive, and only then could he pursue Italy's *sacro egoismo* without restraint. Catapulted upon the diplomatic stage by his personal vanity and the restless activism of his Fascist cohorts, the iron-willed Duce proved surprisingly meek in 1933. Having staked his prestige on the successful conclusion of the pact, he had to accept a wholly emasculated version despite his ingenious versatility and his sonorous promises. Ironically enough, the fate of the Four Power Pact was a striking symbol for Mussolini, the man.

In the long run the most significant feature of the
Four Power Pact consisted in the diplomatic pattern
which evolved during its negotiations. At Hitler's accession to power, the international situation in Europe
was in flux. Initially the powers attempted to continue
the alignment of the 1920's, but slowly the sides reversed and a new, bi-polar constellation took form in
late 1933, to be bridged only once more at Munich.
The deepening chasm between the democracies and
Germany provided the basic pattern until the outbreak
of World War II. Only Mussolini's Italy was an unstable element in the equation, since the Duce continued to crisscross the lines in search of more allur-
ing spoils. As soon as Mussolini would side with
either side irrevocably, the conflict became inevitable, if already his temporizing role in 1933 did not
prevent Hitler from challenging the Western powers.
Only a four-power agreement, in which the interests,
if not the very existence, of some smaller European
nations were sacrificed could produce a semblance of
unity between the Great Powers and could maintain the
uneasy truce for a few more precious months. In 1938
the price for peace was Czechoslovakia, and the agreement reached at Munich was another Four Power Pact.
In this terrible sense Caillaux could claim correctly:
"Its adoption would no doubt have forestalled the war."

"The development of the international relations of
Europe in 1933 had reached the moment of decision
between peace and war, between annihilation or rescue
of human civilization." So wrote a contemporary observer. Is it telescoping history too much to assert
that with Hitler's unpunished withdrawal from Geneva,
his first successful repudiation of the very symbol of
Versailles, the drift into the abyss began? The League
of Nations proved powerless to check it. The Disarmament Conference lay in shambles. There was no basic
community of interest upon which to erect any treaty
structure. A momentary convergence of diverse factors

had produced the proposal and the acceptance of the Four Power Pact. But once resurrected, the Great Power directorate proved unequal to its task. The institutional framework of Europe's organization mattered little while its basic contradictions remained unresolved. Despite Mussolini's histrionic stance, there was more than a grain of truth in his New Year's message of 1934: "In case of failure of revision by the Four Power Pact, his majesty the cannon shall speak!"

APPENDIX

Synoptic Table of Drafts of Four Power Pact

A. Italian draft
of March 4, 1933

B. British draft
of April 1, 1933

C. French draft
of April 10, 1933

No Preamble

No Preamble

Germany, France, Great Britain and Italy, conscious of the special responsibilities imposed on them by their position as permanent members of the Council of the League itself and its members, and of those resulting from their joint signing of the Locarno agreements;

Convinced that the state of malaise which prevails in the world cannot be dispelled except by a strengthening of their solidarity capable of affirming the confidence in Europe in peace;

Faithful to the obligations, which they have assumed under the Covenant of the League of Nations, the Locarno Agreements, and the Briand-Kellogg Pact and referring to the Declaration of No-Resort—to—Force, the principle of which was adopted on March 2 last by the Political Commission of the Disarmament Conference;

Anxious to give full efficacy to all the provisions of the Covenant while conforming to the methods and procedures which are provided for there, from which they do not intend to depart;

Respectful of the rights of each State,

D. German draft of April 20, 1933

Germany,France,Great Britain and Italy, conscious of the special responsibilities imposed on them by their position as permanent members of the Council of the League itself and its members, and of those resulting from their joint signing of the Locarno agreements;

Convinced that the state of malaise which prevails in the world cannot be dispelled except by a strengthening of their solidarity capable of affirming the confidence in Europe in peace;

Faithful to the obligations, which they have assumed under the Covenant of the League of Nations, the Locarno Agreements, and the Briand-Kellogg Pact and referring to the Declaration of No-Resort—to—Force, the principle of which was adopted on March 2 last by the Political Commission of the Disarmament Conference;

Anxious to give full efficacy to all the provisions of the Covenant;

Have agreed on the following provisions:

E. Italian draft of May 13, 1933

Germany,France,Great Britain and Italy, conscious of the special responsibilities imposed on them by their position as permanent members of the Council of the League itself and its members, and of those resulting from their joint signing of the Locarno agreements;

Convinced that the state of malaise which prevails in the world cannot be dispelled except by a strengthening of their solidarity capable of affirming the conficence in Europe in peace;

Faithful to the obligations, which they have assumed under the Covenant of the League of Nations, the Locarno Agreements, and the Briand-Kellogg Pact and referring to the Declaration of No-Resort—to—Force, the principle of which was adopted on March 2 last by the Political Commission of the Disarmament Conference;

Anxious to give full efficacy to all the provisions of the Covenant;

Respectful of the rights of each State, concerning which no disposition can be made without the consent of the interested party;

F. Final draft of June 7, 1933

The President of the French Republic, the President of the German Reich, His Majesty the King of Great Britain,Ireland and the British Dominions beyond the Seas, Emperor of India, and His Majesty the King of Italy;

Conscious of the special responsibilities incumbent upon them as possessing permanent representation on the Council of the League of Nations, where the League itself and its members are concerned, and of the responsibilities resulting from their common signature of the Locarno agreements;

Convinced that the state of disquiet which obtains throughout the world can only be dissipated by reinforcing their solidarity in such a way as to strengthen confidence in peace in Europe;

Faithful to the obligations which they assumed in virtue of the Covenant of the League of Nations, the Locarno Treaties, and the Briand-Kellogg Pact, and taking into account the Declaration of the Renunciation of Force, the principle of which was proclaimed in the declaration signed at Ge-

A. Italian draft (cont.)	B. British draft (cont.)	C. French draft (cont.)
		concerning which no disposition c a n be made without the con- sent of the interested party;
		Have agreed on the following provisions:

- ARTICLE ONE -

The four Western Pow- ers; Italy, France, Ger- many and Great Britain —undertake to carry out between them- selves an effective policy of cooperation with a view to the maintenance of t h e peace in the spirit of	The four Western Pow- ers—France, Germany, Great Britain and Italy —undertake to carry out between them- selves an effective policy of cooperation in order to ensure the maintenance of t h e peace in the spirit of	The High Contracting Parties will consult on all questions which appertain to them and will strive within the f r a m e w o r k of the League of Nations to pursue an effective policy of cooperation a m o n g themselves

D. German draft (cont.)	E. Italian draft (cont.)	F. Final draft (cont.)
	Have agreed on the following provisions:	neva on the 11th December, 1932, by their delegates at the Disarmament Conference and adopted on 2nd March, 1933, by the Political Commission of that Conference;
		Anxious to give full effect to all the provisions of the Covenant of the League of Nations, while conforming to the methods and procedures laid down therein, from which they have no intention of parting;
		Mindful of the rights of every State, which cannot be affected without the consent of the interested party;
		Have resolved to conclude an agreement with these objects, and have appointed as their plenipotentiaries:
		. . . .
		Who, having exchanged their full powers, found in good and due form, have agreed as follows:

- ARTICLE ONE -

D. German draft	E. Italian draft	F. Final draft
The High Contracting Parties will consult on all questions which appertain to them and will strive within the framework of the League of Nations to pursue an effective policy of cooperation among themselves	The High Contracting Parties will concert on all questions which interest the maintenance of peace and which appertain to them, with a view to practicing an effective policy of collaboration in the framework	The High Contracting Parties will consult together as regards all questions which appertain to them. They undertake to make every effort to pursue within the framework of the League of Nations, a

A. Italian draft (cont.)	B. British draft (cont.)	C. French draft (cont.)
the Kellogg Pact and the "No-Force-Pact," and they undertake to act in the sphere of European relations in such a way that this peace policy, if necessary, is adopted by the others.	the Kellogg Pact and the "No-Resort-to-Force-Pact" envisaged by the declaration signed by the above Powers on December 11, 1932.	with a view to maintaining peace.

- ARTICLE TWO -

The four Powers reaffirm in accordance with the provisions of the Covenant of the League of Nations the principle of revision of the Peace Treaties given the existence of conditions which might lead to a conflict between the states. They declare, however, that this principle of revision can be applied only within the framework of the League of Nations and in the spirit of mutual understanding and solidarity of reciprocal interests.	The four Powers confirm that while the provisions of the Covenant of the League of Nations embody a scrupulous respect for all treaty obligations as a means of achieving international peace and security, they also contemplate the possibility of the revision of the Peace Treaties when conditions arise that might lead to a conflict between nations. In order to regulate and define the application of this principle of revision, the four Powers declare that such application should take place through agreements based on the mutual recognition of the interests of all concerned and within the framework of the League of Nations.	The High Contracting Parties, with a view to the possible application in Europe of the Articles of the Covenant, particularly Articles, X, XVI, and XIX decide to examine among themselves, without prejudice to the decisions which can only be taken by the regular organs of the League of Nations any proposal tending to give full efficacy to the methods and procedures provided for by in these articles.

D. German draft (cont.)	E. Italian draft (cont.)	F. Final draft (cont.)
with a view to maintaining peace.	and according to the principles of the Covenant of the League of Nations.	policy of effective co-operation between all Powers with a view to the maintenance of peace.

- ARTICLE TWO -

The four Powers confirm that the obligations of the Covenant demand scrupulous respect for all treaty obligations as a means of ensuring peace and security, but they also recognize the possibility of revision of the Peace Treaties in circumstances that might lead to a conflict among nations. In connection therewith and with a view to the possible application in Europe of the principles enunciated in Articles X (summary), and XIX of the Covenant, they decide to examine among themselves, without prejudice to decisions which can only be taken by the regular organs of the League of Nations, any proposal tending to give full efficacy to these principles.	The High Contracting Parties, with a view to the possible application in Europe of the Articles of the Covenant, notably the Articles X, XVI and XIX, concerning territorial integrity, sanctions and all new examinations of the Peace Treaties, decide to examine among themselves, without prejudice to the decisions which can only be taken by the regular organs of the League of Nations, any proposal tending to give full efficacy to the principles, methods and procedures provided for by these Articles.	In respect of the Covenant of the League of Nations, and particularly of Articles X, XVI and XIX, the High Contracting Parties decide to examine between themselves and without prejudice to decisions which can only be taken by the regular organs of the League of Nations, all proposals relating to methods and procedures calculated to give due effect to those Articles.

A. Italian draft (cont.)	B. British draft (cont.)	C. French draft (cont.)

- ARTICLE THREE -

Italy, France and Great Britain declare that, in case the Disarmament Conference should lead to partial results only, the equality of rights conceded to Germany must have an effective application, and Germany undertakes to implement this equality of rights by stages which shall be the result of successive agreements to be concluded among the four Powers through normal diplomatic channels	It is agreed that the principle of equality of rights as conceded to Germany under the conditions laid down in the Five Power resolution of December 11 must be given practical value.	Renewing in so far as they are concerned their joint declaration of December 11, 1932, the High Contracting Parties see in the recent British draft convention a practical basis of discussion which should permit the Disarmament Conference to work out as quickly as possible a convention assuring a substantial reduction and limitation of armaments with provisions for its subsequent revision with a view to new reductions. Germany for her part recognizes that equality of rights in a system affording security for all nations cannot be realized except by stages in accordance with Article VIII of the Covenant and by virtue of agreements reached to this effect.
The four Powers undertake to conclude similar agreements with regard to "equality" for Austria, Hungary, and Bulgaria.	The four Powers recognize that the draft Disarmament Convention submitted by the United Kingdom delegation on March 16 not only gives effect to this principle, but provides a satisfactory first stage of general disarmament, and they accordingly undertake to recommend it to the Disarmament Conference for acceptance. Germany, for her part, agrees that the principle of equality of rights shall be put into practice by degrees under agreements to which each of the four Powers must be a party.	

D. German draft (cont.)	E. Italian draft (cont.)	F. Final draft (cont.)

- ARTICLE THREE -

The High Contracting Powers undertake to collaborate as quickly as possible with the other powers in a convention ensuring a substantial reduction and limitation of armaments, with provisions for its subsequent revision with a view to a new reduction. In the event that the Disarmament Conference should end with only partial results, France, Great Britain, and Italy declare that the equality of rights accorded to Germany should have an effective application. Germany for her part undertakes for the duration of the first disarmament convention (5 years at the most) to realize this equality of rights only by stages and by virtue of an agreement reached to this effect in relation to the disarmament measures of the other powers. (Analogous arrangements concerning Austria, Hungary, and Bulgaria).	The High Contracting Parties realize that the maintenance of the peace requires the reduction of national armaments to the minimum level which is compatible with national security and that the success of the Disarmament Conference would be the best means to realize this end. They reaffirm their desire to cooperate with the other nations represented there in the effort to elaborate as quickly as possible a convention assuring a substantial reduction and limitation of armaments with provisions for its subsequent revision with a view to new reductions. France, Great Britain, and Italy declare that the principle of equality of rights should have a practical value for Germany and the other states disarmed by the Peace Treaty, and Germany, as far as she is concerned, recognizes that effect cannot be given to this principle of equality of rights except by stages and by virtue of accords to which each of the four powers must be a party.	The High Contracting Parties undertake to make every effort to ensure the success of the Disarmament Conference and, should questions which particularly concern them, remain in suspense on the conclusion of that Conference, they reserve the right to reexamine these questions between themselves with a view to ensuring their solution through appropriate channels.

A. Italian draft (cont.)	B. British draft (cont.)	C. French draft (cont.)

- ARTICLE FOUR -

The four Powers undertake to adopt as much as this is possible, a common line of conduct in all political and non-political, European and extra—European questions as well as with regard to the sphere of colonies.	The application of such a principle of equality of rights to Austria, Hungary, and Bulgaria shall be governed by the same conditions expressed in the case of Germany in the preceding Article and only under agreements to which each of the four Powers must be a party.	The High Contracting Parties affirm in general their desire to consult on all questions of common interest in Europe, particularly on all questions concerning the restoration of its economy, the regulation of which might, without forming the subject of proceedings before the League of Nations, be profitably sought within the framework of the Study Commission for European Union.

- ARTICLE FIVE -

This agreement of understanding and cooperation will, if necessary, be submitted for approval to the Parliaments; its duration shall be for ten years and it shall tacitly be regarded as renewed for the same period of time, unless it is denounced by one of the parties one year before it expires.	The four Powers pledge themselves to cooperate in the work of finding solutions for the economic difficulties which face their respective nations and the world as a whole.	The present accord is concluded for a period of ten years from the exchange of ratifications. If, before the end of the eighth year, none of the High Contracting Parties shall have notified to the others its intention to terminate the agreement, it shall be regarded as renewed and will remain in force indefinitely, each of the Contracting Parties retaining the right to terminate it by denouncing it two years in advance.

D. German draft (cont.)	E. Italian draft (cont.)	F. Final draft (cont.)

- ARTICLE FOUR -

The High Contracting Parties affirm in general their desire to consult on every question of common interest in Europe, particularly on every question concerning the restoriation of its economy.

The High Contracting Parties affirm their desire to consult on all questions of common interest in Europe, particularly on every question concerning the restoration of its economy.

The High Contracting Parties affirm their desire to consult together as regards all economic questions which have a common interest for Europe and particularly for its economic restoration, with a view to seeking within the framework a settlement of the League of Nations.

- ARTICLE FIVE -

The present agreement is concluded for a period of ten years reckoned from the exchange of ratifications. If at the end of the eighth year none of the High Contracting Parties has notified the others of its intention to terminate it, it shall be considered as renewed and shall remain in force indefinitely, the Contracting Parties retaining the right to terminate it by denouncing it two years in advance.

The present agreement is concluded for a period of ten years reckoned from the exchange of ratifications. If at the end of the eighth year none of the High Contracting Parties has notified the others of its intention to terminate it, it shall be considered as renewed and shall remain in force indefinitely, the Contracting Parties retaining the right to terminate it by denouncing it two years in advance.

The present agreement is concluded for a period of ten years reckoned from the exchange of ratifications. If at the end of the eighth year none of the High Contracting Parties has notified the others of its intention to terminate it, it shall be considered as renewed and shall remain in force indefinitely, the Contracting Parties retaining the right to terminate it by denouncing it two years in advance.

| A.   Italian draft | B.   British draft | C.   French draft |
| (cont.) | (cont.) | (cont.) |

- ARTICLE SIX -

The present pact shall be registered at the Secretariat of the League of Nations.

The present agreement of understanding and cooperation will, if necessary, be submitted for the approval of the Parliaments of the Contracting Powers within three months of the date of its signature. Its duration shall be for ten years. If no notice is given before the end of the ninth year by any of the Parties it shall be regarded as renewed for another period of ten years.

The present accord shall be ratified and the signatures shall be exchanged as soon as possible. It shall be registered at the Secretariat of the League of Nations in accordance with the provisions of the Covenant.

- ARTICLE SEVEN -

The present agreement shall be registered in accordance with the Covenant of the League of Nations, at the Secretariat of the League of Nations.

D. German draft (cont.)	E. Italian draft (cont.)	F. Final draft (cont.)

- ARTICLE SIX -

The present accord shall be ratified and the signatures shall be exchanged as soon as possible. It shall be registered at the Secretariat of the League of Nations in accordance with the provisions of the Covenant.	The present accord shall be ratified and the signatures shall be exchanged as soon as possible. It shall be registered at the Secretariat of the League of Nations in accordance with the provisions of the Covenant.	The present agreement, drawn up in English, French, German and Italian, of which the French text prevails in case of divergence, shall be ratified and the ratifications shall be deposited at Rome as soon as possible. The Government of the Kingdom of Italy will deliver to each of the High Contracting Parties a certified copy of the *procès-verbaux* of deposit. The present agreement will enter into force as soon as all the ratifications have been deposited.

It shall be registered at the League of Nations in conformity with the Covenant of the League.

Done at Rome, the 7th June 1933, in a single copy, which will remain deposited in the archives of the Kingdom of Italy, certified copies will be delivered to each of the High Contracting Parties.

In faith of the above mentioned the following plenipotentairies have signed the present agreement:

HENRY DE JOUVENEL
ULRICH VON HASSELL
RONALD GRAHAM
BENITO MUSSOLINI

BIBLIOGRAPHY

I. PRIMARY SOURCES:

1) *Unpublished Documents:*

The German Foreign Office Files contain a large,
if spotty collection on the Four Power Pact. The
present study is based upon the microfilms in
National Archives, Washington, D.C. These provide uneven coverage, since part of the files was
burnt too badly for filming and others were filmed
only selectively. The following files were consulted:

German Foreign Ministry.

II F Abr, Bundle 63/4 Ministerbesprechungen
in Genf, Bd. 1, Serial 7457 / H 176402-
176453
19a, Office of the Reichsminister, Mussolini-
Pakt, vols. I, II, Serial 3170 / D 675724-
676644
Italien Po 4, Viermächtepakt, Serial 6058 H /
E 449635—447501 and Serial 8908 H / E
627734-42
Rom, Geheim 20/2-4, Serial 8910 H / E 621744-
53, Serial 8903 H / E 621666, Serial 8904
H / E 621680.

Abrüstung, Viermächtepakt, Serial 8902 H / E
621659
Viermächtepakt, Handakten Botschafter Koe-
ster, Serial 8906 H / E 621717-20
Pol 2a[1] Deutsch—Italienische Beziehungen,
Bd. 11, Serial 8907 H / E 6217722-6

2) *Published Documents:*

R. Accademia d'Italia, Fondazione A. Volta,
Atti dei Convegni *Il Convegno di scienze
morali e storiche, 14-20 Novembre 1932-
XI.* Tema: L'Europa (Rome, 1933), vol. I.
Berber, Friedrich. *Europäische Politik im
Spiegel der Prager Akten* (Essen, 1941).
Degras, Jane, ed., *Soviet Documents on For-
eign Policy* (London, 1953), vol. III.
France. La Commission chargée d'enquêter
*les évènements survenus en France de
1933 à 1945* (Paris, 1947-1949), vols. I-
IX, ed. by Charles Serre.
France. Journal Officiel de la République
Française. *Annales de la Chambre des
Députés, Débats Parlementaires,* (s.o.,
1933), vols.149-151.
France. Journal Officiel de la République
Française. *Annales du Sénat, Débats Par-
lementaires* (s.o., 1933), vols. 118-119.
France. Ministère des Affaires Étrangères.
*Pacte d'entente et de la collaboration
paraphé à Rome le 7 juin 1933* (Paris,
June 9, 1933).
Germany. *Verhandlungen des Reichstags*
(VIII. Wahlperiode, 1933), vol. 457.
Great Britain. Foreign Office. *British White
Paper* (Command, 4342; June 8, 1933).
Great Britain. Foreign Office. *Documents on
British Foreign Policy, 1919-1945* (Series
C, 1933), vols. IV-V.

Great Britain.   House of Commons, *Parlia-*
mentary Debates (5th series, 1933), vols.
229–281.

Great Britain.   House of Lords, *Parliamen-*
tary Debates (5th series, 1933), vols. 86–
88.

International Military Tribunal. *Trial of the*
Major War Criminals before the Inter-
national Military Tribunal, Nuremberg,
14 November 1945 - 1 October 1946 (Nuremberg, 1947–1949), vols. X, XIX.

Italy. Gran Consiglio del Fascismo. *Il Gran*
Consiglio nei primi dieci anni dell'Era
Fascista (Rome, 1933).

Italy.   Parlamento Nazionale (Legislatura
XXVIII). *Camera dei Deputati, Discussioni*
(Rome, 1934), vols. VII, VIII.

Italy.   Parlamento Nazionale (Legislatura
XXVIII). *Camera dei Senatori, Discus-*
sioni (Rome, 1934), vol. V.

League of Nations. *Records of the Confer-*
ence for the Reduction and the Limitation
of Armaments (Geneva, 1933).

Republic of Poland. Ministry of Foreign Affairs. *Official Documents Concerning*
Polish-German and Polish-Soviet Rela-
tions, 1933-1939 (London, 1941).

U.S. Department of State. *Documents on*
German Foreign Policy 1918-1945 (Series
C, 1933), vols. I-II.

U.S. Department of State. *Foreign Relations*
of the United States: Diplomatic Papers
(1933), vol. I.

Wheeler-Bennett, John W., ed., *Documents*
on International Affairs 1933 (London,
1934).

3) *Collected Works:*

Baynes, Norman H., ed., *The Speeches of Adolf Hitler, April 1922 - August 1939* (London, 1942).

Beck, Josef. *Beiträge zur europäischen Politik: Reden, Erklärungen, Interviews, 1932-1939* (Essen, 1939).

Beneš, Edouard, "La question du directoire européen et la révision des frontières," in *Sources et Documents Tchécoslovaques*, No. 21 (Prague, 1933).

Domarus, Max. *Hitler: Reden und Proklamationen, 1932-1945*. Kommentiert von einem deutschen Zeitgenossen (Würzburg, 1962), vol. I.

Hitler, Adolf. *Hitlers Zweites Buch*, ed. by Gerald L. Weinberg (Stuttgart, 1961).

Hoepli, Ulrico. *Scritti e Discorsi di Benito Mussolini: Edizione Definitiva* (Milan, 1934), vol. VIII.

Litvinov, Maksim M. *Vneshnaia Politika SSSR* (Moscow, 1935).

Sailer, Karl H., ed., *Geheimer Briefwechsel Mussolini-Dollfuss* (Vienna, 1949).

Susmel, Eduardo and Duilio, eds., *Opera Omnia di Benito Mussolini* (Florence, 1958), vols. XXV-XXVI.

4) *Memoirs:*

Aloisi, Pompeo, *Journal, 25 Juillet 1932 - 14 Juin 1936* (Paris, 1957).

Beck, Josef. *Dernier Rapport* (Geneva, 1951).

Beneš, Eduard. *Memoirs of Eduard Beneš*, ed. by Godfrey Lias (London, 1954).

Coudenhove-Kalergi, Count. *An Idea Con - quers the World* (New York, n.d.).

Dirksen, Herbert A. *Moskau—Tokio—London: Erinnerungen und Betrachtungen zu 20 Jahren deutscher Aussenpolitik 1919-1939* (Stuttgart, n.d., probably 1949).

Dodd, William E. and Martha, eds. *Ambassador Dodd's Diary 1933-1938* (New York, (1941).

Eden, Anthony. *Facing the Dictators: The Memoirs of Sir Anthony Eden, Earl of Avon* (Boston, 1962).

François—Poncet, André. *Souvenirs d'une ambassade `a Berlin* (Paris, 1946).

Gamelin, General. *Servir: Le Prologue du drame, 1930-Août 1939* (Paris, 1946).

Geraud, André (pseud. Pertinax). *Les Fossoyeurs: Défaite militaire de la France - Armistice — Contre-révolution* (New York, 1943), vol. I.

Guaraglia, Raffaele. *La Diplomatie difficile* (Paris, 1955).

Herriot, *Jadis: D'une guerre à l'autre, 1914-1936* (Paris, 1952), vol. II.

Lagardelle, Hubert. *Mission à Rome: Mussolini* (Paris, 1955).

Laroche, Jules. *La Pologne de Pilsudski* (Paris, 1953).

Maiskii, Ivan M. *Vospominania Sovetskogo Posla* (Moscow, 1964), vol. II.

Mussolini, Rachele. *La mia Vita con Benito* (Verona, 1948).

Meissner, Otto. *Staatssekretär unter Ebert, Hindenburg, Hitler* (Hamburg, 1950).

Monzie, Anatole de. *Ci-devant* (Paris, 1941).

Nadolny, Rudolf. *Mein Beitrag* (Wiesbaden, 1955).

Paul-Boncour, Joseph. *Entre deux guerres*:

Souvenirs sur la Troisième République (Paris, 1957).

Reynaud, Paul. *Au coeur de la mêlée* (Paris, 1951).

Rheinbaben, Werner Freiherr von. *Viermal Deutschland: Aus dem Erleben eines Seemanns, Diplomaten, Politikers 1895-1954* (Berlin, 1954).

Rintelen, Anton. *Erinnerungen an Österreichs Weg: Versailles,Berchtesgaden, Grossdeutschland* (Munich, 1941).

Roche, Emile. *Caillaux que j'ai connu* (Paris, 1949).

Schmidt, Paul. *Statist auf diplomatischer Bühne, 1923-1945* (Bonn, 1949).

Selby, Walford. *Diplomatic Twilight, 1930-1940* (London, 1953).

Sforza, Carlo. *L'Italia dal 1914 al 1944* (Verona, 1946).

Simon, John Allensbrook. *Retrospect* (London, 1952).

Starhemberg, Ernst Rüdiger. *Between Hitler and Mussolini* (New York, 1942).

Szembeck, Jean. *Journal* (Paris, 1952).

Tardieu, Andre. *L'Heure de la décision* (Paris, 1934).

Temperley, A. C. *The Whispering Gallery of Europe* (London, 1938).

Vansittart, Robert. *The Mist Procession* (London, 1958).

Wilson, Hugh R. *Diplomat Between Wars* (Toronto, 1941).

5) *Newspapers and Periodicals* (March-Oct.,1933):

Christian Century
Current History
Deutsche Allgemeine Zeitung

Europäische Gespräche
Europäische Revue
L 'Europe Nouvelle
Fortnightly Review
L 'Illustration
Izvestia
Le Journal des Débats
Literary Digest
London Daily Herald
London *Times*
New Republic
New Statesman and Nation
New York Times
Nuova Antologia
Pravda
Revue des Deux Mondes
Revue des Vivants (November, 1935; memorial
      issue at the death of its founder, Henry de
      Jouvenel.)
Saturday Review (London)
Spectator
Survey Graphic
Le Temps
Völkischer Beobachter
Vossische Zeitung
World Tomorrow
Zeitschrift für Politik

II. SECONDARY WORKS

1) *Books:*

Adami, Eugenio.   *La Lingua di Mussolini*
      (Modena, 1939).
Airapetian, M. E. and Deborin, G. A.   *Etapi*
      vneshnei politiki SSSR (Moscow, 1961).
Alatri, Paolo. *Le Origini del Fascismo* (Rome,
      1956).

Albrecht-Carrié, René. *France, Europe and the Two World Wars* (New York, 1960).

Albrecht-Carrié, René. *Italy from Napoleon to Mussolini* (New York, 1950).

Arnold, Victor C. *The Little Entente and the Revisionists* (unpublished Ph.D. dissertation at the University of Wisconsin, 1958).

Ball, Margaret M. *Post-War German-Austrian Relations: The Anschluss Movement, 1918-1936* (Stanford, 1937).

Basch, Antonin. *The Danube Basin and the German Economic Sphere* (New York, 1943).

Baumont, Maurice. *La Faillite de la paix, 1918-1939* (Paris, 1951).

Benoist—Mechin, Jaques G. P. M. *Histoire de l'armée allemande, vol. III: L'Essor 1925-1932* (Paris, 1964).

Beer, Max. *Die Auswärtige Politik des dritten Reiches* (Zürich, 1935).

Benedikt, Heinrich, ed., *Geschichte der Republik Österreich* (München, 1954).

Binion, Rudolph. *Defeated Leaders: The Political Fate of Caillaux, Jouvenel and Tardieu* (New York, 1960).

Bonnefous, Edouard. *Histoire politique de la Troisième République* (Paris, 1962), vol. V.

Bonnet, Georges. *Le Quai d'Orsay sous trois Républiques, 1870-1961* (Paris, 1961).

Bracher, K. D., Sauer, W., and Schulz, G. *Die Nationalsozialistische Machtergreifung* (Köln, 1960).

Breyer, Richard. *Das Deutsche Reich und Polen, 1932-1937* (Wiesbaden, 1955).

Bullock, Alan. *Hitler: A Study in Tyranny* (New York, 1960, rev. ed.).

Cameron, Elizabeth R. *Prologue to Appease-ment* (Philadelphia, 1942).

Carr, Edward H. *International Relations between the Two World Wars, 1919-1939* (London, 1947).

Castellan, Georges. *Le Réarmement clandestin du Reich, 1930-1935* (Paris, 1954).

Chabod, Frederico. *A History of Italian Fascism* (London, 1963).

Chambers, F., Grant, C., and Bayley, C. *This Age of Conflict: A Contemporary World History* (New York, 1943).

Chastenet, Jaques. *Histoire de la Troisième République, vol. VI: Le Déclin de la Troisième République, 1931-1938* (Paris, 1962).

Coquet, James de. *Le Procès de Riom* (Paris, 1945).

Craig, Gordon, and Gilbert, Felix. *The Diplomats* (Princeton, 1955).

Davis, John W. *Hitler and the Versailles Settlement* (Unpublished Ph.D. dissertation at the University of Wisconsin, 1964).

Debicki, Roman. *The Foreign Policy of Poland, 1919-1939* (New York, 1962).

Dehio, Ludwig. *Deutschland und die Weltpolitik im zwanzigsten Jahrhundert* (Munich, 1955).

Deierhoi, Tyler. *The Conduct of German Policy at the Disarmament Conference of 1932* (Unpublished Ph.D. dissertation at Duke University, 1963).

Delzell, Charles F. *Mussolini's Enemies: The Italian Anti-Fascist Resistance* (Princeton, 1961).

Duroselle, Jean-Baptiste. *Histoire diplomatique de 1919 à nos jours* (Paris, 1962 ed.)

Eichstadt, Ulrich. *Von Dollfuss zu Hitler:
Geschichte des Anschlusses Österreichs,
1933-1938* (Wiesbaden, 1955).

Fermi, Laura. *Mussolini* (Chicago, 1961).

Ferrero, Guglielmo. *Four Years of Fascism*
(London, 1924).

Furnia, Arthur H. *The Diplomacy of Appeasement: Anglo-French Relations and the
Prelude to World War II* (Washington,
1960).

Freytagh-Loringhoven, Axel. *Deutschlands
Aussenpolitik 1933-1941* (Berlin, 1942).

Gathorne-Hardy, Geoffrey M. *A Short History of International Affairs, 1920-1939*
(London, 1950).

Gayda, Virginio. *Was Will Italien?* (Leipzig, 1941).

Gehl, Jürgen. *Austria, Germany and the Anschluss, 1931-1938* (London, 1963).

Gilbert, Martin and Gott, Richard. *The Appeasers* (Boston, 1963, rev. ed.).

Goldinger, Walter. *Geschichte der Republik
Österreich* (Munich, 1962).

Gravelli, Asvero. *Hitler, Mussolini und die
Revision* (Detmold, n.d., probably 1933).

Gulick, Charles A. *Austria from Hapsburg
to Hitler* (Berkeley, 1948), vol. II.

Halperin, S. William. *Mussolini and Italian
Fascism* (Princeton, 1964).

Hertz, Fredrick. *The Economic Problem of
the Danubian States: A Study in Economic
Nationalism* (London, 1947).

Hibbert, Christopher. *Benito Mussolini: A
Biography* (London, 1962).

Iezzi, Frank. *Selected Political Addresses
of Benito Mussolini* (Unpublished Ph.D.
dissertation at the University of Wisconsin, 1954).

Ivashin, I. F.   *Ocherki istorii vneshnei politiki SSSR* (Moscow, 1958).

Jordan, W. M.   *Great Britain, France and the
German Problem*, *1918–1939*   (London,
1943).

Kerner, Robert J.   *The Balkan Conferences
and the Balkan Entente, 1930-1935* (Berkeley, 1936).

Kertesz, Stephen.   *Diplomacy in a Whirlpool*
(Notre Dame, 1955).

Kieser, Rolf.   *Englands Appeasementpolitik
und der Aufstieg der Dritten Reiches im
Spiegel der britischen Presse*   (1933-
1939) (Winterthur, 1964).

Kirkpatrick, Sir Ivone Elliott.   *Mussolini: A
Study in Power* (New York, 1964).

Kogan, Norman.   *The Politics of Italian Foreign Policy* (New York, 1963).

Kommunisticheskaia Partiia Sovetskogo So-
iuza. Vysshaia partiinaia shkola. *Mezh-
dunarodnye otnoshenia i vneshnaia politika SSSR*, *1917-1960* (Moscow, 1961).

Larmour, Peter.   *The French Radical Party
in the 1930's* (Stanford, 1964).

Lee, Dwight E.   *Ten Years: The World on
the Way to War, 1930-1940* (Boston, 1941).

Ludwig, Emil.   *Mussolinis Gespräche mit
Emil Ludwig* (Berlin, 1932).

Macartney, C. A.   *October Fifteenth:* A History of Modern Hungary, 1929–1945 (Edin-
burgh, 1961 rev. ed.), vol. I.

Macartney, C. A. and Palmer, A. W.   *Independent Eastern Europe* (London, 1962).

Macartney, Maxwell and Cremona, Paul.   *Italy's Foreign and Colonial Policy* (London, 1938).

MacGregor-Hastie, Roy.   *The Day of the Lion:
The Life and Death of Fascist Italy, 1922-
1945* (London, 1963).

Machray, Robert. *The Struggle for the Danube and the Little Entente, 1929-1938* (London, 1938).

Marcovitch, Lazare. *La Politique extérieure de la Yougoslavie* (Paris, 1935).

Medlicott, W. N. *British Foreign Policy since Versailles* (London, 1940).

Megaro, Gaudens. *Mussolini in the Making* (Boston, 1938).

Meinck, Gerhard. *Hitler und die Deutsche Aufrüstung, 1933-1937* (Wiesbaden,1955).

Michaud, Charles. *The French Right and Nazi Germany, 1933-1939* (Durham, 1943).

Miller, Katherine J. *Belgian Foreign Policy between two Wars* (New York, 1951).

Minart, Jaques. *Le Drame du désarmement français: la revanche allemande 1918-1939* (Paris, 1959).

Missiroli, Mario. *La Politica Estera di Mussolini: Dalla Marcia su Roma al Convegno di Monaco, 1922-1938* (Varese, 1939).

Moscow, Institut mezhdunarodnykh otnoshenii. *Istoria mezhdunaronykh otnoshenii i vneshnei politiki SSSR, 1917-1939* (Moscow, 1961), vol. I.

Mouton, Pierre and J. Rinaldi. *Le Ménsonge de Daladier* (Paris, 1942).

Mowat, Charles Loch. *Britain between the Wars, 1918-1940* (London, 1955).

Nolfo, Ennio di. *Mussolini e la Politica Estera Italiana* (Padua, 1960).

Nolte, Ernst. *Der Faschismus in seiner Epoche. Die Action Francaise——Der italianische Faschismus——Der Nationalsozialismus* (Munich, 1963).

Pini, Giorgio. *Geschichte des Faschismus* (Berlin, 1942).

Potemkine, Vladimir. *Histoire de la diplomatie* (Paris, 1947).

Rappard, William E. *The Quest for Peace
since the World War* (Cambridge, 1940).

Rayemaker, O. de. *Belgie's International
Beleid* (Brussels, 1945).

Reynolds, Philip L. *British Foreign Policy
in the Inter-War Years* (London, 1954).

Robertson, Esmonde M. *Hitler's Pre-War
Policy and Military Plans, 1933–1939*
(London, 1963).

Roos, Hans. *Polen und Europa* (Tübingen,
1957).

Rosenberg, Alfred. *Blut und Ehre: Aufsätze
1919-1933* (Munich, 1934).

Roux-Georges. *La Chute de Mussolini*(Paris,
1951).

Rowse, Alfred L. *Appeasement: A Study in
Political Decline, 1933-1939* (New York,
1963).

Sacks, Benjamin. *James Ramsay MacDonald
in Thought and Action*(Albuquerque, 1952).

Salata, Francesco. *Il Patto Mussolini* (Verona, 1933).

Salvatorelli, Luigi. *Il Fascismo nella politica internazionale* (Modena, 1946).

Salvatorelli, Luigi and Mira Giovanni. *Storia
d'Italia nel periodo fascista* (Turin, 1956).

Salvemini, Gaetano. *Mussolini Diplomate*
(Paris, 1952).

Salvemini, Gaetano. *Prelude to World War
II* (New York, 1954).

Sarkotic, Erwin Frhr. v. *Aufbau des Abendlandes: Ein Arbeits plan auf Grund des
Viermächtepaktes* (Wien, 1933).

Schacher, Gerhard. *Central Europe and the
Western World* (London, 1936).

Scott, William E. *Alliance against Hitler*
(Durham, 1962).

Seabury, Paul. *The Wilhelmstrasse: A Study of German Diplomats under the Nazi Regime* (Berkeley, 1954).

Seton-Watson, R. W. *Great Britain and the Dictators* (New York, 1938).

Siebert, Ferdinand. *Italiens Weg in den zweiten Weltkrieg* (Frankfurt, 1962).

Smith, Denis Mack. *Italy* (Ann Arbor, 1959).

Sturzo, Luigi. *Italy and Fascismo* (London, 1926).

Strauss, Emil. *Tschechoslowakische Aussenpolitik: Eine Geschichtliche Einführung* (Prag, 1936).

Tasca, Angelo. *Nascita e avvento del Fascismo* (Fiume, n.d.).

Taylor, A. J. P. *The Origins of the Second World War* (London, 1961).

Toscano, Mario. *Origini e vicende della seconda guerra mondiale* (Milan, 1963).

Toynbee, Arnold, ed., *Survey of International Affairs 1933* (London, 1934).

Vondraceck, F. J. *The Foreign Policy of Czechoslovakia, 1918-1935* (London, 1935).

Villari, Luigi. *Italian Foreign Policy under Mussolini* (New York, 1956).

Walters, Francis P. *A History of the League of Nations* (London, 1952).

Wier, Lauchlin M. *The Tragedy of Ramsay MacDonald* (London, 1938).

Wheeler-Bennett, John W. *The Pipe Dream of Peace* (New York, 1935).

Wierzbowski, Zygmunt. *Pologne 1919-1939* (n.p., n.d.), vol. I (Vie politique et sociale).

Wiskemann, Elizabeth. *The Rome—Berlin Axis* (New York, 1949).

Wolfers, Arnold. *Britain and France between the two Wars* (New York, 1940).

Zuylen, Pierre van. *Les Mains libres: poli-*
tique extérieure de la Belgique, 1914–
1940 (Paris, 1950).

2) *Articles:*

Albrecht-Carrié, René. "Four Power Pacts,
1933–1945." *Journal of Central European*
Affairs (1945), 17–45.

Booms, Hans. "Der Ursprung des 2. Welt-
krieges—Revision oder Expansion?" *Ge-*
schichte in Wissenschaft und Unterricht
(1965), 329–352.

Bracher, Karl D.   "Das Anfangsstadium der
der Hitlerschen Aussenpolitik." *Viertel-*
jahreshefte für Zeitgeschichte (1957),
63–77.

Celovsky, Boris. "Pilsudskis Präventivkrieg
gegen das Nationalsozialistische Deutschland." *Welt als Geschichte* (1954), 53–
70.

Cerruti, V. "Collaborazione internazionale e
ragioni dell'insuccesso della Società delle
Nazioni." *Rivista di studi internazionali*
(1946), 59ff.

Delzell, Charles F.   "Benito Mussolini: A
Guide to Biographical Literature." *Journal*
of Modern History (1963), 339–353.

Festa, Elia. "I biographi di Mussolini."
Nuova Rivista Storica (1961), 467–513.

Gasiorowski, Zygmunt. "Did Pilsudski Attempt to Initiate a Preventive War in 1933?"
Journal of Modern History (1955), 135–
151.

Gasiorowski, Zygmunt. "The German-Polish
Nonaggression Pact of 1934." *Journal for*
Central European Affairs (1955), 3–29.

Grandi, Dino. "The Foreign Policy of the Duce." *Foreign Affairs* (1935), 553-566.

d'Hoop, Jean Marie. "Frankreichs Reaktion auf Hitlers Aussenpolitik 1933-1939." *Geschichte in Wissenschaft und Unterricht* (1964), 211-223.

Jacomini, Francesco. "Il Patto a quattro." *Riuista di studi storici* (1951), 25-66.

Kennedy, A. L. "Lord Simon as Foreign Secretary." *Contemporary Review* (1954), 136-141.

Kent, George O. "Pope Pius XII and Germany: Some Aspects of German—Vatican Relations, 1933-1943." *American Historical Review* (1964), 59-78.

Kluke, Paul. "Nationalsozialistische Europaideologie." *Vierteljahreshefte für Zeitgeschichte* (1955), 240-274.

Knaplund, Paul. "James Ramsay MacDonald." *Saturday Review* (1953), 12.

Legters, Lyman H. "Karl Radek als Sprachrohr des Bolschewismus." *Forschungen zur Osteuropäischen Geschichte* (1959), 196-323.

Lutz, Hermann. "Foreign Policy in the Third Reich." *Current History* (1955), 222-235.

Noether, Emilia P. "Italy Reviews its Fascist Past." *American Historical Review* (1956), 877-899.

Ottenga, Caesare. "Il Concordato fra la Santa Sede e la Germania del 20 luglio 1933." *Nuova Rivista Storica* (1960), 181-205, 382-457.

Pieri, Piero. "La politica estera di Mussolini dal 1922 al 1932." *Nuova Rivista Storica* (1956), 167-174.

Poole, de Witt C. "Light on Nazi Foreign Policy." *Foreign Affairs* (1946), 130-154.

Radek, Karl. "The Bases of Soviet Foreign Policy." *Foreign Affairs* (1934), 193-206.

Roos, Hans. "Die Präventivkriegspläne Pilsudskis von 1933." *Vierteljahreshefte für Zeitgeschichte* (1955), 344-363.

Vogelsang, Thilo. "Hitlers Brief an Reichenau vom 4. Dezember 1932." *Vierteljahreshefte für Zeitgeschichte* (1959), 429-427.

Vogelsang, Thilo. "Neue Dokuments zur Geschichte de Reichswehr, 1930–1933." *Vierteljahreshefte für Zeitgeschichte* (1954), 377-436.

Watson, Steven. "British Lord Chancellors." *History Today* (1955), 234f.

Watt, Donald C. "The German Diplomats and the Nazi Leaders, 1933-1939." *Journal for Central European Affairs* (1955), 148-160.

Abyssinia: and Italy, 3, 50
Albania: and Italy, 10, 11–12
Aloisi, Pompeo, 30*n*, 31*n*, 34,
    38–9, 42*n*, 55, 98*n*, 123, 126,
    183, 217
Anglo–French debates: pact, 38,
    44, 66–71; disarmament plan,
    207–213. *See also* Great
    Britain; France
Anglo–Italian negotiations, 58–
    61
Anschluss, 44, 125, 185, 197*n*.
    See also Austria; Hitler
Appeasement, 113*n*, 119*n*, 224
Austria: crisis of summer 1933,
    6, 91, 182*n*, 187, 188, 195–
    202, 221; inclusion in pact,
    89, 90*n*, 174–5. *See also*
    Anschluss
Austro-fascism, 125, 190, 190*n*,
    193
Axis: Berlin—Rome (fore-
    shadowed), 36, 37, 51, 123,
    192*n*. *See also* Hitler; Mus-
    solini

Balkan Entente, 174*n*, 177*n*, 222
Beck, Josef, 41*n*, 67, 99–104,
    177
Belgium, 93–4, 162, 169, 175
Beneš, Edouard, 41*n*, 67, 95–9,
    101, 145, 162, 176
Berenger, Henry, 31, 119, 132
Bloc national, 83. *See also*
    France

Blomberg, Werner von, 103, 128*n*,
    130*n*, 135, 140*n*, 141, 143,
    144, 154*n*, 208
Blum, Léon, 86
Briand: Study Commission for
    European Unity, 20, 114*n*, 122,
    128, 131, 141, 194*n*
British imperialism: father of
    pact, 41–3*n*, 108–9, 172–3*n*
Brüning, Heinrich, 70, 208*n*
Bulgaria: inclusion in pact, 49,
    116, 129; reaction to pact, 89,
    90*n*, 175; Italian satellite,
    190, 222. *See also* Revision;
    Italy
Bülow, Bernhard von, 51, 127, 130,
    131*n*, 149*n*, 153, 155*n*, 180*n*,
    181*n*, 201–2, 209, 216*n*

Caillaux, Joseph, 90*n*, 119, 226
Cartel des gauches, 83. *See
    also* France
Central Europe, 185, 188, 189,
    190, 191*n*, 194, 221
Cerruti, Vittorio, 48, 51, 52, 142,
    143*n*, 144, 153, 155, 195, 200
Churchill, Sir Winston, 9*n*, 79–
    80, 205, 222
Colonies, 50, 61, 78, 92, 93,
    131*n*, 188
Conference of Ambassadors, 3, 10
Concert of Europe, 3, 5, 49, 91.
    See also Great Power direc-
    torate
Corfu incident, 10

Corporatism: and international
relations, 6, 19, 23, 161, 225
Coudenhove-Kalergi, Richard
Nicolaus von, 20, 191*n*

Daladier, Edouard, 27, 41, 59*n*,
62, 64-5, 67, 84, 88-9, 131*n*,
134*n*, 147*n*, 152, 159, 166,
168*n*, 169, 182, 183, 188,
189*n*, 207, 215, 222, 223;
cabinet: vote of confidence,
27-8, 89, 90*n*, 147, 168-70,
182; insecurity of, 63, 128,
128*n*, 129, 143, 145-6, 151,
164*n*, 168*n*; attitude towards
pact, 65, 67-71, 88, 214-5.
See also France
Danubian problem, 187-195, 219.
See also Central Europe
Davis, Norman, 70, 207, 214
Dirksen, Herbert von, 52*n*, 105,
106
Disarmament Conference: failure
of, 3, 6, 14, 16, 24, 35-6,
48, 49, 113*n*, 116, 117, 124,
134-5, 137*n*, 141, 152, 164,
186*n*, 203-5, 216, 221, 226;
postponement, 40, 115; transfer into four-power framework, 206-7, 214-5. *See also*
MacDonald Plan
Disarmament Convention: draft,
37, 39, 61, 127-9, 136, 139,
207-11
Dollfuss, Engelbert, 91, 125-6,
193, 196*n*, 198*n*
Drummond, Sir Eric, 171-2, 217

Eden, Sir Anthony, 36*n*, 39*n*, 115,
166
Europe: unity, 19-23, 50. *See
also* Mussolini

Fasci, 11, 13, 134
Fascism, 6, 7, 13, 17, 20, 21,
22-3, 30, 45, 162*n*, 191, 225
Fiume question, 9
Five-power conference, 38, 53

Five Power Declaration of December 11, 1932, 14, 36, 61,
68, 116, 124, 151. *See also*
No-Force-Pact
Four Power directorate, 19. *See
also* Great Power directorate;
Concert of Europe
Four-power meeting, 38, 39, 53,
207, 226
Four Power Pact: studies of, 4*n*-
5*n*; meaning of, 5, 60, 100,
160-3, 219-20; origin of, 8,
10, 16, 34-5, 38, 40, 41;
ideological basis of, 16-17,
19-23, 161-2, 225; initial
draft, 34-5, 48-50; formal
proposal of, 47, 48, 54; preamble, 121, 127; conclusion,
139, 141, 144, 148, 157-9,
160-3, 165*n*; final compromise,
141, 148, 149; initialling, 148,
156-9, 160-3, 183-4, 185, 220;
signing, 179, 182, 183, 184*n*,
188*n*; application, 187-194,
195-202, 214; last attempts
to save, 213-8; failure, 210-
8; ratification, 217; historical
significance, 219-227; different drafts of, *see* France;
Great Britain; Germany; Italy
France: reaction to Hitler, 27-8,
32*n*, 37, 146; demand for security, 36, 39, 52, 59, 65, 68,
122, 132; Foreign Office, 120,
150. *See also* Quai d'Orsay
France: and the Four Power Pact,
47, 62-71, 85, 114, 114*n*;
press reaction, 83, 83*n*, 84*n*,
85*n*, 89*n*, 146*n*, 167-8*n*, 202*n*,
213*n*; public opinion, 62-3,
66, 82-3, 112, 146, 221;
Chamber debates on, 84, 85,
86-9, 145, 16-7, 168-9, 214;
Senate debate on, 132; and
British redraft, 119-23; counterdraft, 88, 149; success in
emasculating, 157, 162, 168;
reversal of opinion, 167-8;

exchange of notes with Little Entente, 175-181; *Blue Book*, 177

Franco-German non-aggression pact, 130

Franco-Italian rapprochement, 21, 30-4, 51, 166-9, 179, 187-9, 192*n*, 194-5, 222

Franco-Polish alienation, 104-5, 176-7, 177*n*, 222

Franco-Soviet rapprochement, 31, 174*n*

François-Poncet, André, 26, 130, 130-1*n*, 153*n*, 156*n*

Franklin-Bouillon, Henry, 84, 85, 86, 147, 170

French disarmament plan, 207-211, 208*n*

Geneva Conference, 138, 171. *See also* Disarmament Conference

Geneva, 7, 29, 39, 55, 57, 77, 207, 212. *See also* League of Nations

Geneva Protocol, 55

Geraud, André (*pseud.* Pertinax), 64, 167, 214*n*

Germany: Foreign Office, 51. *See also* Wilhelmstrasse; Concordat, 125; disarmament stand, 208-14; withdrawal from League and Disarmament Conference, 6, 14, 31, 208-18; rearmament, 36, 52, 70, 128*n*, 130*n*, 140, 194*n*, 196, 197, 209-19; equality of rights, 14, 16, 39, 49, 52, 53, 59, 60, 67-8, 77-9, 87, 116, 119, 122, 126-7, 154, 162, 164*n*, 219, 221

Germany and Four Power Pact, 40, 50-3, 74-5, 75*n*; press reaction, 75*n*, 154, 164-5; and British redraft, 117-8; and French draft, 124; counterdraft, 127-8; and Italian draft, 133; Rome draft, 141;

cabinet decision to accept, 141-2, 144; exasperation, 153-6, 156*n*; and French *Blue Book*, 170-80, 181; struggle between diplomats and party, 199-202. *See also* Hitler

Gömbös, Julius, 192, 193

Göring, Hermann, 125, 126, 139, 140, 143, 155, 156*n*, 210, 216

Graham, Sir Ronald, 34, 112*n*, 114, 115, 123, 128, 139, 140, 142, 157, 160, 166, 183, 188, 210, 213*n*, 216*n*

Grandi, Dino, 16*n*, 133*n*, 223, 225

Gravelli, Asvero, 19-22

Great Birtain: Foreign Office, 118. *See also* Whitehall; and Hitler, 28, 196*n*, 220; and revision, 62*n*, 76-9, 82, 220, 221

Great Britain and the Four Power Pact, 40, 47, 58-62, 75-8; acceptance, 59; criticism and modifications, 60-2; press opinion, 76*n*, 165-6, 202-3*n*, 213; Parliamentary debate over, 77-8, 82*n*, 113, 132; role as mediator, 113, 180; redraft, 115-7; initialling, 165-5; *White Paper*, 166; reversal of attitude towards Germany, 80-1, 205, 208*n*, 220-1

Great Power directorate, 3, 4, 5, 10, 16, 20-1*n*, 45, 48, 51, 57, 66, 95, 117, 159, 169, 222, 225

Great Depression, 28, 56, 145, 185

Greece, 91, 174, 222

Habicht, Theo, 196*n*, 198-9*n*, 220

Hailsham, Viscount, 81, 135

Hassell, Ulrich von, 4*n*, 50-1, 52, 90*n*, 105*n*, 112, 117, 123, 124-5, 127, 133, 142*n*, 148, 149*n*, 150*n*, 152, 153*n*, 155, 156, 158, 160, 163*n*, 164*n*, 178*n*, 181, 184*n*, 189, 191-2*n*, 196, 211, 223

Heimwehr, 193*n*, 196*n*
Henderson, Sir Arthur, 203, 212*n*,
    214, 215
Herriot, Edouard, 27, 31, 63, 65,
    66, 87, 114, 120*n*, 129*n*, 131,
    134*n*, 145, 146, 147, 162,
    168; comments on pact, 124*n*,
    145*n*, 170, 170*n*
Hitler, Adolf: seizure of power,
    4, 6, 14, 15, 17, 19, 44*n*, 65,
    205, 220, 224; foreign policy,
    6, 25-6, 195-6, 224; accept-
    ance of pact, 47, 50, 74, 133,
    137-8, 144*n*; and West, 70,
    101, 108*n*, 175; and Musso-
    lini, 74-5, 112, 143-4, 155,
    158-9, 165, 179-80, 182, 184,
    191, 196, 202, 216*n*; and
    Poland, 102-3; peace speech,
    134-8, 139*n*, 142; decision
    to initial, 141, 143-4, 153-6,
    158*n*, 181; anger over French
    Blue Book, 178-183, 188*n*;
    annexation of Austria, 193,
    196-202; withdrawal from
    League and Disarmament
    Conference, 137*n*, 208-18,
    219-20
Hoesch, Leopold von, 37, 80*n*,
    117, 118-9, 130, 135*n*, 210
Hungary: inclusion into pact,
    49, 116, 129; Italian satel-
    lite, 190, 192, 195*n*, 222;
    and pact, 89, 90, 175. *See
    also* Italy; revision

Italy: *sacro egoismo*, 11, 15,
    44, 220, 225; hegemony over
    Central Europe, 192, 193,
    194, 195*n*, 227
Italy and Four Power Pact: com-
    promise draft, 132-3; debates
    on pact, 139; initialling,
    163-4*n*; protest against
    French *Blue Book*, 182, 182*n*;
    demarche in Austrian crisis,

199-202. *See also* Musso-
    lini

Jacomini, Francesco, 4-5*n*, 19,
    25, 35, 43
Japan: withdrawal from League,
    5, 25, 36, 57
Jouvenel, Henry de, 32, 33, 49*n*,
    62*n*, 65, 85, 89*n*, 114, 119,
    120, 121*n*, 123, 128, 140,
    142*n*, 148, 149-52, 159, 160,
    184*n*, 188, 190*n*, 215, 224

Kanya, Koloman von, 90, 175, 192
Kellogg-Briand Pact, 48, 77, 121,
    136
Koester, Roland, 37, 82*n*, 34, 89*n*,
    114*n*, 120*n*, 131*n*, 146*b*, 168*n*,
    174*n*, 179*n*

Labour Party, 28, 76, 79, 79*n*, 81.
    See also Great Britain
Laroche, Jules, 104*n*, 176
Lausanne Conference, 3, 15, 56
League of Nations Covenant, 3,
    52, 56, 58, 59, 65, 87, 94,
    121, 124, 127, 128*n*, 132,
    139, 162, 175, 178, 181, 214;
    Council, 2, 7, 10, 94, 132,
    161, 171; Secretariat, 50,
    191*n*
League of Nations, bankruptcy
    of, 5, 25, 48, 114*n*, 124, 204,
    224, 226; reform, 57, 165*n*,
    206, 223
Léger, Alexis Saint-Léger, 120,
    131*n*, 158*n*, 168*n*, 178, 179*n*,
    180
Lenin, Vladimir I, 173
Little Entente, 15, 29, 44, 69,
    85, 90 , 94-9, 113*n*, 130, 147,
    149, 169, 187, 199, 189*n*, 190,
    195*n*, 222; campaign against
    pact, 96-99, 119, 157; ac-
    quiescence in pact, 98-9, 147-
    9, 160, 175, 178

Litvinov, Maksim, 105-8, 173
Litvonov Protocol, 174, 177, 227
Locarno, Treaties of, 3, 7, 10-
11, 94, 121, 132, 184*n*, 222
London Conference, 171. *See
also* World Economic Con-
ference

MacDonald Plan, 37*n*, 39, 53,
74, 77, 77*n*, 84, 113*n*, 115,
117, 118, 122, 127, 136, 138,
142, 144, 208, 209, 210, 217
MacDonald, James Ramsay, 15,
28, 38, 40, 47, 55-7, 67, 76,
116, 131, 159, 166, 205, 222,
223; and Disarmament Con-
ference, 35, 38, 48, 77, 77*n*;
visit to Rome, 39, 41, 43*n*,
53-62, 77, 163; reaction to
pact, 54, 59, 66, 67-71, 77-
8, 82, 82*n*; correspondence
with Mussolini, 112-4
Marin, Louis, 84, 89, 146, 169
Monzie, Anatole de, 63*n*, 119,
120*n*, 138, 169*n*
Munich Agreements, 4, 7, 105*n*,
110*n*, 222, 226
Mussolini, Benito: diplomacy,
6, 8-15, 44*n*, 46-7, 53, 121,
155, 199, 225; character, 8,
22, 42-4; dislike of League,
9-10; preference for Locarno,
10-11*n*; imperialism, 11, 44;
revisionism, 12-5, 33, 60*n*,
162; and Europe, 19, 20, 22,
44*n*, 162, 218; corporatism,
19-22, 225; motives, 8, 35,
42-5, 144*n*; foreign policy
aims, 48, 219-20; origin of
pact, 8, 10, 16, 34-5, 38,
46; attack on Little Entente,
98; and French draft, 123;
Senate speeches, 154-5,
160-3, 204*n*; popularity, 163-
4, 165, 166, 160, 221; and
World Economic Conference,

186-7*n*; and Danubia, 190,
192-5; disarmament plan, 206;
funeral of pact, 217-8; special position, 44, 53, 112, 199,
202, 226; New Year's message
1934, 227
Mussolini and Hitler, 30, 46-8,
143-4, 179-81, 202-3, 210-11*n*,
216

Nadolny, Rudolf, 38, 40, 52, 132*n*,
209, 210, 211-2
Narkomindel, 106, 173. *See also*
Soviet Union
National Socialism, 4, 6, 7, 17-
8, 21, 25, 30, 71, 74, 162*n*,
191*n*, 193, 197, 198, 220-2
Neurath, Constantin von, 24, 37,
48, 50, 51, 63, 105, 117, 120,
124, 127-33, 135, 140-4, 148,
153-6, 165, 178-81*n*, 182*n*,
200, 207, 210, 211
No-Force-Pact, 48, 68*n*, 77, 121,
122. *See also* Five Power
Declaration

Palazzo Chigi, 124, 129, 132,
148, 153, 153*n*, 158, 159*n*,
180*n*, 181, 214. *See also*
Italy
Palazzo Venetia, 19, 140, 163
Papen, Franz von, 125, 126-7*n*,
135, 153, 156*n*, 208*n*, 215-6
Pan Europa, 20, 24. *See also*
Coudenhove-Kalergi
Parti Radical Socialiste, 31,
63-5, 87-8*n*, 89-90*n*, 135*n*,
207
Paul-Boncour, Joseph, 7, 27, 31-
2, 63*n*, 64-7, 85, 89, 114*n*,
120-3, 132, 135, 140*n*, 149*n*,
157, 168*n*, 176, 180*n*, 189,
194, 195, 215, 221
Permanent diplomatic services,
11, 142*n*, 149*n*, 158-9, 222
Pernot, Maurice, 122*n*, 189, 194*n*

Pilsudski, Josef, 25, 100-5, 176-7, 222

Pius XI, Pope, 91, 172

Poland, 25, 33, 43, 48, 59, 67; and pact, 99-105, 169, 175-7, 218n, 222, 225

Portugal, 91-2

Preventive War: fear of, 25, 44, 48, 101-3, 135, 224

Protocol of procedure, 140n, 141-2, 144

Public opinion in diplomacy, 73-4n, 109-110

Quai d'Orsay, 38, 61, 71, 85, 89, 94, 98, 115, 122, 139, 142, 149, 150, 151, 159, 172, 176, 178-9, 198, 221

Radek, Karel, 105, 107-8, 172-3n

Rapallo, 108, 173

Revision, 7, 13-5, 20-2, 33, 45, 52, 53, 59, 62, 66-8, 77-9, 86-8, 95-9, 107, 116, 118, 124, 126-7, 131-2, 154, 157, 162, 164, 175-9, 192, 103n, 220

Rohan, Prince Karl von, 17. *See also* Volta Congress

Roman Pact. *See* Four Power Pact

Roman Protocols, 195n, 218n, 222

Roosevelt, Franklin D., 92-3, 131, 171n, 186, 214; message, 136, 138-9, 139n, 142

Rosenberg, Alfred, 17, 164-5. *See also* Volta Congress

Rumania, 29, 85, 95-9, 176n, 222

Rumbold, Sir Horace, 24, 105-6, 118n, 149n, 153n, 156n, 173

SA, 18n, 25, 27, 70, 134

Sargent, F. O., 68-9n, 116n, 198n

S.F.I.O., 128-9n, 145, 168n, 170n

Simon, Sir John, 15, 37, 38, 55, 57-8, 67-71, 96, 118-9, 130, 139, 142, 150, 163, 166, 200, 207, 210, 212, 217

South Tyrol, 11, 26

Soviet Union, 9, 14, 26, 31n, 42n, 71, 218n; disapproval of pact, 51, 103-8, 172-3, 186n, 222; historiography of pact, 108n-109n

Spain, 91, 91n, 174

SS, 18n, 134

Starhemberg, Prince Rüdiger von, 190n, 193, 194

State Department, 93, 170-1

Stresa, 190n, 194, 207

Suvich, Fulvio, 16, 35, 52, 53, 112, 129, 139n, 151, 153n, 155n, 180, 181n, 183, 213n. *See also* Palazzo Chigi

Sweden, 91, 173

Syria, 174

Turin speech, 15-6. *See also* Four Power Pact

Tardieu Plan, 63n, 122n, 189n, 192, 222

Temperley, A. C., 39n, 134n

Titulescu, Nicolae, 85, 95-9, 119, 145, 176. *See also* Little Entente

Turkey, 91, 174, 222

Tyrell, Sir William, 41, 85, 146, 150, 197, 220

United States, 92-3, 170-1

Vansittart, Sir Robert, 111, 118-9, 185, 188, 197, 198, 200-1n, 221

Versailles: fight against, 21, 26, 49, 59, 67, 107, 137, 174n, 220; violations of, 27, 70, 135, 199, 201n

Volta Congress (1932), 17-9, 31, 165

Wedgewood, Josiah, 80, 81
Weygand, Maxime, 24, 44. *See also* France; Preventive War
Whitehall, 116, 122, 157, 197, 198, 215, 221. *See also* Great Britain
Wilhelmstrasse, 40, 51, 52-3, 103, 105, 117, 124, 125-9, 133, 140n, 142, 149n, 153n, 155-6, 158, 165n, 178, 180, 181n, 191n, 199, 201, 202, 206. *See also* Germany; Neurath
World Economic Conference, 6, 131, 139, 180n, 182, 186, 196, 219

Yevtitch, M., 95-9, 145, 176
Yugoslavia, 29, 95-9, 176n, 190, 222

LOGMARK EDITIONS

Published for
THE HISTORY DEPARTMENT OF THE UNIVERSITY OF WISCONSIN
Order from the Wisconsin History Foundation,
816 State Street, Madison, Wisconsin 53706

Burgess, Charles O.
NETTIE FOWLER McCORMICK: PROFILE OF AN AMERICAN
PHILANTHROPIST
Moved by ideas of Christian stewardship and humanitarian reform,
the wife of the reaper magnate gave away $8,000,000 during the
last thirty-four years of her intriguing life. Pp. viii, 88. 1962.
[LC 62–34857].   **$3.00**

Byrne, Frank L.
PROPHET OF PROHIBITION: NEAL DOW AND HIS CRUSADE
A new study of the Prohibitionist politician who was responsible for
changing the emphasis of the temperance movement from personal
abstinence to legal prohibition. Pp. viii, 184. 1961. O.P. [LC 61–63120].
$4.00

Chiu, Ping
CHINESE LABOR IN CALIFORNIA, 1850–1880: AN ECONOMIC
STUDY
An analysis of Chinese contributions to the rise of the mining, trans-
portation, farming, construction, and manufacturing industries in the
Far West. Pp. xii, 180. 1963. O. P. [LC 63–63578].   **$3.50**

Costa, Albert B.
MICHEL EUGENE CHEVREUL: PIONEER OF ORGANIC CHEMISTRY
"The significance of science can best be understood if it is considered
historically," is illustrated through an examination of the work of
one of the pioneer organic chemists. Pp. vi, 116. 1962. [LC 62–63148].
$3.50

Dodds, Gordon B., editor
A PYGMY MONOPOLIST: THE LIFE AND DOINGS OF R. D. HUME,
WRITTEN BY HIMSELF AND DEDICATED TO HIS NEIGHBORS
The autobiography of a small-scale monopolist who cornered the
salmon market in the pioneer days of the Pacific Northwest. Pp. viii,
87. Map. 1961. [LC 61–63121].   **$3.00**

Fox, Daniel M.
ENGINES OF CULTURE: PHILANTHROPY AND ART MUSEUMS
A study of the co-operation between public and private philanthropy in the development of art museums in the United States. Pp. vi, 90. 1963. O. P. [LC 63–63372].   Paper **$2.00**

Haeussler, Helmut
GENERAL WILLIAM GROENER AND THE IMPERIAL GERMAN ARMY
The absorbing account of the World War I transportation officer who commanded the German army at the time of its surrender. Groener eventually realized that Germany had to subordinate its ego to the larger interest of Europe. Pp. xiv, 161. 1962. [LC 62–63452]. **$4.00**

Helgeson, Arlan
FARMS IN THE CUTOVER: AGRICULTURAL SETTLEMENT IN NORTH-ERN WISCONSIN
One of the last great efforts to promote individual pioneering failed to settle the stumplands of northern Wisconsin in spite of a colorful "hard-sell" campaign. Pp. viii, 184. Maps. 1962. [LC 62–63453]. **$4.25**

Herz, Henri
MY TRAVELS IN AMERICA. TRANSLATED BY HENRY BERTRAM HILL.
The journal of a French concert pianist in the years 1846–1851. A friendly critic, Herz caricatured American foibles and failings. Pp. vii, 102. 1963. [LC 63–63513].   **$3.00**

Hiebert, Erwin N.
HISTORICAL ROOTS OF THE PRINCIPLE OF THE CONSERVATION OF ENERGY
This study shows "where and how some of the early mechanics treatises came to grips with the energetics notions which, during the nineteenth century, were refined, recast, and eventually incorporated into classical thermodynamics." Pp. vi, 118. 1962. O. P. [LC 62–63146].
                                                                                       $3.50

Hill, Henry Bertram, translator (See Herz, Henri)

Jarausch, Konrad Hugo
THE FOUR POWER PACT, 1933.
An analysis of the attempt made in 1933 to organize the peace of

Europe around a four-power directory of Germany, Italy, France, and England. Pp. x, 265. 1965. [LC 65–64978].   **$4.00**

Jensen, Arthur L.
THE MARITIME COMMERCE OF COLONIAL PHILADELPHIA
An analysis of the rise of a colonial port, the impact of British policy on it, and the role of its merchants in the Revolution. Pp. viii, 312. 1963. O. P. [LC 63–63291].   **$4.75**

Johnson, Roger T.
ROBERT M. LA FOLLETTE, JR., AND THE DECLINE OF THE PROGRESSIVE PARTY IN WISCONSIN
A study in Wisconsin politics from the death of "Fighting Bob" in 1925 to the election of Joseph R. McCarthy in 1946. Pp. x, 195. 1964. O. P. [LC 64–63186].   **$3.50**

Kaldis, William P.
JOHN CAPODISTRIAS AND THE MODERN GREEK STATE
An analysis of the role of administrative machinery in the establishment of a centralized nation state. Pp. viii, 126. 1963. [LC 63–63577].   **$3.00**

Konold, Donald E.
A HISTORY OF AMERICAN MEDICAL ETHICS, 1847–1912
A stimulating analysis of the meaning professional ethics had for medical men, particularly during the crucial years after the formation of the American Medical Association. Pp. viii, 119. 1962. O. P. [LC 62–2711].   **$3.50**

Langsam, Miriam Z.
CHILDREN WEST: A HISTORY OF THE PLACING-OUT SYSTEM OF THE NEW YORK CHILDREN'S AID SOCIETY, 1853–1890
A perceptive study of mid-nineteenth-century attempts to deal with the growing problem of juvenile vagrancy. Pp. x, 91. Tables. 1964. [LC 64–63185].   **$2.25**

Overy, David H., Jr.
WISCONSIN CARPETBAGGERS IN DIXIE
The Reconstruction South is viewed as a "frontier of opportunity" for many graduates of Wisconsin's earlier frontier. Pp. x, 180. 1961. O. P. [LC 61–63122].   **$3.00**

Schlabach, Theron F.
    PENSIONS FOR PROFESSORS
A revealing behind-the-scenes study of the policies, ambitions, and interests of the Carnegie Foundation for the Advancement of Teaching. Pp. vi, 122. 1963. O. P. [LC 63–63136].   **$3.00**

Straka, Gerald M.
    ANGLICAN REACTION TO THE REVOLUTION OF 1688
"Locke becomes irrelevant after one reads the Anglican explanation of the Revolution." A cogent argument that the Anglican Church provided the major contemporary justification of the Glorious Revolution is put forth with considerable wit. Pp. xii, 81. 1962. O. P. [LC 62–63454].
                                                                     $4.25

Vignery, J. Robert
    THE FRENCH REVOLUTION AND THE SCHOOLS: EDUCATIONAL
    POLICIES OF THE MOUNTAIN, 1792–1794.

A revealing study of the development of educational thought and planning accompanying the revolutionary changes in France during the Reign of Terror. Pp. xii, 208. 1965. [LC 65–64979].   **$3.00**

Weill, Herman
    FREDERICK THE GREAT AND SAMUEL VON COCCEJI: A STUDY
    IN THE REFORM OF THE PRUSSIAN JUDICIAL ADMINISTRATION,
    1740–1755
An analysis of the Ministry of Justice and the reformation of the Prussian judicial system under the "Enlightened Despot." Pp. x, 181. 1961. [LC 61–63123].   **$4.00**

White, Donald A.
    LITUS SAXONICUM: THE BRITISH SAXON SHORE IN SCHOLAR-
    SHIP AND HISTORY
A case study of the various historiographical treatments and of the origins of the phrase. Pp. vi, 122. Maps. 1961. [LC 61–63124]. **$3.50**